D0081402

DATE DUE

SOFTWARE
TESTING

A Craftsman's Approach

SOFTWARE TESTING

A Craftsman's Approach

Paul C. Jorgensen, Ph.D.
Department of Computer Science and Information Systems
Grand Valley State University
Allendale, Michigan
and
Software Paradigms
Rockford, Michigan

CRC Press
Boca Raton   New York   London   Tokyo

Library of Congress Cataloging-in-Publication Data

Jorgensen, Paul
    Software testing: a craftsman's approach / by Paul C. Jorgensen.
      p.   cm.
    Includes bibliographical references and index.
    ISBN 0-8493-7345-X (alk. paper)
    1. Computer software—Testing. I. Title
QA76.76.T48J97 1995
005. 1'4--dc20   95-17133
                                                   CIP

No claim to original U.S. Government works
International Standard Book Number 0-8493-7345-X
Library of Congress Card Number 94-17133
Printed in the United States of America 1 2 3 4 5 6 7 8 9 0
Printed on acid-free paper

Preface

We huddled around the door to the conference room, each taking a turn looking through the small window. Inside, a recently hired software designer had spread out source listings on the conference table, and carefully passed a crystal hanging from a long chain over the source code. Every so often, the designer marked a circle in red on the listing. Later, one of my colleagues asked the designer what (s)he had been doing in the conference room. The nonchalant reply: "Finding the bugs in my program." This is a true story, it happened in the mid-1980s when people had high hopes for hidden powers in crystals.

In a sense, the goal of this book is to provide you with a better set of crystals. As the title suggests, I believe that software (and system) testing is a craft, and I think I have some mastery of that craft. Out of a score of years developing telephone switching systems, I spent about a third of that time on testing: defining testing methodologies and standards, coordinating system testing for a major international telephone toll switch, specifying and helping build two test execution tools (now we would call them CASE tools), and a fair amount of plain, hands-on testing. For the past seven years, I have been teaching software engineering at the university graduate level. My academic research centers on specification and testing. Adherents to the Oxford Method claim that you never really learn something until you have to teach it — I think they're right. The students in my graduate course on testing are all full-time employees in local industries. Believe me, they keep you honest. This book is an outgrowth of my lectures and projects in that class.

I think of myself as a Software Engineer, but when I compare the level of precision and depth of knowledge prevalent in my field to those of more traditional engineering disciplines, I am uncomfortable with the term. While much of software development is subjective (and even artistic), software testing, by its very nature, admits to and supports strong mathematical and logical considerations. A colleague and I were returning to our project in Italy when Myers' book, *The Art of Software Testing* , first came out. On the way to the airport, we stopped by the MIT bookstore and bought one of the early copies. In the intervening fifteen years, I believe we have moved software testing from an Art to a Craft. I had originally planned to title this book "The Craft of Software Testing", but as I neared the final chapters, another book with that title appeared. Maybe that's confirmation that software testing is becoming a craft. There's still a way to go before it is a science.

Part of any craft is knowing the capabilities and limitations of both the tools and the medium. A good woodworker has a variety of tools and, depending on the item being made and the wood being used, knows which tool is the most appropriate. For testers to reach such a level, the background material in Part I is essential. Of all the phases of the traditional Waterfall Model of the software development life cycle, testing is the most amenable to precise analysis. Elevating software testing to a craft requires that the testing craftsperson must know the basic tools. To this end, Chapters 3 and 4 provide mathematical background which is used freely in the remainder of the text.

Mathematics is a descriptive device that helps us better understand software to be tested. Precise notation, by itself, is not enough. We must also have good technique and judgment, to identify appropriate testing methods and to apply them well. These are the goals of Parts II and III, which deal with fundamental functional and structural testing techniques. These techniques are applied to the continuing examples, which are described in Chapter 2. In Part IV, we apply these techniques to the integration and system levels of testing, and to object-oriented testing. At these levels, we are more concerned with what to test than how to test it, so the discussion moves toward requirements specification. Part IV concludes with an examination of testing interactions in a software controlled system, with a short discussion of client-server systems.

It is ironic that a book on testing contains faults. Despite the conscientious efforts of reviewers and editors, I am confident that faults persist in this text. Those that remain are my responsibility.

In 1977, I attended a testing seminar given by Edward Miller, who has since become one of the luminaries in software testing circles. In that seminar, Miller went to great lengths to convince us that testing need not be bothersome drudgery, but can be a very creative, interesting part of software development. My goal for you, the reader of this book, is that you will become a testing craftsperson, and that you will be able to derive the sense of pride and pleasure that a true craftsperson realizes from a job well done.

Paul C. Jorgensen
Rockford, Michigan
January, 1995

Contents

Part I A Mathematical Context 1

Chapter 1 3

1.1 Basic Definitions 3
1.2 Test Cases 4
1.3 Insights from a Venn Diagram 5
1.4 Identifying Test Cases 7
1.4.1   Functional Testing 7
1.4.2 Structural Testing 8
1.4.3 The Functional Versus Structural Debate 9
1.5 Error and Fault Taxonomies 10
1.6. Levels of Testing 10

Chapter 2 15

2.1 The Triangle Problem 15
2.1.1 Problem Statement 15
2.1.2 Discussion 15
2.1.3 Traditional Implementation 16
2.1.4 Structured Implementation 17
2.2 The NextDate Function 19
2.2.1 Problem Statement 19
2.2.2 Discussion 19
2.2.3 Implementation 19
2.3 The Commission Problem 20
2.3.1 Problem statement 20
2.3.2 Discussion 20
2.3.3 Implementation 21
2.4 The SATM System..22
2.4.1 Problem Statement 22
2.4.2 Discussion 23
2.5 Saturn Windshield Wiper Controller 24

Chapter 3 27

3.1 Set Theory...27
3.1.1 Set Membership 27
3.1.2 Set Definition 28
3.1.3 The Empty Set 28
3.1.4 Venn Diagrams 29
3.1.5 Set operations 29
3.1.6 Set Relations 31
3.1.7 Set Partitions 31
3.1.8 Set Identities 32
3.2 Functions 32
3.2.1 Domain and Range 32
3.2.2 Function Types 33
3.2.3 Function Composition 33
3.3 Relations 34
3.3.1 Relations Among Sets 35

3.3.2 Relations on a Single Set 36
3.4 Propositional Logic 36
3.4.1 Logical Operators 37
3.4.2 Logical Expressions 37
3.4.3 Logical Equivalence 37
3.5 Probability Theory 38

Chapter 4 41

4.1 Graphs 41
4.1.1 Degree of a Node 42
4.1.2 Incidence Matrices 42
4.1.3 Adjacency Matrices 43
4.1.4 Paths 43
4.1.5 Connectedness 44
4.1.6 Condensation Graphs 44
4.1.7 Cyclomatic Number 44
4.2 Directed Graphs 45
4.2.1 Indegrees and Outdegrees 46
4.2.2 Types of Nodes 46
4.2.3 Adjacency Matrix of a Directed Graph 46
4.2.4 Paths and Semi-Paths 47
4.2.5 Reachability Matrix 47
4.2.6 N-Connectedness 47
4.2.7 Strong Components 48
4.3 Graphs for Testing 49
4.3.1 Program Graphs 49
4.3.2 Finite State Machines 50
4.3.3 Petri Nets 52

Part II Functional Testing 55

Chapter 5 57

5.1 Boundary Value Analysis 57
5.1.1 Generalizing Boundary Value Analysis 59
5.1.2 Limitations of Boundary Value Analysis 59
5.2 Robustness Testing 59
5.3 Worst Case Testing 60
5.4 Special Value Testing 60
5.5 Examples 61
5.5.1 Test Cases for the Triangle Problem 61
5.5.2 Test Cases for the NextDate Problem 65
5.5.3 Test Cases for the Commission Problem 67
5.6 Guidelines for Boundary value Testing 67

Chapter 6 71

6.1 Equivalence Classes 71
6.1.1 Weak Equivalence Class Testing 72
6.1.2 Strong Equivalence Class Testing 72
6.1.3 Traditional Equivalence Class Testing 73
6.2 Equivalence Class Test Cases for the Triangle Problem 73
6.3 Equivalence Class Test Cases for the NextDate Function 74
6.4 Equivalence Class Test Cases for the Commission Problem 77
6.5 Guidelines and Observations 79

Chapter 7 81

7.1 Decision Tables 81
7.1.2 Technique 82
7.2 Test Cases for the Triangle Problem 85
7.3 Test Cases for the NextDate Function 86
7.4 Test Cases for the Commission Problem 90
7.5 Guidelines and Observations 92

Chapter 8 93

8.1 Selected Test Cases 93
8.1.1 Triangle Program Test Cases 93
8.1.2 NextDate Problem Test Cases 95
8.1.3 Commission Problem Test Cases 99
8.2 Testing Effort 100
8.3 Testing Efficiency 102
8.4 Testing Effectiveness 103
8.5 Guidelines 103

Part III Structural Testing 105

Chapter 9 107

9.1 DD-Paths 109
9.2 Test Coverage Metrics 111
9.2.1 Metric Based Testing 112
9.2.2. Test Coverage Analyzers 114
9.3 Basis Path Testing 114
9.3.1 McCabe's Basis Path Method 114
9.3.2 Observations on McCabe's Basis Path Method 117
9.3.3 Essential Complexity 118
9.4 Guidelines and Observations 120

Chapter 10 123

10.1 Define/Use Testing 123
10.1.1 Example 124
10.1.2 Du-path Test Coverage Metrics 129
10.2 Slice-Based Testing 131
10.2.1 Example 133
10.2.2 Style and Technique 135
10.3 Guidelines and Observations 137

Chapter 11 139

11.1 Gaps and Redundancies 139
11.2 Metrics for Method Comparison 145
11.2.1 Comparing Functional Testing Methods 145
11.2.2 Comparing Structural Testing Metrics 147
11.3 Functional-Structural Hybrid Testing 149
11.4 Closure 155

Part IV Integration and System Testing 157

Chapter 12 159

12.1 Traditional View of Testing Levels 159
12.2 Alternative Life Cycle Models 160
12.2.1 Waterfall Spin-offs 161

12.2.2 Specification Based Models 162
12.2.3 An Object-Oriented Life Cycle Model 163
12.3 Formulations of the SATM System 164
12.3.1 SATM with Structured Analysis 164
12.3.3 Object-oriented Formulation of SATM 173
12.4 Separating Integration and System Testing 173
12.4.1 Structural Insights 174
12.4.2 Behavioral Insights 175

Chapter 13 177

13.1 A Closer Look at the SATM System 177
13.2 Decomposition Based Integration 178
13.2.1 Top-Down Integration 180
13.2.2 Bottom-up Integration 181
13.2.3 Sandwich Integration 181
13.2.4 Pros and Cons 181
13.3 Call Graph Based Integration 181
13.3.1 Pair-wise Integration 182
13.3.2 Neighborhood Integration 182
13.3.3 Pros and Cons 183
13.4 Path Based Integration 183
13.4.1 New and Extended Concepts 183
13.4.2 MM-Paths and ASFs in the SATM System 186
13.4.3 Pros and Cons 188

Chapter 14 191

14.1 Threads 191
14.1.1 Thread Possibilities 192
14.1.2 Thread Definitions 192
14.2 Basis Concepts for Requirements Specification 193
14.2.1 Data 193
14.2.2 Actions 194
14.2.3 Ports 194
14.2.4 Events 194
14.2.5 Threads 194
14.2.6 Relationships Among Basis Concepts 194
14.2.7 Modeling with the Basis Concepts 195
14.3 Finding Threads 196
14.4 Structural Strategies for Thread Testing 200
14.4.1 Bottom-up Threads 200
14.4.2 Node and Edge Coverage Metrics 201
14.5 Functional Strategies for Thread Testing 201
14.5.1 Event-based Thread Testing 203
14.5.2 Port-based Thread Testing 203
14.5.3 Data-based Thread Testing 204
14.6 SATM Test Threads 205
14.7 System Testing Guidelines 210
14.7.1 Pseudo-structural System Testing 210
14.7.2 Operational Profiles 210
14.7.3 Progression vs. Regression Testing 211

Chapter 15 213

15.1 Object Orientation 213
15.2 Issues Raised by Object Orientation 214

15.2.1 Levels of Testing 214
15.2.2 Object Composition 215
15.2.3 Esoteric Object Features 218
15.3 Framework for Object-Oriented Testing 218
15.4 Object-Oriented Testing of the SATM System 219
15.5 Guidelines for Object-oriented Testing 223

Chapter 16 227

16.1 Context of Interaction 227
16.2 A Petri Net Model for Interactions 228
16.3 A Taxonomy of Interactions 231
16.3.1 Static Interactions in a Single Processor 231
16.3.2 Static Interactions in Multiple Processors 232
16.3.3 Dynamic Interactions in a Single Processor 233
16.3.4 Dynamic Interactions in Multiple Processors 238
16.4 Interaction, Composition, and Determinism 242
16.5 Client-Server Testing 243

References 247

Index 251

Dedication

To Carol, Kirsten, and Katia.

Part I

A Mathematical Context

A Perspective on Testing

Why do we test? There are two main reasons: to make a judgment about quality or acceptability, and to discover problems. We test because we know that we are fallible — this is especially true in the domain of software and software controlled systems. The goal of this chapter is to create a perspective (or context) on software testing. We will operate within this context for the remainder of the text.

1.1 BASIC DEFINITIONS

Much of testing literature is mired in confusing (and sometimes inconsistent) terminology, probably because testing technology has evolved over decades and via scores of writers. The terminology here (and throughout this book) is taken from standards developed by the Institute of Electronics and Electrical Engineers Computer Society. To get started let's look at a useful progression of terms [IEEE 83].

Error
People make errors. A good synonym is "mistake". When people make mistakes while coding, we call these mistakes "bugs". Errors tend to propagate; a requirements error may be magnified during design, and amplified still more during coding.

Fault
A fault is the result of an error. It is more precise to say that a fault is the representation of an error, where representation is the mode of expression, such as narrative text, dataflow diagrams, hierarchy charts, source code, and so on. "Defect" is a good synonym for fault; so is "bug". Faults can be elusive. When a designer makes an error of omission, the resulting fault is that something is missing that should be present in the representation. This suggests a useful refinement; to borrow from the Church, we might speak of faults of commission and faults of omission. A fault of commission occurs when we enter something into a representation that is incorrect. Faults of omission occur when we fail to enter correct information. Of these two types, faults of omission are more difficult to detect and resolve.

Failure
A failure occurs when a fault executes. Two subtleties arise here: one is that failures only occur in an executable representation, which is usually taken to be source code, or more precisely, loaded object code. The second subtlety is that this definition relates failures only to faults of commission. How can we deal with "failures" that correspond to faults of omission? We can push this still further: what about faults that never happen to execute, or maybe don't execute for a long time? The Michaelangelo virus is an example of such a fault. It doesn't execute until Michelangelo's birthday, March 6. Reviews prevent many failures by finding faults, in fact, well done reviews can find faults of omission.

Incident

When a failure occurs, it may or may not be readily apparent to the user (or customer or tester). An incident is the symptom(s) associated with a failure that alerts the user to the occurrence of a failure.

Test

Testing is obviously concerned with errors, faults, failures, and incidents. A test is the act of exercising software with test cases. There are two distinct goals of a test: either to find failures, or to demonstrate correct execution.

Test Case

A test case has an identity, and is associated with a program behavior. A test case also has a set of inputs, a list of expected outputs.

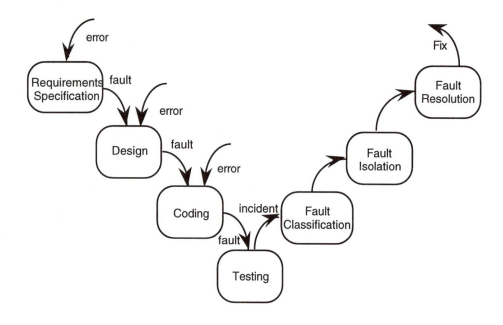

Figure 1.1 A Testing Life Cycle

Figure 1.1 portrays a life cycle model for testing. Notice that, in the development phases, there are three opportunities for errors to be made, resulting in faults that propagate through the remainder of the development. One prominent tester summarizes this life cycle as follows: the first three phases are "Putting Bugs IN", the testing phase is Finding Bugs, and the last three phases are "Getting Bugs OUT" [Poston 90]. The Fault Resolution step is another opportunity for errors (and new faults). When a "fix" causes formerly correct software to misbehave, the fix is deficient. We'll revisit this when we discuss regression testing.

From this sequence of terms, we see that test cases occupy a central position in testing. The process of testing can be subdivided into separate steps: test planning, test case development, running test cases, and evaluating test results. The focus of this book is how to identify useful sets of test cases.

1.2 TEST CASES

The essence of software testing is to determine a set of test cases for the item being tested. Before going on, we need to clarify what information should be in a test case. The most obvious information is inputs; inputs are really of two types: pre-conditions (circumstances that hold prior to test case execution) and the actual inputs that were identified by some testing method. The next most obvious part of a test case is the expected outputs; again, there are two types: post conditions and actual outputs. The output portion of a test case is frequently overlooked. Unfortunate, because this is often the hard part. Suppose, for example, you were testing software that determined an optimal route for an aircraft, given certain FAA air corridor constraints and the weather data for a flight day. How would you know what the optimal route really is? There have been various responses to this problem. The academic response is to postulate the existence of an oracle, who "knows all the answers". One industrial response to this problem is known as Reference Testing, where the system is tested in the presence of expert users, and these experts make judgments as to whether or not outputs of an executed set of test case inputs are acceptable.

The act of testing entails establishing the necessary pre-conditions, providing the test case inputs, observing the outputs, and then comparing these with the expected outputs to determine whether or not the test passed.

Test Case ID

Purpose

Pre-Conditions

Inputs

Expected Outputs

Post-Conditions

Execution History
Date   Result   Version   Run By

Figure 1.2   Typical Test Case Information

The remaining information (see Fig. 1.2) in a well-developed test case primarily supports testing management. Test cases should have an identity, and a reason for being (requirements tracing is a fine reason). It is also useful to record the execution history of a test case, including when and by whom it was run, the pass/fail result of each execution, and the version (of software) on which it was run. From all of this, it should be clear that test cases are valuable — at least as valuable as source code. Test cases need to be developed, reviewed, used, managed, and saved.

1.3 INSIGHTS FROM A VENN DIAGRAM

Testing is fundamentally concerned with behavior; and behavior is orthogonal to the structural view common to software (and system) developers. A quick differentiation is that the structural view focuses on "what it is" and the behavioral view considers "what it does". One of the continuing sources of difficulty for testers is that the base documents are usually written by and for developers, and therefore the emphasis is on structural, rather than behavioral, information. In this section, we develop a simple Venn diagram which clarifies several nagging questions about testing.

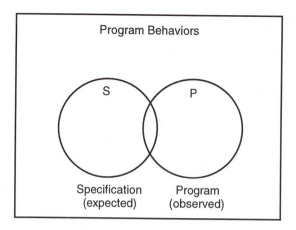

Figure 1.3 Specified and Implemented Program Behaviors

Consider a Universe of program behaviors. (Notice that we are forcing attention on the essence of testing.) Given a program and its specification, consider the set S of specified behaviors, and the set P of programmed behaviors. Figure 1.3 shows the relationship between our universe of discourse and the specified and programmed behaviors. Of all the possible program behaviors, the specified ones are in the circle labeled S; and all those behaviors actually programmed (note the slight difference between P and U, the Universe) are in P. With this diagram, we can see more clearly the problems that confront a tester. What if there are specified behaviors that have not been programmed? In our earlier terminology, these are faults of omission. Similarly, what if there are programmed (implemented) behaviors that have not been specified? These correspond to faults of commission, and to errors which occurred after the specification was complete. The intersection of S and P (the football shaped region) is the "correct" portion, that is behaviors that are both specified and implemented. A very good view of testing is that it is the determination of the extent of program behavior that is both specified and implemented. (As a sidelight, note that "correctness" only has meaning with respect to a specification and an implementation. It is a relative term, not an absolute.)

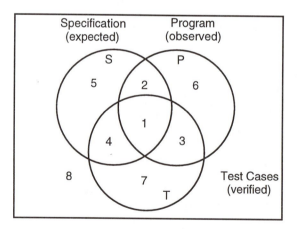

Figure 1.4 Specified, Implemented, and Tested Behaviors

The new circle in Fig. 1.4 is for Test Cases. Notice there is a slight discrepancy with our Universe of Discourse, the set of program behaviors. Since a test case causes a program behavior, the mathematicians might forgive us. Now, consider the relationships among the sets S, P, and T. There may be specified behaviors that are not tested (regions 2 and 5), specified behaviors that are tested (regions 1 and 4), and test cases that correspond to unspecified behaviors (regions 3 and 7).

Similarly, there may be programmed behaviors that are not tested (regions 2 and 6), programmed behaviors that are tested (regions 1 and 3), and test cases that correspond to unprogrammed behaviors (regions 4 and 7). Each of these regions is important. If there are specified behaviors for which there are no test cases, the testing is necessarily incomplete. If there are test cases that correspond to unspecified behaviors, two possibilities arise: either such a test case is unwarranted, or the specification is deficient. (In my experience, good testers often postulate test cases of this latter type. This is a fine reason to have good testers participate in specification and design reviews.)

We are already at a point where we can see some possibilities for testing as a craft: what can a tester do to make the region where these sets all intersect (region 1) be as large as possible? Another way to get at this is to ask how the test cases in the set T are identified. The short answer is that test cases are identified by a testing method. This framework gives us a way to compare the effectiveness of diverse testing methods, as we shall see in chapters 8 and 11.

1.4 IDENTIFYING TEST CASES

There are two fundamental approaches to identifying test cases; these are known as functional and structural testing. Each of these approaches has several distinct test case identification methods, more commonly called testing methods.

1.4.1 FUNCTIONAL TESTING

Functional testing is based on the view that any program can be considered to be a function that maps values from its input domain to values in its output range. (Function, domain, and range are defined in Chapter 3.) This notion is commonly used in engineering, when systems are considered to be "black boxes". This leads to the term Black Box Testing, in which the content (implementation) of a black box is not known, and the function of the black box is understood completely in terms of its inputs and outputs. In *Zen and The Art of Motorcycle Maintenance* , Pirsig refers to this as "romantic" comprehension [Pirsig 73]. Many times, we operate very effectively with black box knowledge; in fact this is central to object orientation. As an example, most people successfully operate automobiles with only black box knowledge.

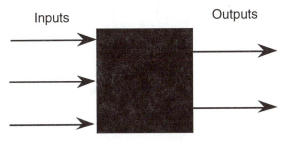

Figure 1.5 An Engineer's Black Box

With the functional approach to test case identification, the only information that is used is the specification of the software. There are two distinct advantages to functional test cases: they are independent of how the software is implemented, so if the implementation changes, the test cases are still useful, and test case development can occur in parallel with the implementation, thereby reducing overall project development interval. On the negative side, functional test cases frequently suffer from two problems: there can be significant redundancies among test cases, and this is compounded by the possibility of gaps of untested software.

Figure 1.6 shows the results of test cases identified by two functional methods. Method A identifies a larger set of test cases than does Method B. Notice that, for both methods, the set of test cases is completely contained within the set of specified behavior. Since functional methods are based on the specified behavior, it is hard to imagine these methods identifying behaviors that are not specified. In Chapter 8 we will see direct comparisons of test cases generated by various functional methods for the examples defined in Chapter 2.

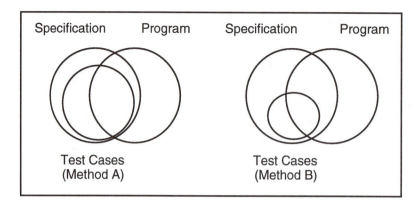

Figure 1.6 Comparing Functional Test Case Identification Methods

In Part II we will examine the mainline approaches to functional testing, including Boundary Value Analysis, Robustness Testing, Worst Case Analysis, Special Value Testing, Input (Domain) Equivalence Classes, Output (Range) Equivalence Classes, and Decision Table Based Testing. The common thread running through these techniques is that all are based on definitional information of the item being tested. The mathematical background presented in Chapter 3 applies primarily to the functional approaches.

1.4.2 STRUCTURAL TESTING

Structural testing is the other fundamental approach to test case identification. To contrast it with Functional Testing, it is sometimes called White Box (or even Clear Box) Testing. The clear box metaphor is probably more appropriate, because the essential difference is that the implementation (of the Black Box) is known and used to identify test cases. Being able to "see inside" the black box allows the tester to identify test cases based on how the function is actually implemented.

Structural Testing has been the subject of some fairly strong theory. To really understand structural testing, the concepts of linear graph theory (Chapter 4) are essential. With these concepts, the tester can rigorously describe exactly what is being tested. Because of its strong theoretical basis, structural testing lends itself to the definition and use of test coverage metrics. Test coverage metrics provide a way to explicitly state the extent to which a software item has been tested, and this in turn, makes testing management more meaningful.

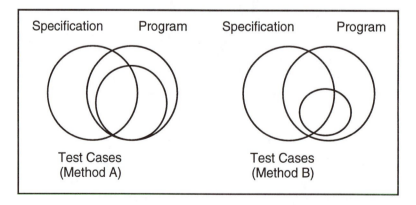

Figure 1.7 Comparing Structural Test Case Identification Methods

Figure 1.7 shows the results of test cases identified by two structural methods. As before, Method A identifies a larger set of test cases than does Method B. Is a larger set of test cases necessarily better? An excellent question, and structural testing provides important ways to develop an answer. Notice that, for both methods, the set of test cases is completely contained within the set of programmed behavior. Since structural methods are based on the program, it is hard to imagine these methods identifying behaviors that are not programmed. It is easy to imagine, however, that a set of structural test cases is relatively small with respect to the full set of programmed behaviors. At the end of Part III, we will see direct comparisons of test cases generated by various structural methods.

1.4.3   THE FUNCTIONAL VERSUS STRUCTURAL DEBATE

Given two fundamentally different approaches to test case identification, the natural question is which is better? If you read much of the literature, you will find strong adherents to either choice. Referring to structural testing, Robert Poston writes: "this tool has been wasting tester's time since the 1970s. . . [it] does not support good software testing practice and should not be in the testers tool kit" [Poston 91]. In defense of structural testing, Edward Miller [Miller 91] writes: "Branch coverage [a structural test coverage metric], if attained at the 85 percent or better level, tends to identify twice the number of defects that would have been found by 'intuitive' [functional] testing."

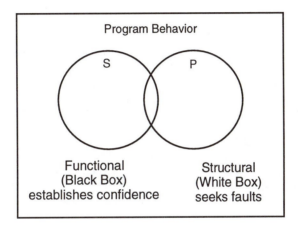

Figure 1.8   Sources of Test Cases

    The Venn diagrams we developed earlier yield a strong resolution to this debate. Recall that the goal of the two approaches is to identify test cases. Functional testing uses only the specification to identify test cases, while structural testing uses the program source code (implementation) as the basis of test case identification. Our earlier discussion forces the conclusion that neither approach, taken by itself, is sufficient. Consider program behaviors: if all specified behaviors have not been implemented, structural test cases will never be able to recognize this. Conversely, if the program implements behaviors that have not been specified, this will never be revealed by functional test cases. (A virus is a good example of such unspecified behavior.) The quick answer is that both approaches are needed; the testing craftsperson's answer is that a judicious combination will provide the confidence of functional testing and the measurement of structural testing. Earlier, we asserted that functional testing often suffers from twin problems of redundancies and gaps. When functional test cases are executed in combination with structural test coverage metrics, both of these problems can be recognized and resolved.

    The Venn diagram view of testing provides one final insight. What is the relationship between the set T of test cases and the sets S and P of specified and implemented behaviors? Clearly, the test cases in T are determined by the test case identification method used. A very good question to ask is how appropriate (or effective) is this method? We can close a loop with an earlier part of our discussion. Recall the causal trail from error to fault, failure, and incident. If we know what kind of errors we are prone to make, and if we know what kinds of faults are likely to reside in the software to be tested, we can use this to employ more appropriate test case identification methods. This is the point at which testing really becomes a craft.

1.5 ERROR AND FAULT TAXONOMIES

Our definitions of error and fault hinge on the distinction between process and product: process refers to how we do something, and product is the end result of a process. The point at which testing and Software Quality Assurance meet is that SQA typically tries to improve the product by improving the process. In that sense, testing is clearly more product oriented. SQA is more concerned with reducing errors endemic in the development process, while testing is more concerned with discovering faults in a product. Both disciplines benefit from a clearer definition of types of faults. Faults can be classified in several ways: the development phase where the corresponding error occurred, the consequences of corresponding failures, difficulty to resolve, risk of no resolution, and so on. My favorite is based on anomaly occurrence: one time only, intermittent, recurring, or repeatable. Figure 1.9 contains a fault taxonomy [Beizer 84] that distinguishes faults by the severity of their consequences.

1. Mild	Misspelled word
2. Moderate	Misleading or redundant information
3. Annoying	Truncated names, bill for $0.00
4. Disturbing	Some transaction(s) not processed
5. Serious	Lose a transaction
6. Very Serious	Incorrect transaction execution
7. Extreme	Frequent "Very Serious" errors
8. Intolerable	Database corruption
9. Catastrophic	System shut down
10. Infectious	Shut down that spreads to others

Figure 1.9 Faults Classified by Severity

For a comprehensive treatment of types of faults, see [IEEE 93]; the IEEE Standard Classification for Software Anomalies. (A software anomaly is defined in that document as "a departure fro the expected", which is pretty close to our definition.) The IEEE standard defines a detailed anomaly resolution process built around four phases (another life cycle): recognition, investigation, action, and disposition. Some of the more useful anomalies are given in Tables 1 through 5; most of these are from the IEEE standard, but I have added some of my favorites.

1.6. LEVELS OF TESTING

Thus far we have said nothing about one of the key concepts of testing — levels of abstraction. Levels of testing echo the levels of abstraction found in the Waterfall Model of the software development life cycle. While this model has its drawbacks, it is useful for testing as a means of identifying distinct levels of testing, and for clarifying the objectives that pertain to each level. A diagrammatic variation of the Waterfall Model is given in Figure 1.10; this variation emphasizes the correspondence between testing and design levels. Notice that, especially in terms of functional testing, the three levels of definition (specification, preliminary design, and detailed design) correspond directly to three levels of testing —

Table 1   Input/Output Faults

Type	Instances
Input	correct input not accepted
	incorrect input accepted
	description wrong or missing
	parameters wrong or missing
Output	wrong format
	wrong result
	correct result at wrong time (too early, too late)
	incomplete or missing result
	spurious result
	spelling/grammar
	cosmetic

Table 2   Logic Faults

missing case(s)
duplicate case(s)
extreme condition neglected
misinterpretation
missing condition
extraneous condition(s)
test of wrong variable
incorrect loop iteration
wrong operator (e.g., < instead of ≤)

Table 3   Computation Faults

incorrect algorithm
missing computation
incorrect operand
incorrect operation
parenthesis error
insufficient precision (round-off, truncation)
wrong built-in function

unit, integration, and system testing. The levels of testing also raise the question of testing order: bottom up, top down, or some other possibility. (We'll get to that question in Chapter 13.)

There is a practical relationship between levels of testing and functional and structural testing. Most practitioners agree that structural testing is most appropriate at the unit level, while functional testing is most appropriate at the system level. While this is generally true, it is also a likely consequence of the base information produced during the requirements specification, preliminary design, and detailed design

Table 4   Interface Faults

incorrect interrupt handling
I/O timing
call to wrong procedure
call to non-existent procedure
parameter mismatch (type, number)
incompatible types
superfluous inclusion

Table 5   Data Faults

incorrect initialization
incorrect storage/access
wrong flag/index value
incorrect packing/unpacking
wrong variable used
wrong data reference
scaling or units error
incorrect data dimension
incorrect subscript
incorrect type
incorrect data scope
sensor data out of limits
off by one
inconsistent data

phases. The constructs defined for structural testing make the most sense at the unit level; and similar constructs are only now becoming available for the integration and system levels of testing. We develop such structures in Part IV to support structural testing at the integration and system levels for both traditional and object-oriented software.

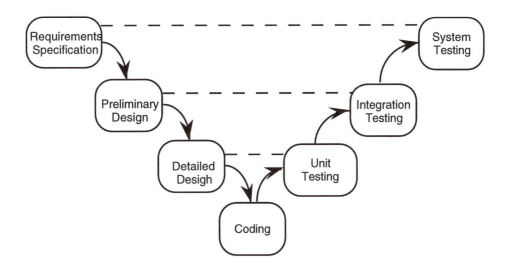

Figure 1.10 Levels of Abstraction and Testing in the Waterfall Model

EXERCISES

1. Make a Venn Diagram that reflects a part of one of the great confessions of the Catholic Church: "... we have left undone that which we ought to have done, and we have done that which we ought not to have done..."
2. Describe each of the eight regions in Figure 1.4.
3. One of the folk tales of software lore describes a disgruntled employee who writes a payroll program. The program contains logic that checks for the employee's identification number before producing paychecks. If the employee is ever terminated, the program creates havoc. Discuss this situation in terms of the error, fault, failure pattern, and decide which form of testing would be appropriate.

Chapter 2

Examples

Three examples will be used throughout in Parts II and III to illustrate the various unit testing methods. They are: the Triangle Problem (a venerable example in testing circles), a logically complex function, NextDate, and an example that typifies MIS testing, known here as the Commission Problem. Taken together, these examples raise most of the issues that testing craftspersons will encounter. The discussion of integration and system testing in Part IV uses two examples; a simplified version of an automated teller machine, known here as the Simple ATM System (SATM), and the windshield wiper control device from the Saturn automobile.

For the purposes of structural testing, TurboPascal implementations of the three unit level examples are given in this chapter. System level descriptions of the SATM system and the Saturn Windshield Wiper system, namely an E/R diagram, a set of dataflow diagrams, and a Finite State Machine description, are given in Part IV.

2.1 THE TRIANGLE PROBLEM

The year of this writing marks the twentieth anniversary of publications using the Triangle Problem as an example. Some of the more notable entries in this generation of testing literature are [Gruenberger 73], [Brown 75], [Myers 79], [Pressman 82 (and the second and third editions], [Clarke 83], [Clarke 84], [Chellappa 87], and [Hetzel 88]. There are probably others, but this list should suffice.

2.1.1 PROBLEM STATEMENT

The Triangle Program accepts three integers as input; these are taken to be sides of a triangle. The output of the program is the type of triangle determined by the three sides: Equilateral, Isosceles, Scalene, or NotATriangle. Sometimes this problem is extended to include right triangles as a fifth type; we will use this extension in some of the exercises.

2.1.2 DISCUSSION

Perhaps one of the reasons for the longevity of this example is that, among other things, it typifies some of the incomplete definition that impairs communication among customers, developers, and testers. This specification presumes the developers know some details about triangles, in particular the Triangle Property: the sum of any pair of sides must be strictly greater than the third side. If a, b, and c denote the three integer sides, then the triangle property is mathematically stated as three inequalities: $a < b + c$, $b < a + c$, and $c < a + b$. If any one of these fails to be true, the integers a, b, and c do not constitute sides of a triangle. If all three sides are equal, they constitute an equilateral triangle; if exactly one pair of sides is equal, they form an isosceles triangle; and if no pair of sides is equal, they constitute a scalene triangle. A good tester might further clarify the problem statement by putting limits on the lengths of the sides. What response would we expect if we presented the program with the sides -5, -4, -3? We will require that all sides be at least 1, and while we are at it, we may as well declare some upper limit, say 20,000. (Some languages, like Pascal, have an automatic limit, called MAXINT, which is the largest binary integer representable in a certain number of bits.)

2.1.3 TRADITIONAL IMPLEMENTATION

The "traditional" implementation of this grandfather of all examples has a rather FORTRAN-like style. The flowchart for this implementation appears in Figure 2.1. The flowchart box numbers correspond to comment numbers in the (FORTRAN-like) TurboPascal program given next. (These numbers correspond exactly to those in [Pressman 82].) I don't really like this implementation very much, so a more structured implementation is given in section 2.1.4.

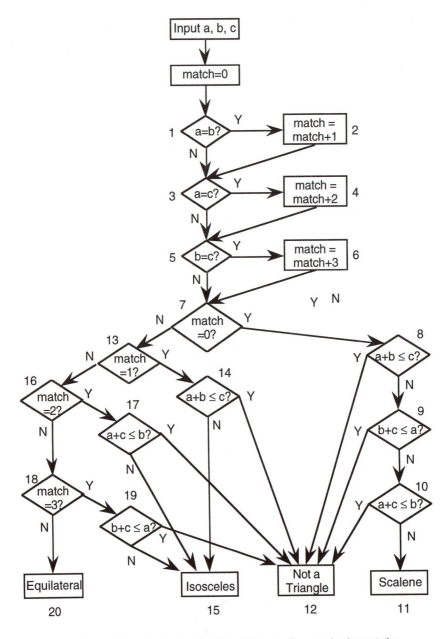

Figure 2.1 Flowchart for the Traditional Triangle Program Implementation

The variable match is used to record equality among pairs of the sides. There is a classical intricacy of the FORTRAN style connected with the variable match: notice that all three tests for the triangle property do not occur. If two sides are equal, say a and c, it is only necessary to compare a+c with b. (Since b must be greater than zero, a + b must be greater than c, because c equals a.) This observation clearly reduces the amount of comparisons that must be made. The efficiency of this version is obtained at the expense of clarity (and ease of testing!).

We will find this version useful later in Part III when we discuss infeasible program execution paths. That is the best reason for retaining this version.

```
PROGRAM triangle1  (input,output);
VAR
    a,  b,  c,  match  :INTEGER;
BEGIN
    writeln('Enter  3  integers  which  are  sides  of  a  triangle');
    readln(a,b,c);
    writeln('Side  A  is  ',a);
    writeln('Side  B  is  ',b);
    writeln('Side  C  is  ',c);
    match  := 0;
    IF  a  =  b                                                    {1  }
    THEN    match  :=  match  +  1;                                {2  }
    IF  a  =  c                                                    {3  }
    THEN    match  :=  match  +  2;                                {4  }
    IF  b  =  c                                                    {5  }
    THEN    match  :=  match  +  3;                                {6  }
    IF  match  =  0                                                {7  }
    THEN  IF  (a+b)<=c                                             {8  }
            THEN  writeln('Not  a  Triangle')                      {12.1}
            ELSE  IF  (b+c)<=a                                     {9  }
                    THEN  writeln('Not  a  Triangle')              {12.2}
                    ELSE  IF  (a+c)<=b                             {10  }
                            THEN  writeln('Not  a  Triangle')      {12.3}
                            ELSE  writeln ('Triangle  is  Scalene') {11  }
    ELSE  IF  match=1                                              {13  }
            THEN  IF  (a+c)<=b                                     {14  }
                    THEN  writeln('Not  a  Triangle')             {12.4}
                    ELSE  writeln ('Triangle  is  Isosceles')      {15.1}
            ELSE  IF  match=2                                      {16  }
                    THEN  IF  (a+c)<=b                             {17  }
                            THEN  writeln('Not  a  Triangle')      {12.5}
                            ELSE  writeln ('Triangle  is  Isosceles {15.2}
                    ELSE  IF  match=3                              {18  }
                            THEN  IF  (b+c)<=a                     {19  }
                                    THEN  writeln('Not  a  Triangle') {12.6}
                                    ELSE  writeln ('Triangle  is  Isosceles'{15.3}
                            ELSE  writeln ('Triangle  is  Equilateral'); {20  }
END.
```

Notice that there are six ways to reach the Not A Triangle box (12.1 - 12.6) and there are three ways to reach the Isosceles box (15.1 - 15.3).

2.1.4 STRUCTURED IMPLEMENTATION

Figure 2.2 is a dataflow diagram description of the triangle program. We could implement it as a main program with the four indicated procedures. Since we will use this example later for unit testing, the four procedures have been merged into one TurboPascal program. Comment lines relate sections of the code to the decomposition given in Figure 2.2.

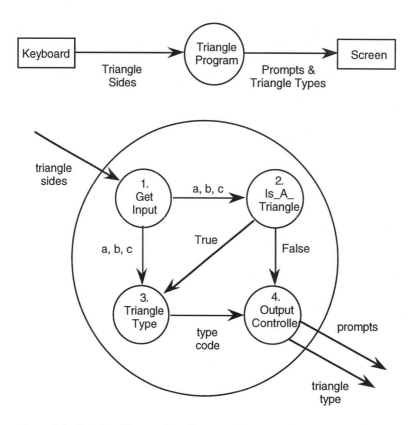

Figure 2.2 Dataflow Diagram for a Structured Triangle Program Implementation

```
PROGRAM triangle2 (input,output);
VAR
     a, b, c       : INTEGER;
     IsATriangle   : BOOLEAN;
BEGIN
{Function 1:  Get Input}
     writeln('Enter 3 integers which are sides of a triangle');
     readln(a,b,c);
     writeln('Side A is ',a);
     writeln('Side B is ',b);
     writeln('Side C is ',c);
{Function 2:  Is A Triangle?}
     IF (a < b + c) AND (b < a + c) AND (c < a + b)
     THEN IsATriangle := TRUE
     ELSE IsATriangle := FALSE ;
{Function 3:  Determine Triangle Type}
     IF IsATriangle
     THEN IF (a = b) AND (b = c)
          THEN writeln ('Triangle is Equilateral');
          ELSE IF (a <> b) AND (a <> c) AND (b <> c)
               THEN writeln ('Triangle is Scalene');
               ELSE writeln ('Triangle is Isosceles')
     ELSE writeln('Not a Triangle');
{Note: Function 4, the Output Controller, has been merged into
clauses in Function 3.}
END.
```

2.2 THE NEXTDATE FUNCTION

The complexity in the Triangle Program is due to relationships between inputs and correct outputs. We will use the NextDate function to illustrate a different kind of complexity — logical relationships among the input variables themselves.

2.2.1 PROBLEM STATEMENT

NextDate is a function of three variables: month, day, and year. It returns the date of the day after the input date. The month, day, and year variables have numerical values: with $1 \leq month \leq 12$, $1 \leq day \leq 31$, and $1812 \leq year \leq 2012$.

2.2.2 DISCUSSION

There are two sources of complexity in the NextDate function: the just mentioned complexity of the input domain, and the rule that distinguishes common years from leap years. Since a year is 365.2422 days long, leap years are used for the "extra day" problem. If we declared a leap year every fourth year, there would be a slight error. The Gregorian Calendar (instituted by Pope Gregory in 1582) resolves this by adjusting leap years on century years. Thus a year is a leap year if it is divisible by 4, unless it is a century year. Century years are leap years only if they are multiples of 400 [Inglis 61], [ISO 91], so 1992, 1996, and 2000 are leap years, while the year 1900 is a common year.

The NextDate function also illustrates a sidelight of software testing. Many times, we find examples of Zipf's Law, which states that 80% of the activity occurs in 20% of the space. Notice how much of the source code is devoted to leap year considerations.

2.2.3 IMPLEMENTATION

```
PROGRAM NextDate (INPUT,OUTPUT);
TYPE        monthType = 1..12;
            dayType   = 1..31;
            yearType  = 1812..2012;
            dateType  = record
                month : monthType;
                day   : dayType;
                year  : yearType;
            end; (*dateType record *)
VAR         today, tomorrow :dateType;
BEGIN (*NextDate*)
writeln ('Enter today''s date in the form MM DD YYYY');
readln (today.month, today.day, today.year);
tomorrow := today;
WITH today DO
    CASE month OF
    1,3,5,7,8,10:  IF day < 31 THEN tomorrow.day := day + 1
                   ELSE Begin
                            tomorrow.day := 1;
                            tomorrow.month := month + 1
                        End;
    4,6,9,11    :  IF day < 30 THEN tomorrow.day := day + 1
                   ELSE Begin
                            tomorrow.day := 1;
                            tomorrow.month := month + 1
                        End;
    12:  IF day < 31 THEN tomorrow.day := day + 1
         ELSE Begin
                  tomorrow.day := 1;
                  tomorrow.month := 1;
                  IF year = 2012
                    THEN Writeln ('2012 is over')
                    ELSE tomorrow.year := year + 1
              End;
```

```
    2:     IF day < 28    THEN tomorrow.day := day + 1
           ELSE IF    day = 28
               THEN IF ((year MOD 4)=0) AND ((year MOD 400)<>0)
                    THEN tomorrow.day := 29 {leap year}
                    ELSE Begin             {common year}
                              tomorrow.day := 1;
                              tomorrow.month := 3;
                         End
           ELSE IF    day = 29
               THEN Begin
                         tomorrow.day := 1;
                         tomorrow.month := 3;
                    End;
               ELSE writeln('Cannot have Feb.', day);
       End;(*CASE month*)
End; (*WITH today*)
Writeln ('Tomorrow''s date is', tomorrow.month:3,
       tomorrow.day:3, tomorrow.year:5);
END.   (*NextDate*)
```

2.3 THE COMMISSION PROBLEM

Our third example is more typical of commercial computing. It contains a mix of computation and decision making, so it leads to interesting testing questions.

2.3.1 PROBLEM STATEMENT

Rifle salespersons in the Arizona Territory sold rifle locks, stocks, and barrels made by a gunsmith in Missouri. Locks cost $45.00, stocks cost $30.00, and barrels cost $25.00. Salespersons had to sell at least one complete rifle per month, and production limits are such that the most one salesperson could sell in a month is 70 locks, 80 stocks, and 90 barrels. Each rifle salesperson sent a telegram to the Missouri company with the total order for each town (s)he visits; salespersons visit at least one town per month, but travel difficulties made ten towns the upper limit. At the end of each month, the company computed commissions as follows: 10% on sales up to $1000, 15% on the next $800, and 20% on any sales in excess of $1800. The company had four salespersons. The telegrams from each salesperson were sorted into piles (by person) and at the end of each month a datafile is prepared, containing the salesperson's name, followed by one line for each telegram order, showing the number of locks, stocks, and barrels in that order. At the end of the sales data lines, there is an entry of "-1" in the position where the number of locks would be to signal the end of input for that salesperson. The program produces a monthly sales report that gives the salesperson's name, the total number of locks, stocks, and barrels sold, the salesperson's total dollar sales, and finally his/her commission.

2.3.2 DISCUSSION

This example is somewhat contrived to make the arithmetic quickly visible to the reader. It might be more realistic to consider some other additive function of several variables, such as various calculations found in filling out a US 1040 income tax form. (We'll stay with rifles.)

This problem separates into two distinct pieces: the input data portion, which deals with records of sales in individual towns, and the commission calculation portion, which computes the salesperson's commission as a function of the total number of locks, stocks, and barrels sold. The functional view of the entire problem is that the salesperson's commission is a function of the telegrams:

$$F(telegrams) = commission$$

This decomposes naturally into three subfunctions:

$$F1(telegrams) = (locks, stocks, barrels)$$
$$F2(locks, stocks, barrels) = sales$$
$$F3(sales) = commission$$

We will refer to the Commission Problem as the composition of F2 and F3, and refer to the entire example as the Lock, Stock, and Barrel problem.

2.3.3 IMPLEMENTATION

```
PROGRAM Lock_Stock_and_Barrel  (INPUT,OUTPUT);
CONST
      lock_price = 45.0;
      stock_price = 30.0;
      barrel_price = 25.0;
TYPE
      STRING_30 = string[30];  {Salesman's Name}
VAR
      locks, stocks, barrels, num_locks, num_stocks,
      num_barrels, salesman_index, order_index : INTEGER;
      sales, commission : REAL;
      salesman : STRING_30;
BEGIN {program Lock_Stock_and_Barrel}
FOR   salesman_index := 1 TO 4 DO
      BEGIN
            readln(salesman);
            writeln ('Salesman is ', salesman);
            num_locks := 0;
            num_stocks := 0;
            num_barrels := 0;
            READ(locks);
            WHILE locks <> -1 DO
                  BEGIN
                        readln(stocks, barrels);
                        num_locks := num_locks + locks;
                        num_stocks := num_stocks + stocks;
                        num_barrels := num_barrels + barrels;
                        READ(locks);
                  END; {WHILE locks}
            readln;
            writeln('Sales for ',salesman);
            writeln('Locks sold: ', num_locks);
            writeln('Stocks sold: ', num_stocks);
            writeln('Barrels sold: ', num_barrels);
            sales := lock_price*num_locks + stock_price*num_stocks
                  + barrel_price * num_barrels;
            writeln('Total sales: ', sales:8:2);
            writeln;
            IF (sales > 1800.0)
            THEN  BEGIN
                        commission := 0.10 * 1000.0
                        commission := commission + 0.15 * 800.0
                        commission := commission + 0.20*(sales-1800.0)
                  END;
            ELSE IF (sales > 1000.0)
                  THEN  BEGIN
                              commission := 0.10 * 1000.0
                              commission := commission + 0.15 *
(sales - 1000.0)
                        END;
                  ELSE commission := 0.10 * sales;
      writeln('Commission is $',commission:6:2);
END;  {FOR salesman}
```

```
END.    {program Lock_Stock_and_Barrel}
PROGRAM Commission (INPUT,OUTPUT);
CONST
        lock_price = 45.0;
        stock_price = 30.0;
        barrel_price = 25.0;
TYPE
        STRING_30 = string[30]; {Salesman's Name}
VAR
        locks, stocks, barrels, num_locks, num_stocks,
        num_barrels, salesman_index, order_index : INTEGER;
        sales, commission : REAL;
        salesman : STRING_30;
BEGIN {program Commission}
writeln('Enter the number of locks, stocks, and barrels);
readln(locks,stocks, barrels);
sales := lock_price * num_locks + stock_price * num_stocks + barrel_price
* num_barrels;
writeln('Total sales: ', sales:8:2);
IF (sales > 1800.0)
THEN  BEGIN
              commission := 0.10 * 1000.0
              commission := commission + 0.15 * 800.0
              commission := commission + 0.20*(sales-1800.0)
      END;
ELSE  IF (sales > 1000.0)
      THEN  BEGIN
                    commission := 0.10 * 1000.0
                    commission := commission + 0.15 * (sales - 1000.0)
            END;
      ELSE commission := 0.10 * sales;
      writeln('Commission is $',commission:6:2);
END.    {program Commission}
```

2.4 THE SATM SYSTEM

To better discuss the issues of integration and sytem testing, we need an example with larger scope. The automated teller machine described here is a refinement of that in [Topper 93]; it contains an interesting variety of functionality and interactions. Although it typifies real-time systems, practitioners in the commercial EDP domain are finding that even traditional COBOL systems have many of the problems usually associated with real-time systems.

2.4.1 PROBLEM STATEMENT

The SATM system communicates with bank customers via the fifteen screens shown in Figure 2.4. Using a terminal with features as shown in Figure 2.3, SATM customers can select any of three transaction types: deposits, withdrawals, and balance inquiries, and these can be done on two types of accounts, checking and savings.

When a bank customer arrives at an SATM station, screen 1 is displayed. The bank customer accesses the SATM system with a plastic card encoded with a Personal Account Number (PAN), which is a key to an internal customer account file, containing, among other things, the customer's name and account information. If the customer's PAN matches the information in the customer account file, the system presents screen 2 to the customer. If the customer's PAN is not found, screen 4 is displayed, and the card is kept.

At screen 2, the customer is prompted to enter his/her Personal Identification Number (PIN). If the PIN is correct (i.e., matches the information in the customer account file), the system displays screen 5;

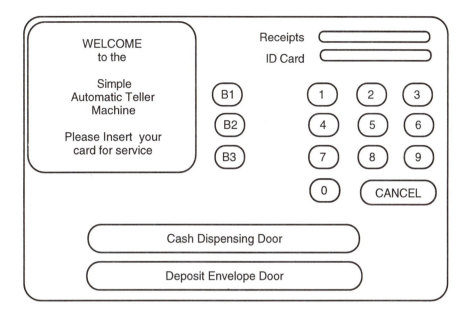

Figure 2.3 The SATM Terminal

otherwise, screen 3 is displayed. The customer has three chances to get the PIN correct; after three failures, screen 4 is displayed, and the card is kept.

On entry to screen 5, the system adds two pieces of information to the customer's account file: the current date, and an increment to the number of ATM sessions. The customer selects the desired transaction from the options shown on screen 5; then the system immediately displays screen 6, where the customer chooses the account to which the selected transaction will be applied.

If **balance** is requested, the system checks the local ATM file for any unposted transactions, and reconciles these with the beginning balance for that day from the customer account file. Screen 14 is then displayed.

If **deposit** is requested, the status of the Deposit Envelope slot is determined from a field in the Terminal Control File. If no problem is known, the system displays screen 7 to get the transaction amount. If there is a problem with the deposit envelope slot, the system displays screen 12. Once the deposit amount has been entered, the system displays screen 13, accepts the deposit envelope, and processes the deposit. The deposit amount is entered as an unposted amount in the local ATM file, and the count of deposits per month is incremented. Both of these (and other information) are processed by the Master ATM (centralized) system once per day. The system then displays screen 14.

If **withdrawal** is requested, the system checks the status (jammed or free) of the withdrawal chute in the Terminal Control File. If jammed, screen 10 is displayed, otherwise, screen 7 is displayed so the customer can enter the withdrawal amount. Once the withdrawal amount is entered, the system checks the Terminal Status File to see if it has enough money to dispense. If it does not, screen 9 is displayed; otherwise the withdrawal is processed. The system checks the customer balance (as described in the Balance request transaction), and if there are insufficient funds, screen 8 is displayed. If the account balance is sufficient, screen 11 is displayed, and the money is dispensed. The withdrawal amount is written to the unposted local ATM file, and the count of withdrawals per month in incremented. The balance is printed on the transaction receipt as it is for a balance request transaction. After the cash has been removed, the system displays screen 14.

When the No button is pressed in screens 10, 12, or 14, the system presents screen 15 and returns the customer's ATM card. Once the card is removed from the card slot, screen 1 is displayed. When the Yes button is pressed in screens 10, 12, or 14, the system presents screen 5 so the customer can select additional transactions.

2.4.2 DISCUSSION

There is a surprising amount of information "buried" in the system description just given. For instance, if you read it closely, you can infer that the terminal only contains ten dollar bills (see screen 7). This

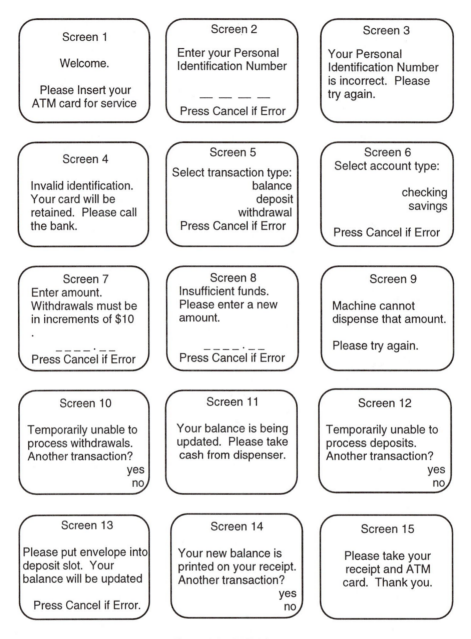

Figure 2.4 SATM Screens

textual definition is probably more precise than what is usually encountered in practice. The example is deliberately simple (hence the name).

A plethora of questions could be resolved by a list of assumptions. For example, is there a borrowing limit? What keeps a customer from taking out more than his actual balance if he goes to several ATM terminals? There are lots of "start up" questions: how much cash is initially in the machine? How are new customers added to the system? These, and other "real world" refinements, are eliminated to maintain simplicity.

2.5 SATURN WINDSHIELD WIPER CONTROLLER

The windshield wiper on the Saturn automobile (at least on the 1992 models) is controlled by a lever with a dial. The lever has four positions, OFF, INT (for intermittent), LOW, and HIGH, and the dial has three positions, numbered simply 1, 2, and 3. The dial positions indicate three intermittent speeds, and the dial position is relevant only when the lever is at the INT position. The decision table below shows the windshield wiper speeds (in wipes per minute) for the lever and dial positions.

Lever	OFF	INT	INT	INT	LOW	HIGH
Dial	n/a	1	2	3	n/a	n/a
Wiper	0	4	6	12	30	60

ACKNOWLEDGMENT

Mr. John Meyer, a graduate student at Grand Valley State University, provided the reference to resolve the question of whether or not the year 2000 is a leap year.

EXERCISES

1. Revisit the traditional Triangle Program flowchart in Figure 2.1. Can the variable match ever have the value of 4? Of 5? Is it ever possible to "execute" the following sequence of numbered boxes: 1, 2, 5, 6 ?
2. Recall the discussion from Chapter 1 about the relationship between the specification and the implementation of a program. If you study the implementation of NextDate carefully, you will see a problem. Look at the CASE clause for 30 day months (4, 6, 9, 11). There is no special action for day = 31. Discuss whether or not this implementation is "correct". Repeat this discussion for the treatment of values of day ≥ 29 in the CASE clause for February.
3. In Chapter 1, we mentioned that part of a test case is the expected output. What would you use as the expected output for a NextDate test case of June 31, 1812? Why?
4. One common addition to the Triangle Problem is to check for right triangles. Three sides constitute a right triangle if the Pythagorean Relationship is satisfied:

$$c^2 = a^2 + b^2$$

   This change makes it convenient to require that the sides be presented in increasing order, i.e., $a \leq b \leq c$. Extend the Triangle2 program to include thr right triangle feature. We will use this extension in the exercise sections in Parts II and III.
5. What will the triangle program do for the sides -3, -3, 5? Discuss this in terms of the considerations we made in Chapter 1.
6. The function YesterDate is the inverse of NextDate. Given a month, day, year, YesterDate returns the date of the day before. Develop a program (in your favorite programming language) for YesterDate. We will also use this as a continuing exercise.
7. Since the Gregorian calendar was instituted in 1582 a.d., calculate the first year in which the current leap year system will result in a full extra day.

Chapter 3

Discrete Math for Testers

More than any other life cycle activity, testing lends itself to mathematical description and analysis. In this chapter and in the next, testers will find the mathematics they need. Following the craftsperson metaphor, the mathematical topics presented here are tools, and a testing craftsperson should know how to use them well. With these tools, a tester gains rigor, precision, and efficiency—all of which improve testing. The "for testers" part of the chapter title is important: this chapter is written for testers who either have a sketchy math background or who have forgotten some of the basics. Serious mathematicians (or maybe just those who take themselves seriously) will likely be annoyed by the informal discussion here. If you are already comfortable with the topics in this chapter, skip to the next chapter and start right in on graph theory.

In general, discrete mathematics is more applicable to functional testing, while graph theory pertains more to structural testing. "Discrete" raises a question: what might be indiscreet about mathematics? The mathematical antonym is continuous, as in the calculus, which software developers (and testers) seldom use. Discrete math includes set theory, functions, relations, propositional logic, and probability theory, each of which is discussed here.

3.1 SET THEORY

How embarrassing to admit, after all the lofty expiation of rigor and precision, that there is no explicit definition of a set. This is really a nuisance, since set theory is central to these two chapters on math. At this point, mathematicians make an important distinction: naive versus axiomatic set theory. In naive set theory, a set is recognized as a primitive term, much like point and line are primitive concepts in geometry. Here are some synonyms for "set": collection, group, bunch, . . ., you get the idea. The important thing about a set is that it lets us refer to several things as a group, or whole. For example, we might wish to refer to the set of months that have exactly 30 days (we need this set when we test the NextDate function from Chapter 2). In set theory notation, we write

$$M1 = \{\text{April, June, September, November}\}$$

and we read this notation as "M1 is the set whose elements are the months April, June, September, November."

3.1.1 SET MEMBERSHIP

The items in a set are called *elements* or *members* of the set, and this relationship is denoted by the symbol $\in$. Thus we could write April $\in$ M1. When something is not a member of a set, we use the symbol $\notin$, so we might write December $\notin$ M1.

3.1.2 SET DEFINITION

There are three ways to define a set: by simply listing its elements, by giving a decision rule, or by constructing a set from other sets. The listing option works well for sets with just a few elements, and also for sets in which the elements obey an obvious pattern. We might define the set of years in the NextDate program as follows:

$$Y = \{ 1812, 1813, 1814, \ldots, 2011, 2012 \}$$

When we define a set by listing its elements, the order of the elements is irrelevant. We will see why when we discuss set equality. The decision rule approach is more complicated, and this complexity carries both advantages and penalties. We could define the years for NextDate as

$$Y = \{ \text{ year: } 1812 \leq \text{year} \leq 2012 \}$$

which reads "Y is the set of all years such that (the colon is "such that") the years are between 1812 and 2012 inclusive". When a decision rule is used to define a set, the rule must be unambiguous. Given any possible value of year, we can therefore determine whether or not that year is in our set Y.

The advantage of defining sets with decision rules is that the unambiguity requirement forces clarity. Experienced testers have encountered "untestable requirements". Many times, the reason that such requirements cannot be tested boils down to an ambiguous decision rule. In our Triangle Program, for example, suppose we defined a set

$$N = \{ \text{ t : t is a nearly equilateral triangle } \}$$

We might say that the triangle with sides (500, 500, 501) is an element of N, but how would we treat the triangles with sides (50, 50, 51) or (5, 5, 6)?

A second advantage of defining sets with decision rules is that we might be interested in sets whose elements are difficult to list. In the Lock, Stock, and Barrel problem, for example, we might be interested in the set

$$S = \{ \text{ sales : the 15\% commission rate applies to the sale } \}$$

We cannot easily write down the elements of this set, but given a particular value for sale, we can easily apply the decision rule.

The main disadvantage of decision rules is that they can become logically complex, particularly when they are expressed with the predicate calculus quantifiers $\exists$ ("there exists") and $\forall$ ("for all"). If everyone understands this notation, the precision is helpful; too often customers are overwhelmed by statements with these quantifiers. A second problem with decision rules has to do with self reference. This is interesting, but it really has very little application for testers. The problem arises when a decision rule refers to itself, which is a circularity. As an example, the Barber of Seville "is the man who shaves everyone who does not shave himself".

3.1.3 THE EMPTY SET

The empty set, denoted by the symbol $\varnothing$, occupies a special place in set theory. The empty set contains no elements. At this point, mathematicians will digress to prove a bunch of facts about empty sets:

- the empty set is unique, that is, there cannot be two empty sets. (We'll take their word for it.)
- $\varnothing$, $\{\varnothing\}$, $\{\{\varnothing\}\}$, .. are all different sets (we won't need this).

It is useful to note that when a set is defined by a decision rule that is always false, the set is empty. For instance,

$$\varnothing = \{ \text{ year : } 2012 \leq \text{year} \leq 1812 \}$$

3.1.4 VENN DIAGRAMS

Sets are commonly pictured by Venn Diagrams, as we did in Chapter 1, when we discussed sets of specified and programmed behaviors. In a Venn diagram, a set is depicted as a circle, and points in the interior of the circle correspond to elements of the set. Then we might draw our set M1 of 30-day months as in Figure 3.1.

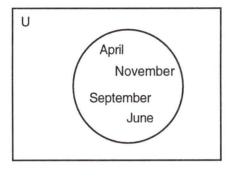

Figure 3.1   Venn Diagram of the Set of 30-day Months

Venn diagrams communicate various set relationships in an intuitive way, but there are some picky questions. What about finite versus infinite sets? Both can be drawn as Venn diagrams; in the case of finite sets we cannot assume that every interior point corresponds to a set element. We won't need to worry about this, but it is helpful to know the limitations. Sometimes we will find it helpful to label specific elements. Another sticky point has to do with the empty set. How do we show that a set, or maybe a portion of a set, is empty? The common answer is to shade empty regions, but this is often contradicted by other uses in which shading is used to highlight regions of interest. The best practice is to provide a legend that clarifies the intended meaning of shaded areas.

It is often helpful to think of all the sets in a discussion as being subsets of some larger set, known as the Universe of Discourse. We did this in Chapter 1 when we chose the set of all program behaviors as our universe of discourse. The universe of discourse can usually be guessed from given sets. In Figure 3.1, most people would take the universe of discourse to be the set of all months in a year. Testers should be aware that many times assumed universes of discourse are sources of confusion. As such, they constitute a subtle point of miscommunication between customers and developers.

3.1.5 SET OPERATIONS

Much of the expressive power of set theory comes from basic operations on sets: union, intersection, and complement. There are other handy operations: relative complement, symmetric difference, and Cartesian product. Each of these is defined next. In each of these definitions, we begin with two sets, A and B, contained in some universe of discourse U. The definitions use logical connectives from the propositional calculus: and ($\wedge$), or ($\vee$), exclusive or ($\oplus$), and not ($\neg$).

Definition
Given sets A and B,

- their ***union*** is the set $A \cup B = \{ x : x \in A \vee x \in B \}$
- their ***intersection*** is the set $A \cap B = \{ x : x \in A \wedge x \in B \}$
- the ***complement*** of A is the set $A' = \{ x : x \notin A \}$
- the ***relative complement*** of B with respect to A is the set
  $A - B = \{ x : x \in A \wedge x \notin B \}$
- the ***symmetric difference*** of A and B is the set $A \oplus B = \{ x : x \in A \oplus x \in B \}$

Venn diagrams for these sets are shown in Figure 3.2.

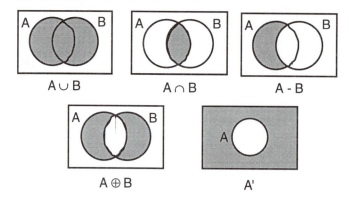

Figure 3.2 Venn Diagrams of Basic Sets

The intuitive expressive power of Venn diagrams is very useful for describing relationships among test cases and among items to be tested. Looking at the Venn diagrams in Figure 3.2, we might guess that

$$A \oplus B = (A \cup B) - (A \cap B).$$

This is the case, and we could prove it with propositional logic.

Venn diagrams are used elsewhere in software development: together with directed graphs, they are the basis of the StateCharts notation [Harel 88], which is among the most rigorous specification techniques supported by CASE technology. StateCharts are also the control notation chosen for the OMT object-oriented methodology [Rumbaugh 91].

The Cartesian product (also known as the cross product) of two sets is more complex; it depends on the notion of ordered pairs, which are two element sets in which the order of the elements is important. The usual notation for ordered and unordered pairs is:

$$\text{unordered pair:} \quad (a, b)$$
$$\text{ordered pair:} \quad < a, b >$$

The difference is that, for a ≠ b,

$$(a, b) = (b, a), \text{ but}$$
$$< a, b > \neq < b, a >$$

This distinction is important to the material in Chapter 4; as we shall see, the fundamental difference between ordinary and directed graphs is exactly the difference between unordered and ordered pairs.

Definition
The *Cartesian Product* of two sets A and B is the set A × B = {< x, y >:x ∈ A ∧ x ∈ B}.

Venn diagrams do not show Cartesian products, so we'll look at a short example. The Cartesian product of the sets A = { 1, 2, 3 } and B = { w, x, y, z } is the set

$$A \times B = \{ < 1, w >, < 1, x >, < 1, y >, < 1, z >, < 2, w >, < 2, x >,$$
$$< 2, y >, < 2, z >, < 3, w >, < 3, x >, < 3, y >, < 3, z >, \}$$

The Cartesian product has an intuitive connection with arithmetic. The cardinality of a set A is the number of elements in A, and is denoted by |A|. (Some authors prefer Card(A).) For sets A and B, |A×B| = |A| x |B|. When we study functional testing in Chapter 5, we will use the Cartesian product to describe test cases for programs with several input variables. The multiplicative property of the Cartesian product means that this form of testing generates a very large number of test cases.

3.1.6 SET RELATIONS

We use set operations to construct interesting new sets from existing sets. When we do, we often would like to know something about the way the new and the old sets are related. Given two sets, A and B, we define three fundamental set relationships:

Definition
A is a ***subset*** of B, written $A \subseteq B$, if and only if (iff) $a \in A \Rightarrow a \in B$,
A is a ***proper subset*** of B, written $A \subset B$, iff $A \subseteq B \land B - A \neq \emptyset$,
A and B are ***equal*** sets, written $A = B$, iff $A \subseteq B \land B \subseteq A$.

In plain English, set A is a subset of set B if every element of A is also an element of B. In order to be a proper subset of B, A must be a subset of B and there must be some element in B that is not an element of A. Finally, the sets A and B are equal if each is a subset of the other.

3.1.7 SET PARTITIONS

A partition of a set is a very special situation that is extremely important for testers. Partitions have several analogs in everyday life: we might put up partitions to partition an office area into individual offices (note the sloppiness of natural language here); we also encounter political partitions when a state is divided up into legislative districts. In both of these, notice that the sense of "partition" is to divide up a whole into pieces such that everything is in some piece, and nothing is left out. More formally:

Definition
Given a set B, and a set of subsets A1, A2, . . . , An of B, the subsets are a ***partition*** of B iff

1. $A1 \cup A2 \cup \ldots \cup An = B$, and
2. $i \neq j \Rightarrow Ai \cap Aj = \emptyset$

Since a partition is a set of subsets, we frequently refer to individual subsets as "elements of the partition".

The two parts of this definition are important for testers. The first part guarantees that every element of B is in some subset, while the second part guarantees that no element of B is in two of the subsets. This corresponds well with the legislative districts example: everyone is represented by some legislator, and nobody is represented by two legislators. A picture puzzle is another good example of a partition, in fact, Venn diagrams of partitions are often drawn like puzzles, as in Figure 3.3.

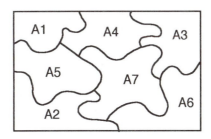

Figure 3.3 Venn Diagram of a Partition

Partitions are helpful to testers because the two definitional properties yield important assurances: completeness (everything is somewhere), and non-redundancy. When we study functional testing, we shall see that its inherent weakness is the vulnerability to both gaps and redundancies: some things may remain untested, while others are tested repeatedly. One of the problems centers on finding an appropriate partition. In the Triangle Program, for example, the universe of discourse is the set of all triplets of positive integers. (Note that this is actually a Cartesian product of the set of positive integers with itself three times.) We might partition this universe three ways:

- into triangles and non-triangles
- into equilateral, isosceles, scalene, and non-triangles
- into equilateral, isosceles, scalene, right, and non-triangles

At first, these partitions seem okay, but there is a problem with the last partition. The sets of scalene and right triangles are not disjoint (the triangle with sides 3,4,5 is a right triangle that is scalene.)

3.1.8 SET IDENTITIES

Set operations and relations, when taken together, yield an important class of set identities, which can be used to algebraically simplify complex set expressions. Math students usually have to derive all these; we'll just list them and (occasionally) use them.

Name	Expression
Identity Laws	$A \cup \varnothing = A$ $A \cap U = A$
Domination Laws	$A \cup U = U$ $A \cap \varnothing = \varnothing$
Idempotent Laws	$A \cup A = A$ $A \cap A = A$
Complementation Law	$(A')' = A$
Commutative Laws	$A \cup B = B \cup A$ $A \cap B = B \cap A$
Associative Laws	$A \cup (B \cup C) = (A \cup B) \cup C$ $A \cap (B \cap C) = (A \cap B) \cap C$
Distributive Laws	$A \cup (B \cap C) = (A \cup B) \cap (A \cup C)$ $A \cap (B \cup C) = (A \cap B) \cup (A \cap C)$
DeMorgan's Laws	$(A \cup B)' = A' \cap B'$ $(A \cap B)' = A' \cup B'$

3.2 FUNCTIONS

Functions are a central notion to software development and testing. The whole functional decomposition paradigm, for example, implicitly uses the mathematical notion of a function. We make this notion explicit here because all of functional testing is based on it.

Informally, a function associates elements of sets. In the NextDate program, for example, the function of a given date is the date of the following day, and in the triangle problem, the function of three input integers is the kind of triangle formed by sides with those lengths. In the Lock, Stock, and Barrel problem, the salesperson's commission is a function of sales, which in turn, is a function of the number of locks, stocks, and barrels sold. Functions in the ATM system are much more complex; not surprisingly, this will add complexity to the testing.

Any program can be thought of as a function that associates its outputs with its inputs. In the mathematical formulation of a function, the inputs are the domain and the outputs are the range of the function.

Definition

Given sets A and B, a *function* f is a subset of $A \times B$ such that, for a_i, $a_j \in A$, b_i, $b_j \in B$, and $f(a_i) = b_i$, $f(a_j) = b_j$, $b_i \neq b_j \Rightarrow a_i \neq a_j$.

Since formal definitions like the one above are notoriously terse, let's take a closer look. The inputs to the function f are elements of the set A, and the outputs of f are elements of B. What the definition says is that the function f is "well behaved" in the sense that an element in A is never associated with more than one element of B.

3.2.1 DOMAIN AND RANGE

In the definition just given, the set A is the *domain* of the function f, and the set B is the *range* . Because input and output have a "natural" order, it is an easy step to say that a function f is really a set of ordered pairs in which the first element is from the domain and the second element is from the range. Here are two common notations for function:

$$f: A \rightarrow B$$
$$f \subseteq A \times B$$

We haven't put any restrictions on the sets A and B is this definition. We could have A = B (as in the NextDate program), and A could be a Cartesian product of other sets (as in the Triangle program and the Lock, Stock, And Barrel program).

3.2.2 FUNCTION TYPES

Functions are further described by particulars of the mapping. In the definition below, we start with a function f: A $\rightarrow$ B , and we define the set

$$f(A) = \{ b_i \in B : b_i = f(a_i) \text{ for some } a_i \in A \}$$

This set is sometimes called the image of A under f.

Definition

- f is a function from A **onto** B iff f(A) = B,
- f is a function from A **into** B iff f(A) $\subset$ B, (note the proper subset here!)
- f is a **one-to-one** function from A to B iff, for all a_i , $a_j \in$ A, $a_i \neq a_j \Rightarrow f(a_i) \neq f(a_j)$.

Back to plain English, if f is a function from A onto B, we know that every element of B is associated with some element of A. If f is a function from A into B, we know that there is at least one element of B that is not associated with an element of A. Finally, one-to-one functions guarantee a form of uniqueness: distinct domain elements are never mapped to the same range element. (Notice this is the inverse of the "well behaved" attribute described earlier.) If a function is not one-to-one, it is many-to-one; that is, more than one domain element can be mapped to the same range element. In these terms, the "well-behaved" requirement prohibits functions from being one-to-many. Testers familiar with relational databases will recognize that all of these possibilities (one-to-one, one-to-many, many-to-one, and many-to-many are allowed for relations).

Referring again to our testing examples, suppose we take A, B, and C to be sets of dates for the NextDate program, where

$$A = \{ \text{ date : 1 January 1812} \leq \text{date} \leq \text{31 December 2012}\}$$
$$B = \{ \text{ date : 2 January 1812} \leq \text{date} \leq \text{1 January 2013}\}$$
$$C = A \cup B$$

Now   NextDate: A $\rightarrow$ B is a one-to-one, onto function,
and   NextDate: A $\rightarrow$ C is a one-to-one, into function.

It makes no sense for NextDate to be many-to-one, but it is easy to see how the Triangle problem can be many-to-one. When a function is one-to-one and onto, such as NextDate: A $\rightarrow$ B above, each element of the domain corresponds to exactly one element of the range, and conversely, each element of the range corresponds to exactly one element of the domain. When this happens, it is always possible to find an inverse function (see the YesterDate problem in Chapter 2) that is one-to-one from the range back to the domain.

All of this is important for testing. The into versus onto distinction has implications for domain and range based functional testing, and one-to-one functions require much more testing than many-to-one functions.

3.2.3 FUNCTION COMPOSITION

Suppose we have sets and functions such that the range of one is the domain of the next:

$$f : A \rightarrow B$$
$$g : B \rightarrow C$$
$$h : C \rightarrow D$$

When this occurs, we can compose the functions. To do this, let's refer to specific elements of the domain and range sets a $\in$ A, b $\in$ B, c $\in$ C, d $\in$ D, and suppose that f(a) = b, g(b) = c, and h(c) = d. Now the composition of functions h, g, and f is:

$$h \circ g \circ f(a) = h(g(f(a)))$$
$$= h(g(b))$$
$$= h(c)$$
$$= d$$

Function composition is a very common practice in software development; it is inherent on the process of defining procedures and subroutines. We have an example of it in the Lock, Stock, and Barrel program, in which

f1(telegram) = (locks, stocks, barrels)
f2((locks, stocks, barrels)) = sales
f3(sales) = commission

Composed chains of functions can be problematic for testers, particularly when the range of one function is a proper subset of the domain of the "next" function in the chain. Figure 3.4 shows how this can happen in a program defined by a dataflow diagram.

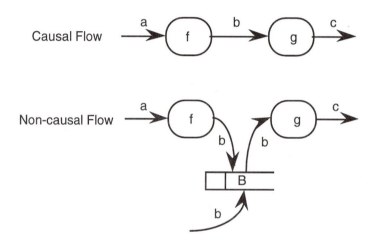

Figure 3.4   Causal and Non-causal Flows in a Dataflow Diagram

In the causal flow, the composition g ∘ f(a) (which we know to be g(b), which yields c) is a rather assembly-line like process. In the non-causal flow, the possibility of more than one source of b values for the datastore B raises two problems for testers. Multiple sources of b values might raise problems of domain/range compatibility, and even if this is not a problem, there might be timing anomalies with respect to b values. (What if g used an "old" b value?)

There is a special case of composition that helps testers in a curious way. Recall we discussed how one-to-one onto functions always have an inverse function. It turns out that this inverse function is unique and is guaranteed to exist (again, the math folks would prove this). If f is a one-to-one function from A onto B, we denote its unique inverse by f^{-1}. It turns out that for a ∈ A and b ∈ B, $f^{-1} \circ f(a) = a$ and f ∘ $f^{-1}(b) = b$. The NextDate and YesterDate programs are such inverses. The way this helps testers is that, for a given function, its inverse acts as a "cross-check", and this can often expedite the identification of functional test cases.

3.3 RELATIONS

Functions are a special case of a relation: both are subsets of some Cartesian product, but in the case of functions, we have the "well-behaved" requirement that says that a domain element cannot be associated with more than one range element. This is borne out in everyday usage: when we say something "is a function" of something else, our intent is that there is a deterministic relationship present. Not all relationships are strictly functional. Consider the mapping between a set of patients and a set of physicians. One patient may be treated by several physicians, and one physician may treat several patients, a many-to-many mapping.

3.3.1 RELATIONS AMONG SETS
Let's start with a definition.

Definition
Given two sets A and B, a **relation** R is a subset of the Cartesian product A × B.

Two notations are popular; when we wish to speak about the entire relation, we usually just write R $\subseteq$ A × B; for specific elements $a_i \in$ A , $b_i \in$ B , we write a_i R b_i. Most math texts omit treatment of relations; we are interested in them because they are essential to both data modeling and object-oriented analysis.

Next, we have to explain an overloaded term — cardinality. Recall that as it applies to sets, cardinality refers to the number of elements in a set. Since a relation is also a set, we might expect that the cardinality of a relation refers to how many ordered pairs are in the set R $\subseteq$ A × B . Unfortunately, this is not the case.

Definition
Given two sets A and B, a relation R $\subseteq$ A × B, the **cardinality** of relation R is:

- **one-to-one** iff R is a one-to-one function from A to B,
- **many-to-one** iff R is a many-to-one function from A to B,
- **one-to-many** iff at least one element a $\in$ A is in two ordered pairs in R, that is (a, b_i) $\in$ R and (a, b_j) $\in$ R,
- **many-to-many** iff at least one element a $\in$ A is in two ordered pairs in R, that is (a, b_i) $\in$ R and (a, b_j) $\in$ R . and at least one element b $\in$ B is in two ordered pairs in R, that is (a_i , b) $\in$ R and (a_j , b) $\in$ R.

The distinction between functions into and onto their range has an analog in relations — the notion of participation.

Definition
Given two sets A and B, a relation R $\subseteq$ A × B, the **participation** of relation R is:

- **total** iff every element of A is in some ordered pair in R,
- **partial** iff some element of A is not in some ordered pair in R,
- **onto** iff every element of B is in some ordered pair in R,
- **into** iff some element of B is not in some ordered pair in R.

In plain English, a relation is total if it applies to every element of A, and partial if it does not apply to every element. Another term for this distinction is *mandatory* versus *optional* participation. Similarly, a relation is onto if it applies to every element of B, and into if it does not. The parallelism between total/ partial and onto/into is curious, and deserves special mention here. From the standpoint of relational database theory, there is no reason for this; in fact, there is a compelling reason to avoid this distinction. Data modeling is essentially declarative, while process modeling is essentially imperative. The parallel sets of terms force a direction on relations, when in fact there is no need for the directionality. Part of this is a likely holdover from the fact that Cartesian products consist of ordered pairs, which clearly have a first and second element.

So far, we have only considered relations between two sets. Extending relations to three or more sets is more complicated than simply the Cartesian product. Suppose, for example, we had three sets, A, B, and C, and a relation R $\subseteq$ A × B × C. Do we intend the relation to be strictly among three elements, or is it between one element and an ordered pair (there would be three possibilities here)? This line of thinking also needs to be applied to the definitions of cardinality and participation. It is straightforward for participation, but cardinality is essentially a binary property. (Suppose, for example the relation is one-to-one from A to B, and is many-to-one from A to C.) We discussed a three-way relation in Chapter 1, when we examined the relationships among specified, implemented, and tested program behaviors. We would like to have some form of totality between test cases and specification-implementation pairs; we will revisit this when we study functional and structural testing.

Testers need to be concerned with the definitions of relations because they bear directly on software properties to be tested. The onto/into distinction, for example, bears directly on what we will call output based functional testing. The mandatory-optional distinction is the essence of exception handling, which also has implications for testers.

3.3.2 RELATIONS ON A SINGLE SET

There are two important mathematical relations that are both defined on a single set: ordering relations and equivalence relations. Both are defined with respect to specific properties of relations.

Let A be a set, and let $R \subseteq A \times A$ be a relation defined on A, with <a,a>, <a,b>, <b,a>, <b,c>, and <a, c> ∈ R . There are four special attributes of relations:

Definition
A relation $R \subseteq A \times A$ is

- *reflexive* iff for all a ∈ A , <a, a> ∈ R,
- *symmetric* iff <a, b> ∈ R ⇒ <b, a> ∈ R,
- *anti-symmetric* <a, b>, <b, a> ∈ R ⇒ a=b,
- *transitive* iff <a, b>, <b, c> ∈ R ⇒ <a, c> ∈ R.

Family relationships are nice examples of these properties. You might want to think about the following relationships, and decide for yourself which attributes apply: brother of, sibling of, ancestor of. Now we can define the two important relations.

Definition
A relation $R \subseteq A \times A$ is an *ordering relation* if R is reflexive, anti-symmetric, and transitive.

Ordering relations have a sense of direction; some common ordering relations are Older than, ≥, ⇒, and Ancestor of. (The reflexive part usually requires some fudging—we really should say Not Younger Than and Not a Descendant of.) Ordering relations are a common occurrence in software: data access techniques, hashing codes, tree structures, and arrays are all situations where ordering relations are used.

The power set of a given set is the set of all subsets of the given set. The power set of the set A is denoted P(A). The subset relation ⊆ is an ordering relation on P(A), because it is reflexive (any set is trivially a subset of itself), it is anti-symmetric (the definition of set equality), and it is transitive.

Definition
A relation $R \subseteq A \times A$ is an *equivalence relation* if R is reflexive, symmetric, and transitive.

Mathematics is full of equivalence relations: equality and congruence are two quick examples. There is a very important connection between equivalence relations and partitions of a set. Suppose we have some partition A1, A2, . . . , An of a set B, and we say that two elements b1 and b2 of B are related (i.e., b1 R b2) if b1 and b2 are in the same partition element. This relation is reflexive (any element is in its own partition), it is symmetric (if b1 and b2 are in a partition element, then b2 and b1 are), and it is transitive (if b1 and b2 are in the same set, and if b2 and b3 are in the same set, then b1 and b3 are in the same set). The relation defined from the partition is called the equivalence relation *induced by* the partition. The converse process works in the same way. If we start with an equivalence relation defined on a set, we can define a subsets according to elements that are related to each other. This turns out to be a partition, and is called the partition *induced by* the equivalence relation. The sets in this partition are known as *equivalence classes* . The end result is that partitions and equivalence relations are interchangeable, and this becomes a powerful concept for testers. Recall that the two properties of a partition are notions of completeness and non-redundancy. When translated into testing situations, these notions allow testers to make powerful, absolute statements about the extent to which a software item has been tested. In addition, great efficiency follows from testing just one element of an equivalence class, and assuming that the remaining elements would behave similarly.

3.4 PROPOSITIONAL LOGIC

We have already been using propositional logic notation; if you were perplexed by this usage before definition, you're not alone. Set theory and propositional logic have a chicken and egg relationship — it's hard to decide which should be discussed first. Just as sets are taken as primitive terms, and are therefore not defined, we take propositions to be primitive terms. A proposition is a sentence that is either true or false, and we call these the truth values of the proposition. Furthermore, propositions are unambiguous: given a proposition, it is always possible to tell whether it is true or false. The sentence "Mathematics is difficult" wouldn't qualify as a proposition because of the ambiguity. We usually denote propositions with lower case letters p, q, and r. Propositional logic has operations, expressions, and identities that are very similar to (in fact they are isomorphic) set theory.

3.4.1 LOGICAL OPERATORS

Logical operators (also known as logical connectives or operations) are defined in terms of their effect on the truth values of the propositions to which they are applied. This is easy, since there are only two values: T (for true) and F (for false). Arithmetic operators could also be defined this way, (in fact that is how they are taught to children) but the tables become too large. The three basic logical operators are and ($\wedge$), or ($\vee$), and not ($\neg$); these are sometimes called conjunction, disjunction, and negation. Negation is the only unary (one operand) logical operator; the others are all binary.

p	q	p $\wedge$ q	p $\vee$ q	$\neg$ p
T	T	T	T	F
T	F	F	T	F
F	T	F	T	T
F	F	F	F	T

Conjunction and disjunction are familiar in everyday life: a conjunction is true only when all components are true, and a disjunction is true if at least one component is true. Negations also behaves as we expect. There are two other common connectives, exclusive or ($\oplus$) and if-then ($\rightarrow$); they are defined as follows:

p	q	p $\oplus$ q	p $\rightarrow$ q
T	T	F	T
T	F	T	F
F	T	T	T
F	F	F	T

An exclusive-or is true only when one of the propositions is true, while a disjunction (or inclusive or) is true also when both propositions are true. The if-then connective usually causes the most difficulty. The easy view is that this is just a definition, but since the other connectives all transfer nicely to natural language, we have similar expectations for if-then. The quick answer is that the if-then connective is closely related to the process of deduction: in a valid deductive syllogism, we can say "if premises, then conclusion" and the if-then statement will be a tautology.

3.4.2 LOGICAL EXPRESSIONS

We use logical operators to build logical expressions in exactly the same way that we use arithmetic operators to build algebraic expressions. We can specify the order in which operators are applied with the usual conventions on parentheses, or we can employ a precedence order (negation first, then conjunction followed by disjunction). Given a logical expression, we can always find its truth table by "building up" to it following the order determined by the parentheses. For example, the expression $\neg((p \rightarrow q) \wedge (q \rightarrow p))$ has the following truth table:

p	q	p $\rightarrow$ q	q $\rightarrow$ p	(p$\rightarrow$q)$\wedge$((q$\rightarrow$p)	$\neg$((p$\rightarrow$q)$\wedge$((q$\rightarrow$p))
T	T	T	T	T	F
T	F	F	T	F	T
F	T	T	F	F	T
F	F	T	T	T	F

3.4.3 LOGICAL EQUIVALENCE

The notions of arithmetic equality and identical sets have analogs in propositional logic. Notice that the expressions $\neg((p \rightarrow q) \wedge (q \rightarrow p))$ and $p \oplus q$ have identical truth tables. This means that, no matter what truth values are given to the base propositions p and q, these expressions will always have the same truth value. There are several ways to define this property, we use the simplest.

Definition
Two propositions p and q are *logically equivalent* (denoted p$\Leftrightarrow$q) iff their truth tables are identical.

By the way, the curious "iff" abbreviation we have been using for "if and only if" is sometimes called the bi-conditional, so the proposition p iff q is really $(p \rightarrow q) \wedge (q \rightarrow p)$, which is denoted $p \leftrightarrow q$.

Definition

A proposition that is always true is a **_tautology_**; a proposition that is always false is a **_contradiction_**.

In order to be a tautology or a contradiction, a proposition must contain at least one connective and two or more primitive propositions. We sometimes denote a tautology as a proposition T, and a contradiction as a proposition F. We can now state several laws that are direct analogs of the ones we had for sets.

Law	Expression
Identity	$p \wedge T \Leftrightarrow p$ $p \vee F \Leftrightarrow p$
Domination	$p \vee T \Leftrightarrow T$ $p \wedge F \Leftrightarrow F$
Idempotent	$p \wedge p \Leftrightarrow p$ $p \vee p \Leftrightarrow p$
Complementation	$\neg(\neg p) \Leftrightarrow p$
Commutative	$p \wedge q \Leftrightarrow q \wedge p$ $p \vee q \Leftrightarrow q \vee p$
Associative	$p \wedge (q \wedge r) \Leftrightarrow (p \wedge q) \wedge r$ $p \vee (q \vee r) \Leftrightarrow (p \vee q) \vee r$
Distributive	$p \wedge (q \vee r) \Leftrightarrow (p \wedge q) \vee (p \wedge r)$ $p \vee (q \wedge r) \Leftrightarrow (p \vee q) \wedge (p \vee r)$
DeMorgan's	$\neg(p \wedge q) \Leftrightarrow \neg p \vee \neg q$ $\neg(p \vee q) \Leftrightarrow \neg p \wedge \neg q$

3.5 PROBABILITY THEORY

We will have two occasions to use probability theory in our study of software testing: one deals with the probability that a particular path of statements executes, and the other generalizes this to a popular industrial concept called an "operational profile" (see chapter 14). Because of this limited use, we'll only cover the rudiments here.

As with both set theory and propositional logic, we start out with a primitive concept — the probability of an event. Here is the definition provided by a contemporary textbook [Rosen 91]: "The probability of an event E, which is a subset of a finite sample space S of equally likely outcomes, is $p(E) = |E| / |S|$." This definition hinges on the idea of an experiment that results in an outcome, the sample space is the set of all possible outcomes, and an event is a subset of outcomes. This definition is circular: what are "equally likely" outcomes? We assume these have equal probabilities, but then probability is defined in terms of itself.

The French mathematical Laplace had a reasonable working definition of probability two centuries ago. To paraphrase it, the probability that something occurs is the number of favorable ways it can occur divided by the total number of ways (favorable and unfavorable). Laplace's definition works well when we are concerned with drawing colored marbles out of a bag (probability folks are unusually concerned with their marbles, maybe there's a lesson here), but it doesn't extend well to situations in which it's hard to enumerate the various possibilities.

We will use our (refurbished) capabilities in set theory and propositional logic to arrive at a more cohesive formulation. As testers, we will be concerned with things that happen; we'll call these events, and say that the set of all events is our Universe of Discourse. Next, we will devise propositions about events, such that the propositions refer to elements in the universe of discourse. Now, for some universe U and some proposition p about elements of U, we make a definition:

Definition

The *truth set* T of a proposition p, written T(p), is the set of all elements in the universe U for which p is true.

Since propositions are either true or false, a proposition p divides the universe of discourse into two sets, T(p) and (T(p))', where T(p) $\cup$ (T(p))' = U. Notice that (T(p))' is the same as T($\neg$p). Truth sets facilitate a clear mapping among set theory, propositional logic, and probability theory.

Definition

The *probability* that a proposition p is true, denoted Pr(p), is |T(p)| / |U|.

With this definition, Laplace's "number of favorable ways" becomes the cardinality of the truth set T(p), and the total number of ways becomes the cardinality of the universe of discourse. This forces one more connection: since the truth set of a tautology is the universe of discourse, and the truth set of a contradiction is the empty set, the probabilities of $\varnothing$ and U are, respectively, 0 and 1.

The NextDate problem is a good source of examples. Consider the month variable, and the proposition

$$p(m): \text{m is a 30-day month}$$

The universe of discourse is the set U = {Jan., Feb., .. , Dec.}, and the truth set of p(m) is the set

$$T(p(m)) = \{\text{Apr., June, Sept., Nov.}\}$$

Now, the probability that a given month is a 30-day month is

$$Pr(p(m) = |T(p(m))|/|U| = 4/12.$$

There's a subtlety in the role of the universe of discourse; this is part of the craft of using probability theory in testing — choosing the right universe. Suppose we want to know the probability that a month is February. The quick answer: 1/12. Now, suppose we wan the probability of a month with exactly 29 days. Less easy — we need a universe that includes both leap years and non-leap years. We could use congruence arithmetic, and choose a universe that consists of months in a period of four consecutive years, say 1991, 1992, 1993, and 1994. This universe would contain 48 "months", and in this universe, the probability of a 29-day month is 1/48. Another possibility would be to use the full two century range of the NextDate program, in which the year 2000 is not a leap year. This would slightly reduce the probability of a 29-day month. One conclusion: getting the right universe is important. A bigger conclusion: it's even more important to avoid "shifting universes".

Here are some facts about probabilities that we will use without proof. They refer to a given universe, propositions p and q, with truth sets T(p) and T(q).

1. Pr($\neg$p) = 1 - Pr(p)
2. Pr(p $\wedge$ q) = Pr(p) x Pr(q)
3. Pr(p $\vee$ q) = Pr(p) + Pr(q) - Pr(p $\wedge$ q)

These facts, together with the tables of set theory and propositional identities, provide a strong algebraic capability to manipulate probability expressions.

EXERCISES

1. There is a very deep connection (an isomorphism) between set operations and the logical connectives in the propositional logic.

Operation	Propositional Logic	Set Theory
disjunction	Or	Union
conjunction	And	Intersection
negation	Not	Complement
	Exclusive Or	Symmetric Difference

    a. Express $A \oplus B$ in words.

    b. Express $(A \cup B) - (A \cap B)$ in words.

    c. Convince yourself that $A \oplus B$ and $(A \cup B) - (A \cap B)$ are the same set.

    d. Is it true that $A \oplus B = (A - B) \cup (B - A)$?

    e. What name would you give to the blank entry in the table above?

2. In many parts of the US, real estate taxes are levied by different taxing bodies, for example, a school district, a fire protection district, a township, and so on. Discuss whether these taxing bodies form a partition of a state.

4

Graph Theory for Testers

Graph theory is a branch of topology, which is sometimes referred to as "rubber sheet geometry". Curious, because the rubber sheet parts of topology have little to do with graph theory; furthermore, the graphs in graph theory do not involve axes, scales, points and curves as you might expect. Whatever the origin of the term, graph theory is probably the most useful part of mathematics for computer science — far more useful than the calculus — yet it is not commonly taught. Our excursion into graph theory will follow a "pure math" spirit: definitions are as devoid of specific interpretations as possible. Postponing interpretations results in maximum latitude in interpretations later, much like well-defined abstract data types promote re-use.

There are two basic kinds of graphs, undirected and directed. Since the latter are a special case of the former, we begin with undirected graphs. This will allow us to inherit many concepts when we get to directed graphs.

4.1 GRAPHS

A graph (also known as a linear graph) is an abstract mathematical structure defined from two sets, a set of nodes and a set of edges that form connections between nodes. A computer network is a fine example of a graph. More formally,

Definition
A *graph* G = (V, E) is composed of a finite (and non-empty) set $V = \{n_1, n_2, \ldots, n_m\}$ of nodes, and a set $E = \{e_1, e_2, \ldots, e_p\}$ of edges, where each edge $e_k = \{n_i, n_j\}$ for some nodes $n_i, n_j \in V$.

Recall from chapter 3 that the set $\{n_i, n_j\}$ is an unordered pair, which we sometimes write as (n_i, n_j). Nodes are sometimes called vertices, edges are sometimes called arcs, and we sometimes call nodes the endpoints of an arc. The common visual form of a graph shows nodes as circles, and edges as lines connecting pairs of nodes, as in Figure 4.1. We will use this figure as a continuing example, so take a minute to become familiar with it.

In the graph in Figure 4.1 the node and edge sets are:

$$V = \{ n_1, n_2, n_3, n_4, n_5, n_6, n_7\}$$
$$E = \{ e_1, e_2, e_3, e_4, e_5\}$$
$$= \{(n_1, n_2), (n_1, n_4), (n_3, n_4), (n_2, n_5), (n_4, n_6)\}$$

To define a particular graph, we must first define a set of nodes, and then define a set of edges between pairs of nodes. We will usually think of nodes as program statements, and we will have various kinds of edges, representing, for instance, flow of control or define/use relationships.

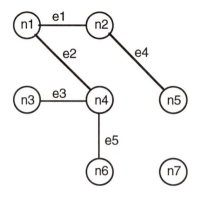

Figure 4.1   A Graph with Seven Nodes and Five Edges.

4.1.1 DEGREE OF A NODE

Definition

The *degree of a node* in a graph is the number of edges that have that node as an endpoint. We write deg(n) for the degree of node n.

We might say that the degree of a node indicates its "popularity" in a graph. In fact, social scientists use graphs to describe social interactions, in which nodes are people, edges often refer to things like "friendship", "communicates with", and so on. If we make a graph in which objects are nodes and edges are messages, the degree of a node (object) indicates the extent of integration testing that is appropriate for the object.

The degrees of the nodes in Figure 4.1 are:

$$deg(n_1) = 2$$
$$deg(n_2) = 2$$
$$deg(n_3) = 1$$
$$deg(n_4) = 3$$
$$deg(n_5) = 1$$
$$deg(n_6) = 1$$
$$deg(n_7) = 0$$

4.1.2 INCIDENCE MATRICES

Graphs need not be represented pictorially — they can be fully represented in an incidence matrix. This concept becomes very useful for testers, so we will formalize it here. When graphs are given a specific interpretation, the incidence matrix always provides useful information for the new interpretation.

Definition

The *incidence matrix* of a graph G = (V, E) with m nodes and n edges is an m x n matrix, where the element in row i, column j is a 1 if and only if node i is an endpoint of edge j, otherwise the element is 0.

The incidence matrix of the graph in Figure 4.1 is:

	e_1	e_2	e_3	e_4	e_5
n_1	1	1	0	0	0
n_2	1	0	0	1	0
n_3	0	0	1	0	0
n_4	0	1	1	0	1
n_5	0	0	0	1	0
n_6	0	0	0	0	1
n_7	0	0	0	0	0

We can make some observations about a graph by examining its incidence matrix. First, notice that the sum of the entries in any column is 2; that's because every edge has exactly two endpoints. If a column sum in an incidence matrix is ever something other than 2, there's a mistake somewhere. Thus forming column sums is a form of integrity checking similar in spirit to that of parity checks. Next, we see that the row sum is the degree of the node. When the degree of a node is zero, as it is for node n_7, we say the node is isolated. (This might correspond to unreachable code, or to objects that are included but never used.)

4.1.3 ADJACENCY MATRICES

The adjacency matrix of a graph is a useful supplement to the incidence matrix. Because adjacency matrices deal with connections, they are the basis of many later graph theory concepts.

Definition
The *adjacency matrix* of a graph $G = (V, E)$ with m nodes is an m x m matrix, where the element in row i, column j is a 1 if and only if there is an edge between node i and node j, otherwise the element is 0.

The adjacency matrix is symmetric (element i,j always equals element j,i), and a row sum is the degree of the node (as it was in the incidence matrix).

The adjacency matrix of the graph in Figure 4.1 is:

	n1	n2	n3	n4	n5	n6	n7
n_1	0	1	0	1	0	0	0
n_2	1	0	0	0	1	0	0
n_3	0	0	0	1	0	0	0
n_4	1	0	1	0	0	1	0
n_5	0	1	0	0	0	0	0
n_6	0	0	0	1	0	0	0
n_7	0	0	0	0	0	0	0

4.1.4 PATHS

As a preview of how we will use graph theory, the structural approaches to testing (see Part III) all center on types of paths in a program. Here we define (interpretation free) paths in a graph.

Definition
A *path* is a sequence of edges such that, for any adjacent pair of edges e_i, e_j in the sequence, the edges share a common (node) endpoint.

Paths can be described either as sequences of edges, or as sequences of nodes; the node sequence choice is more common.

Here are some paths in the graph in Figure 4.1:

Path	Node Sequence	Edge Sequence
between n_1 and n_5	n_1, n_2 , n_5	e_1, e_4
between n_6 and n_5	$n_6, n_4 , n_1 , n_2, n_5$	e_5, e_2 , e_1 , e_4
between n_3 and n_2	n_3, n_4 , n_1 , n_2	e_3 , e_2 , e_1
between n_1 and n_5	n_1, n_2 , n_5	e_1, e_4

Paths can be generated directly from the adjacency matrix of a graph using a binary form of matrix multiplication and addition. In our continuing example, edge e_1 is between nodes n_1 and n_2, and edge e_4 is between nodes n_2 and n_5. In the product of the adjacency matrix with itself, the element in position (1, 2) forms a product with the element in position (2, 5), yielding an element in position (1, 5), which corresponds to the two-edge path between n_1 and n_5. If we multiplied the product matrix by the original adjacency matrix again, we would get all three edge paths, and so on. At this point, the pure math folks go into a long digression to determine the length of the longest path in a graph; we won't bother. Instead, we focus our interest on the fact that paths connect "distant" parts of a graph.

The graph in Figure 4.1 predisposes a problem. It is not completely general, since it doesn't show all the situations that might occur in a graph. In particular, there are no paths in which a node occurs twice in the path. If it did, the path would be a loop (or circuit). We could create a circuit by adding an edge between nodes n_3 and n_6.

4.1.5 CONNECTEDNESS

Paths let us speak about nodes that are connected; this leads to a powerful simplification device that is very important for testers.

Definition
Nodes n_i and n_j are **connected** if and only if they are in the same path.

"Connectedness" is an equivalence relation (see Chapter 3) on the node set of a graph. To see this, we can check the three defining properties of equivalence relations:

1. Connectedness is reflexive, because every node is obviously in a path of length 0 with itself.
2. Connectedness is symmetric, because if nodes n_i and n_j are in a path, then nodes n_j and n_i are in the same path.
3. Connectedness is transitive (see the discussion of adjacency matrix multiplication for paths of length 2).

Since equivalence relations induce a partition (see Chapter 3 if you need a reminder), we are guaranteed that connectedness defines a partition on the node set of a graph. This permits the definition of components of a graph:

Definition
A **component** of a graph is a maximal set of connected nodes.

Nodes in the equivalence classes are components of the graph. The classes are maximal due to the transitivity part of the equivalence relation. There are two components in the graph in Figure 4.1: $\{n_1, n_2, n_3, n_4, n_5, n_6\}$ and $\{n_7\}$.

4.1.6 CONDENSATION GRAPHS

We are finally in a position to formalize an important simplification mechanism for testers.

Definition
Given a graph $G = (V, E)$, its **condensation graph** is formed by replacing each component by a condensing node.

Developing the condensation graph of a given graph is an unambiguous (i.e., algorithmic) process. We use the adjacency matrix to identify path connectivity, and then use the equivalence relation to identify components. The absolute nature of this process is important: the condensation graph of a given graph is unique. This implies that the resulting simplification represents an important aspect of the original graph. The components in our continuing example are $S_1 = \{ n_1, n_2, n_3, n_4, n_5, n_6 \}$ and $S_2 = \{ n_7 \}$.

There can be no edges in a condensation graph of an ordinary (undirected) graph. Two reasons why:

1. Edges have individual nodes as endpoints, not sets of nodes. (Here we can finally use the distinction between n_7 and $\{ n_7 \}$.)
2. Even if we fudge the definition of edge to ignore this distinction, a possible edge would mean that nodes from two different components were connected, hence in a path, hence in the same (maximal!) component.

The implication for testing is that components are independent in an important way, thus they can be tested separately.

4.1.7 CYCLOMATIC NUMBER

There is another property of graphs that has deep implications for testing: cyclomatic complexity.

Definition
The **cyclomatic number of a graph** G is given by $V(G) = e - n + p$,
where:

- e is the number of edges in G,
- n is the number of nodes in G, and
- p is the number of components in G.

V(G) is the number of distinct regions in a graph. One formulation of structural testing postulates the notion of basis paths in a program, from which all other paths can be derived, and shows that the cyclomatic number of the program graph (see the end of this chapter) is the number of these basis elements.

The cyclomatic number of our example graph is V(G) = 5 - 7 + 2 = 0. When we use cyclomatic complexity in testing, we will (usually) have strongly connected graphs; this will generate graphs with larger cyclomatic complexity.

4.2 DIRECTED GRAPHS

Directed graphs are a slight refinement to ordinary graphs: edges acquire a sense of direction. Symbolically, the unordered pairs (n_i, n_j) become ordered pairs $<n_i, n_j>$, and we speak of a directed edge going from node n_i to n_j, rather than being between the nodes.

Definition
A *directed graph* (or digraph) D = (V, E) consists of a finite set V = $\{n_1, n_2, ...,n_m \}$ of nodes , and a set E = $\{e_1, e_2,...,e_p \}$ of edges, where each edge $e_k = <n_i, n_j>$ is an ordered pair of nodes $n_i, n_j \in$ V.

In the directed edge $e_k = <n_i, n_j >$, n_i is the initial (or start) node, and n_j is the terminal (or finish) node. Edges in directed graphs fit naturally with many software concepts: sequential behavior, imperative programming languages, time-ordered events, define/reference pairings, messages, function and procedure calls, and so on. Given this, you might ask why we spent (wasted?) so much time on ordinary graphs. The difference between ordinary and directed graphs is very analogous to the difference between declarative and imperative programming languages. In imperative languages (e.g., COBOL, FORTRAN, Pascal, C, Ada) the sequential order of source language statements determines the execution time order of compiled code. This is not true for declarative languages (such as Prologue). The most common declarative situation for most software developers is Entity/Relationship modeling. In an E/R model, we choose entities as nodes, and identify relationships as edges. (If a relationship involves three or more entities, we need the notion of a "hyper-edge" that has three or more endpoints.) The resulting graph of an E/R model is more properly interpreted as an ordinary graph. Good E/R modeling practice suppresses the sequential thinking that directed graphs would promote.

When testing a program written in a declarative language, the only concepts available to the tester are those that follow from ordinary graphs. Fortunately, most software is developed in imperative languages, so testers usually have the full power of directed graphs at their disposal.

The next series of definitions roughly parallels the ones for ordinary graphs. We modify our now familiar continuing example to the one shown in Figure 4.2.

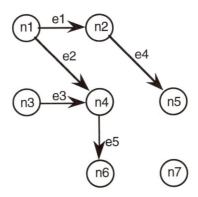

Figure 4.2 A Directed Graph

We have the same node set V = $\{ n_1, n_2, n_3, n_4, n_5, n_6, n_7\}$, and the edge set appears to be the same: E = $\{e_1, e_2, e_3, e_4, e_5\}$. The difference is that the edges are now ordered pairs of nodes in V.

$$E = \{<n_1, n_2>, <n_1, n_4>, <n_3, n_4>, <n_2, n_5>, <n_4, n_6>\}$$

4.2.1 INDEGREES AND OUTDEGREES

The degree of a node in an ordinary graph is refined to reflect direction, as follows.

Definition

The **indegree of a node** in a directed graph is the number of distinct edges that have the node as a terminal node. We write indeg(n) for the indegree of node n.

The **outdegree of a node** in a directed graph is the number of distinct edges that have the node as an start point. We write outdeg(n) for the outdegree of node n.

The nodes in the digraph in Figure 4.2 have the following indegrees and outdegrees:

$$\text{indeg}(n_1) = 0 \ \text{outdeg}(n_1) = 2$$
$$\text{indeg}(n_2) = 1 \ \text{outdeg}(n_2) = 1$$
$$\text{indeg}(n_3) = 0 \ \text{outdeg}(n_3) = 1$$
$$\text{indeg}(n_4) = 2 \ \text{outdeg}(n_4) = 1$$
$$\text{indeg}(n_5) = 1 \ \text{outdeg}(n_5) = 0$$
$$\text{indeg}(n_6) = 1 \ \text{outdeg}(n_6) = 0$$
$$\text{indeg}(n_7) = 0 \ \text{outdeg}(n_7) = 0$$

Ordinary and directed graphs meet through definitions that relate obvious correspondences, such as deg(n) = indeg(n) + outdeg(n)

4.2.2 TYPES OF NODES

The added descriptive power of directed graphs lets us define different kinds of nodes:

Definition

A node with indegree = 0 is a **source node**.

A node with outdegree = 0 is a **sink node**.

A node with indegree $\neq$ 0 and outdegree $\neq$ 0 is a **transfer node**.

Source and sink nodes constitute the external boundary of a graph. If we made a directed graph of a context diagram (from a set of dataflow diagrams produced by Structured Analysis), the external entities would be source and sink nodes.

In our continuing example, n1, n3, and n7 are source nodes, n5, n6, and n7 are sink nodes, and n2 and n4 are transfer (also known as interior) nodes. A node that is both a source and a sink node is an isolated node.

4.2.3 ADJACENCY MATRIX OF A DIRECTED GRAPH

As we might expect, the addition of direction to edges changes the definition of the adjacency matrix of a directed graph. (It also changes the incidence matrix, but this matrix is seldom used in conjunction with digraphs.)

Definition

The **adjacency matrix** of a directed graph D = (V, E) with m nodes is an m x m matrix A = (a(i, j)) , where a(i, j) is a 1 if and only if there is an edge from node i and node j, otherwise the element is 0.

The adjacency matrix of a directed graph is not necessarily symmetric . A row sum is the outdegree of the node; a column sum is the indegree of a node. The adjacency matrix of our continuing example is

	n1	n2	n3	n4	n5	n6	n7
n_1	0	1	0	1	0	0	0
n_2	0	0	0	0	1	0	0
n_3	0	0	0	1	0	0	0
n_4	0	0	0	0	0	1	0
n_5	0	0	0	0	0	0	0
n_6	0	0	0	0	0	0	0
n_7	0	0	0	0	0	0	0

One common use of directed graphs is to record family relationships, in which siblings, cousins, and so on are connected by an ancestor, and parents, grandparents, and so on are connected by a descendant. Entries in powers of the adjacency matrix now show existence of directed paths.

4.2.4 PATHS AND SEMI-PATHS

Direction permits a more precise meaning to paths that connect nodes in a directed graph. As a handy analogy, you may think in terms of one-way and two-way streets.

Definition

A *(directed) path* is a sequence of edges such that, for any adjacent pair of edges e_i, e_j, in the sequence, the terminal node of the first edge is the initial node of the second edge.
A *cycle* is a directed path that begins and ends at the same node.
A *(directed) semi-path* is a sequence of edges such that, for at least one adjacent pair of edges e_i, e_i in the sequence, the initial node of the first edge is the initial node of the second edge or the terminal node of the first edge is the terminal node of the second edge.

Directed paths are sometimes called chains; we will use this concept in Chapter 9. Our continuing example contains the following paths and semi-paths (not all are listed):

There is a path from n_1 to n_6;
there is a semi-path between n_1 and n_3;
there is a semi-path between n_2 and n_4; and
there is a semi-path between n_5 and n_6.

4.2.5 REACHABILITY MATRIX

When we model an application with a digraph, we often ask questions that deal with paths that let us reach (or "get to") certain nodes. This is an extremely useful capability, and is made possible by the reachability matrix of a digraph.

Definition

The *reachability matrix of a directed graph* D = (V, E) with m nodes is an m x m matrix R = (r(i, j)), where r(i, j) is a 1 if and only if there is a path from node i and node j, otherwise the element is 0.

The reachability matrix of a directed graph D can be calculated from the adjacency matrix A as follows:

$$R = I + A + A^2 + A^3 + ... + A^k,$$

where k is the length of the longest path in D, and I is the identity matrix. The reachability matrix for our continuing example is

	n1	n2	n3	n4	n5	n6	n7
n_1	0	1	0	1	1	1	0
n_2	0	0	0	0	1	0	0
n_3	0	0	0	1	0	1	0
n_4	0	0	0	0	0	1	0
n_5	0	0	0	0	0	0	0
n_6	0	0	0	0	0	0	0
n_7	0	0	0	0	0	0	0

The reachability matrix tells us that nodes n_2, n_4, n_5, and n_6 can be reached from n_1, node n_5 can be reached from n_2, and so on.

4.2.6 N-CONNECTEDNESS

Connectedness of ordinary graphs extends to a rich, highly explanatory concept for digraphs.

Definition

Two nodes n_i and n_j in a directed graph are:

- **0-connected** iff there is no path between n_i and n_j,
- **1-connected** iff there is a semi-path but no path between n_i and n_j,
- **2-connected** iff there is a path between n_i and n_j,
- **3-connected** iff there is a path from n_j to n_i and a path from n_i to n_j.

There are no other degrees of connectedness.

   We need to modify our continuing example to show 3-connectedness. The change is the addition of a new edge e_6 from n_6 to n_3, so the graph contains a cycle.

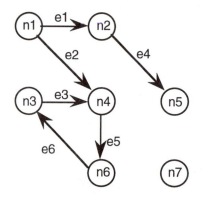

Figure 4.3   A Directed Graph with a Cycle.

With this change, we have the following instances of n-connectivity in Figure 4.3 (not all are listed):

n_1 and n_7 are 0-connected
n_2 and n_6 are 1-connected
n_1 and n_6 are 2-connected
n_3 and n_6 are 3-connected

   If we picture directed edges as one-way streets, you can't get from n_2 to n_6.

4.2.7 STRONG COMPONENTS

The analogy continues. We get two equivalence relations from n-connectedness: 1-connectedness yields what we might call "weak connection", and this in turn yields weak components. (These turn out to be the same as we had for ordinary graphs, which is what should happen, because 1-connectedness effectively ignores direction.) The second equivalence relation, based on 3-connectedness, is more interesting. As before, the equivalence relation induces a partition on the node set of a digraph, but the condensation graph is quite different. Nodes that previously were 0-, 1-, or 2-connected remain so. The 3-connected nodes become the strong components.

Definition

A **strong component of a directed graph** is a maximal set of 3-connected nodes.

   In our amended example, the strong components are the sets { n_3, n_4, n_6} and {n_7}. The condensation graph for our amended example is shown in Figure 4.4.

   Strong components let us simplify by removing loops and isolated nodes. While this is not as dramatic as the simplification we had in ordinary graphs, it does solve a major testing problem. Notice that the condensation graph of a digraph will never contain a loop. (If it did, the loop would have been condensed by the maximal aspect of the partition.) These graphs have a special name: directed acyclic graphs, sometimes written as a DAG.

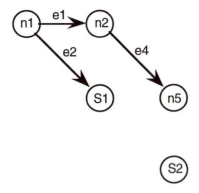

Figure 4.4 Condensation Graph of the Digraph in Figure 4.3

Many papers on structured testing make quite a point of showing how relatively simple programs can have millions of distinct execution paths. The intent of these discussions is to convince us that exhaustive testing is exactly that — exhaustive. The large number of execution paths comes from nested loops. Since condensation graphs eliminate loops (or at least condense them down to a single node), we can use this as a strategy to simplify situations that otherwise are computationally untenable.

4.3 GRAPHS FOR TESTING

We conclude this chapter with three special graphs that are widely used for testing. The first of these, the program graph, is used primarily at the unit testing level. The other two, finite state machines and Petri nets, are best used to describe system level behavior, although they can be used at lower levels of testing.

4.3.1 PROGRAM GRAPHS

At the beginning of this chapter, we made a point of avoiding interpretations .on the graph theory definitions to preserve latitude in later applications. Here we give the most common use of graph theory in software testing, the program graph. To better connect with existing testing literature, the traditional definition is given, followed by an improved definition.

Definition
Given a program written in an imperative programming language, its **program graph** is a directed graph in which:

1. (Traditional Definition)
   Nodes are program statements, and edges represent flow of control (there is an edge from node i to node j iff the statement corresponding to node j can be executed immediately after the statement corresponding to node i).
2. (Improved Definition)
   Nodes are either entire statements or fragments of a statement, and edges represent flow of control (there is an edge from node i to node j iff the statement or statement fragment corresponding to node j can be executed immediately after the statement or statement fragment corresponding to node i).

Since it will be cumbersome to always say "statement or statement fragment", we adopt the convention that a statement fragment can be an entire statement. The directed graph formulation of a program enables very precise description of testing aspects of the program. For one thing, there is a very satisfying connection between this formulation and the precepts of structured programming. The basic structured programming constructs (sequence, selection, and repetition) all have clear directed graphs, as shown in Figure 4.5

When these constructs are used in a structured program, the corresponding graphs are either nested or concatenated. The single entrance and single exit criteria result in unique source and sink nodes in the program graph. In fact, the old (non-structured) "spaghetti code" resulted in very complex program

Sequence   If-Then-Else   Case

If-Then   Pre-test Loop   Post-test Loop

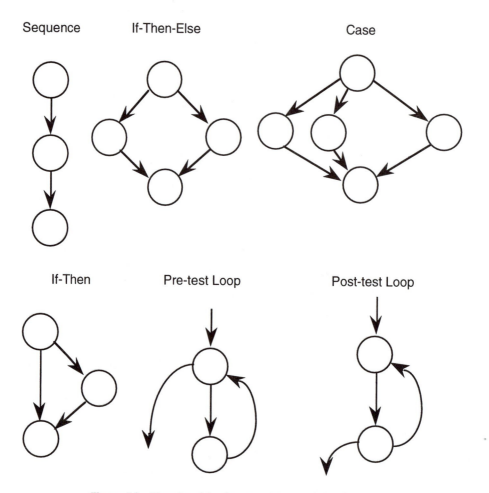

Figure 4.5 Digraphs of the Structured Programming Constructs

graphs. GOTO statements, for example, introduce edges, and when these are used to branch into or out of loops, the resulting program graphs become even more complex. One of the pioneering analysts of this is Thomas McCabe, who popularized the cyclomatic number of a graph as an indicator of program complexity [McCabe76]. When a program executes, the statements that execute comprise a path in the program graph. Loops and decisions greatly increase the number of possible paths, and therefore similarly increase the need for testing.

One of the problems with program graphs is how to treat non-executable statements, such as comments and data declaration statements. The simplest answer is to ignore them. A second problem has to do with the difference between topologically possible and semantically feasible paths. We will discuss this in more detail in Part III.

4.3.2 FINITE STATE MACHINES

Finite state machines have become a fairly standard notation for requirements specification. All the real-time extensions of Structured Analysis use some form of finite state machine, and nearly all forms of object-oriented analysis require them. A finite state machine is a directed graph in which states are nodes, and transitions are edges. Source and sink states become initial and terminal nodes, paths are modeled as paths, and so on. Most finite state machine notations add information to the edges (transitions) to indicate the cause of the transition and actions that occur as a result of the transition. More formally:

Definition

A *Finite State Machine* (abbreviated FSM) is a directed graph (S, T, Ev, Act), in which S is a set of nodes (states), T is a set of edges (transitions), and Ev and Act are sets of events and actions that are associated with the transitions in T.

Figure 4.6 is a finite state machine for the PIN try portion of the SATM system. This machine contains five states (Idle, Awaiting First PIN Try, and so on) and eight transitions, which are shown as edges. The labels on the transitions follow a convention that the "numerator" is the event that causes the transition, and the "denominator" is the action that is associated with the transition. The events are mandatory — transitions don't just happen, but the actions are optional. Finite state machines are simple ways to represent situations in which a variety of events may occur, and their occurrence has different consequences. In the PIN entry portion of the SATM system, for example, a customer has three chances to enter the correct PIN digits. If the correct PIN is entered on the first try, the SATM system exhibits the output action of displaying screen 5 (which invites the customer to choose a transaction type). If an incorrect PIN is entered, the machine goes to a different state, one in which it awaits a second PIN attempt. Notice that the same events and actions occur on the transitions from the Awaiting Second PIN Try state. This is the way finite state machines can keep a history of past events.

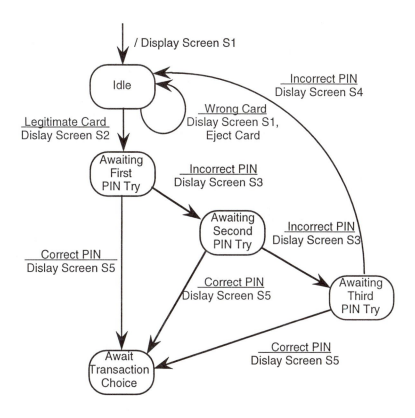

Figure 4.6   Finite State Machine for PIN Tries

Finite state machines can be executed, but a few conventions are needed first. One is the notion of the active state. We speak of a system being "in" a certain state; when the system is modeled as a finite state machine, the active state refers to the state "we are in". Another convention is that finite state machines may have an initial state, which is the state that is active when a finite state machine is first entered. (The Idle state is the initial state in Figure 4.6; this is indicated by the transition that comes from nowhere. Final states are recognized by the absence of outgoing transitions.) Exactly one state can be active at any time. We also think of transitions as instantaneous occurrences, and the events that cause transitions also occur one at a time. To execute a finite state machine, we start with an initial state, and provide a sequence of events that cause state transitions. As each event occurs, the transition changes the active state, and a new event occurs. In this way, a sequence of events selects a path of states (or equivalently, of transitions) through the machine.

4.3.3 PETRI NETS

Petri nets were the topic of Carl Adam Petri's Ph.D. dissertation in 1963; today they are the accepted model for protocols and other applications involving concurrency and distributed processing. Petri nets are a special form of directed graph: a bipartitie directed graph. (A bipartite graph has two sets of nodes, V_1 and V_2, and a set of edges E, with the restriction that every edge has its initial node on one of the sets V_1, V_2, and its terminal node in the other set.) In a Petri net, one of the sets is referred to as "places", and the other is referred to as "transitions". These sets are usually denoted as P and T, respectively. Places are inputs to and outputs of transitions; the input and output relationships are functions, and they are usually denoted as In and Out, as in the following definition.

Definition
A *Petri net* is a bipartite directed graph (P, T, In, Out), in which P and T are disjoint sets of nodes, and In and Out are sets of edges, where In $\subseteq$ P $\times$ T, and Out $\subseteq$ T $\times$ P.

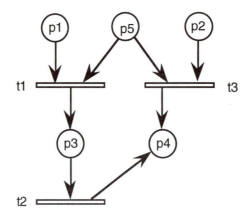

Figure 4.7 A Petri Net

For the sample Petri net in Figure 4.7, the sets P, T, In, and Out and are

P = { p1, p2, p3, p4, p5}
T = { t1, t2, t3}
In = {<p1, t1>, <p5, t1>, <p5, t3>, <p2, t3>, <p3, t2>}
Out = {<t1, p3>, <t2, p4>, <t3, p4>}

Petri nets are executable, in more interesting ways than finite state machines. The next few definitions lead us to Petri net execution.

Definition
A *marked Petri net* is a 5-tuple (P, T, In, Out, M) in which (P, T, In, Out) is a Petri net and M is a set of mappings of places to positive integers.

The set M is called the marking set of the Petri net. Elements of M are n-tuples, where n is the number of places in the set P. For the Petri net in Figure 4.7, the set M contains elements of the form <n1, n2, n3, n4, n5>, where the n's are the integers associated with the respective places. The number associated with a place refers to the number of tokens that are said to be "in" the place. Tokens are abstractions that can be interpreted in modeling situations. For example, tokens might refer to the number of times a place has been used, or the number of things in a place, or whether the place is true. Figure 4.8 shown a marked Petri net.

The marking tuple for the marked Petri net in Figure 4.8 is <1, 1, 0, 2, 0>. We need the concept of tokens to make two essential definitions.

Definition
A transition in a Petri net is *enabled* if there is at least one token in each of its input places.

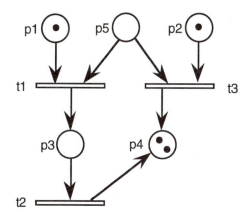

Figure 4.8 A Marked Petri Net

There are no enabled transitions in the marked Petri net in Figure 4.8. If we put a token in place p3, then transition t2 would be enabled.

Definition
When an enabled Petri net transition *fires*, one token is removed from each of its input places, and one token is added to each of its output places.

In Figure 4.9, transition t2 is enabled in the upper net, and it has been fired in the lower net.
The marking set for the net in Figure 4.9 contains two tuples; the first shows the net when t2 is enabled, and the second shows the net after t2 has fired.

$$M = \{<1, 1, 1, 2, 0>, <1, 1, 0, 3, 0>\}$$

Tokens may be created or destroyed by transition firings. Under special conditions, the total number of tokens in a net never changes; such nets are called conservative. We usually won't worry about token conservation. Markings let us execute Petri nets in much the same way that we execute finite state machines. (It turns out that finite state machines are a special case of Petri nets.) Suppose we had a different marking of the net in Figure 4.7; in this new marking places p1, p2, and p5 are all marked. With such a marking, transitions t1 and t3 are both enabled. If we choose to fire transition t1, the token in place p5 is removed, and t3 is no longer enabled. Similarly, if we choose to fire t3, we disable t1. This pattern is known as Petri net conflict, more specifically, we say that transitions t1 and t3 are in conflict with respect to place p5. Petri net conflict exhibits an interesting form of interaction between two transitions; we will revisit this (and other) interactions in Chapter 16.

EXERCISES

1. Propose a definition for the length of a path in a graph.
2. What loop(s) is/are created if an edge is added between nodes n_5 and n_6 in the graph in Figure 4.1?
3. Convince yourself that 3-connectedness is an equivalence relation on the nodes of a digraph.
4. Compute the cyclomatic complexity for each of the structured programming constructs in Figure 4.5.
5. The digraphs below were obtained by adding nodes and edges to the digraph in Figure 4.3. Compute the cyclomatic complexity of each new digraph, and explain how the changes affected the complexity.

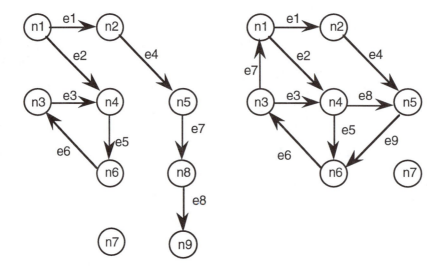

6. Suppose we make a graph in which nodes are people and edges correspond to some form of social interaction, such as "talks to" or socialized with". Find graph theory concepts that correspond to social concepts such as popularity, cliques, and hermits.

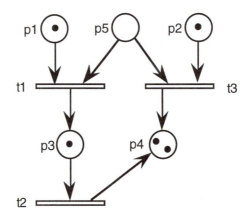

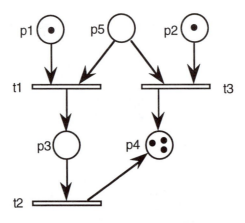

Figure 4.9 Before and After Firing t2

Part II

Functional Testing

Chapter 5

Boundary Value Testing

In Chapter 3, we saw that a function maps values from one set (its domain) to values in another set (its range), and that the domain and range can be cross products of other sets. Any program can be considered to be a function in the sense that program inputs form its domain, and program outputs form its range. Boundary value testing is the best known functional testing technique. In this (and the next two) chapter(s), we examine how to use knowledge of the functional nature of a program to identify test cases for the program. Historically, this form of testing has focused on the input domain, but it is often a good supplement to apply many of these techniques to develop range-based test cases.

5.1 BOUNDARY VALUE ANALYSIS

For the sake of comprehensible drawings, the discussion relates to a function, F, of two variables x_1 and x_2 . When the function F is implemented as a program, the input variables x_1 and x_2 will have some (possibly unstated) boundaries:

$$a \leq x_1 \leq b$$

$$c \leq x_2 \leq d.$$

Unfortunately, the intervals [a, b] and [c, d] are referred to as the ranges of x_1 and x_2 , so right away, we have an overloaded term. The intended meaning will always be clear from its context. Strongly typed languages (such as Ada and Pascal) permit explicit definition of such variable ranges. In fact, part of the historical reason for strong typing was to prevent programmers from making the kind of errors that result in faults that are easily revealed by boundary value testing. Other languages (such as COBOL, FOR-TRAN, and C) are not strongly typed, so boundary value testing is more appropriate for programs coded in such languages. The input space (domain) of our function F is shown in Figure 5.1. Any point within the shaded rectangle is a legitimate input to the function F.

Boundary value analysis focuses on the boundary of the input space to identify test cases. The rationale behind boundary value testing is that errors tend to occur near the extreme values of an input variable. The US. Army (CECOM) made a study of its software, and found that a surprising portion of faults turned out to be boundary value faults. Loop conditions, for example, may test for < when they should test for ≤, and counters often are "off by one". The desktop publishing program in which this manuscript was typed has an interesting boundary value problem. There are two modes of textual display: a scrolling view in which new pages are indicated by a dotted line, and a page view which displays a full page image showing where the text is placed on the page, together with headers and footers. If the cursor is at the last line of a page and new text is added, an anomaly occurs: in the first mode, the new line(s) simply appear, and the dotted line (page break) is adjusted. In the page display mode, however, the new text is lost — it doesn't appear on either page.

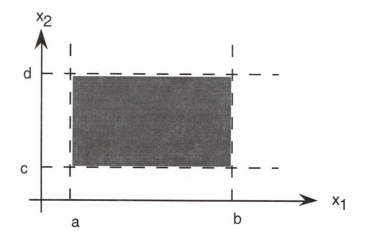

Figure 5.1 Input Domain of a Function of Two Variables

The basic idea of boundary value analysis is to use input variable values at their minimum, just above the minimum, a nominal value, just below their maximum, and at their maximum. There is a commercially available testing tool (named T) that generates such test cases for a properly specified program. This tool has been successfully integrated with two popular front-end CASE tools (Teamwork from Cadre Systems, and Software Through Pictures from Interactive Development Environments). The T tool refers to these values as min, min+, nom, max- and max; we will use this convention here.

The next part of boundary value analysis is based on a critical assumption; it's known as the "single fault" assumption in reliability theory. This says that failures are only rarely the result of the simultaneous occurrence of two (or more) faults. Thus the boundary value analysis test cases are obtained by holding the values of all but one variable at their nominal values, and letting that variable assume its extreme values. The boundary value analysis test cases for our function F of two variables are:

$$\{ <x_{1nom}, x_{2min} >, <x_{1nom}, x_{2min+} >, <x_{1nom}, x_{2nom} >, <x_{1nom}, x_{2max-} >,$$
$$<x_{1nom}, x_{2max} >, <x_{1min}, x_{2nom} >, <x_{1min+}, x_{2nom} >, <x_{1nom}, x_{2nom} >,$$
$$<x_{1max-}, x_{2nom} >, <x_{1max}, x_{2nom} > \}$$

These are illustrated in Figure 5.2.

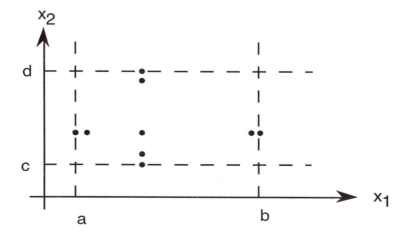

Figure 5.2 Boundary Value Analysis Test Cases for a Function of Two Variables

5.1.1 GENERALIZING BOUNDARY VALUE ANALYSIS

The basic boundary value analysis technique can be generalized in two ways: by the number of variables, and by the kinds of ranges. Generalizing the number of variables is easy: if we have a function of n variables, we hold all but one at the nominal values, and let the remaining variable assume the min, min+, nom, max- and max values, and repeat this for each variable. Thus for a function of n variables, boundary value analysis yields 4n + 1 test cases.

Generalizing ranges depends on the nature (or more precisely, the type) of the variables themselves. In the NextDate function, for example, we have variables for the month, the day, and the year. In a FORTRAN-like language, we would most likely encode these, so that January would correspond to 1, February to 2, and so on. In a language that supports user defined types (like Pascal), we could define the variable month as an enumerated type {Jan., Feb., . . . , Dec.}. Either way, the values for min, min+, nom, max- and max are clear from the context. When a variable has discrete, bounded values, as the variables in the commission problem have, the min, min+, nom, max- and max are also easily determined. When there are no explicit bounds, as in the triangle problem, we usually have to create "artificial" bounds. The lower bound of side lengths is clearly 1 (a negative side length is silly), but what might we do for an upper bound? By default, the largest representable integer (called MAXINT in some languages) is one possibility, or we might impose an arbitrary upper limit such as 200 or 2000.

Boundary value analysis doesn't make much sense for Boolean variables; the extreme values are TRUE and FALSE, but there is no clear choice for the remaining three. We will see in Chapter 7 that Boolean variables lend themselves to decision table-based testing. Logical variables also present a problem for boundary value analysis. In the ATM example, a customer's Personal Identification Number (PIN) is a logical variable, as is the transaction type (deposit, withdrawal, or inquiry). We could "go through the motions" of boundary value analysis testing for such variables, but the exercise is not very satisfying to the "tester's intuition".

5.1.2 LIMITATIONS OF BOUNDARY VALUE ANALYSIS

Boundary value analysis works well when the program to be tested is a function of several independent variables that represent bounded physical quantities. The key words here are *independent* and *physical quantities* . A quick look at the boundary value analysis test cases for NextDate (in section 5.5) shows them to be inadequate. There is very little stress on February and on leap years, for example. The real problem here is that there are interesting dependencies among the month, day, and year variables. Boundary value analysis presumes the variables to be truly independent. Even so, boundary value analysis happens to catch end-of-month and end-of-year faults. Boundary value analysis test cases are derived from the extrema of bounded, independent variables that refer to physical quantities, with no consideration of the nature of the function, nor of the semantic meaning of the variables. We see boundary value analysis test cases to be rudimentary, in the sense that they are obtained with very little insight and imagination. As with so many things, you get what you pay for.

The physical quantity criterion is equally important. When a variable refers to a physical quantity, such as temperature, pressure, air speed, angle of attack, load, and so forth, physical boundaries can be extremely important. (In an interesting example of this, Sky Harbor International Airport in Phoenix had to close on June 26, 1992 because the air temperature was 122 °F. Aircraft pilots were unable to make certain instrument settings before take-off: the instruments could only accept a maximum air temperature of 120 °F.) In another case, a medical analysis system uses stepper motors to position a carousel of samples to be analyzed. It turns out that the mechanics of moving the carousel back to the starting cell often causes the robot arm to miss the first cell.

As an example of logical (versus physical) variables, we might look at PINs or telephone numbers. It's hard to imagine what faults might be revealed by PINs of 0000, 0001, 5000, 9998, and 9999.

5.2 ROBUSTNESS TESTING

Robustness testing is a simple extension of boundary value analysis: in addition to the five boundary value analysis values of a variable, we see what happens when the extrema are exceeded with a value slightly greater than the maximum (max+) and a value slightly less than the minimum (min-). Robustness test cases for our continuing example are shown in Figure 5.3.

Most of the discussion of boundary value analysis applies directly to robustness testing, especially the generalizations and limitations. The most interesting part of robustness testing is not with the inputs, but with the expected outputs. What happens when a physical quantity exceeds its maximum? If it is the angle of attack of an airplane wing, the aircraft might stall. If it's the load capacity of a public elevator, we hope nothing special would happen. If it's a date, like May 32, we would expect an error message. The main value of robustness testing is that it forces attention on exception handling. With strongly typed languages, robustness testing may be very awkward. In Pascal, for example, if a variable is defined to be within a certain range, values outside that range result in run-time errors that abort normal execution. This raises an interesting question of implementation philosophy: is it better to perform explicit range checking and use exception handling to deal with "robust values", or is it better to stay with strong typing? The exception handling choice mandates robustness testing.

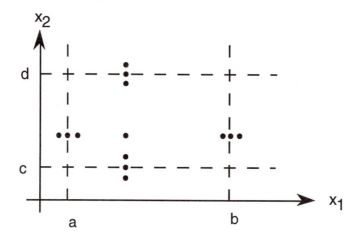

Figure 5.3 Robustness Test Cases for a Function of Two Variables

5.3 WORST CASE TESTING

Boundary value analysis, as we said earlier, makes the single fault assumption of reliability theory. Rejecting this assumption means that we are interested in what happens when more than one variable has an extreme value. In electronic circuit analysis, this is called "worst case analysis"; we use that idea here to generate worst case test cases. For each variable, we start with the five element set that contains the min, min+, nom, max- and max values. We then take the Cartesian product (see Chapter 3) of these sets to generate test cases. The result of the two-variable version of this is shown in Figure 5.4.

Worst case testing is clearly more thorough in the sense that boundary value analysis test cases are a proper subset of worst case test cases. It also represents much more effort: worst case testing for a function of n variables generates 5^n test cases, as opposed to $4n+1$ test cases for boundary value analysis.

Worst case testing follows the generalization pattern we saw for boundary value analysis. It also has the same limitations, particularly those related to independence. Probably the best application for worst case testing is where physical variables have numerous interactions, and where failure of the function is extremely costly. For really paranoid testing, we could go to robust worst case testing. This involves the Cartesian product of the seven element sets we used in robustness testing. Figure 5.5 shows the robust worst case test cases for our two variable function.

5.4 SPECIAL VALUE TESTING

Special value testing is probably the most widely practiced form of functional testing. It also is the most intuitive and the least uniform. Special value testing occurs when a tester uses his/her domain knowledge, experience with similar programs, and information about "soft spots" to devise test cases. We might also call this "ad hoc testing" or "seat of the pants/skirt" testing. There are no guidelines, other than to use "best engineering judgment." As a result, special value testing is very dependent on the abilities of the tester.

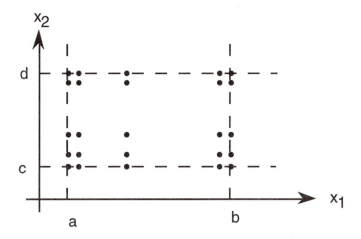

Figure 5.4   Worst Case Test Cases for a Function of Two Variables

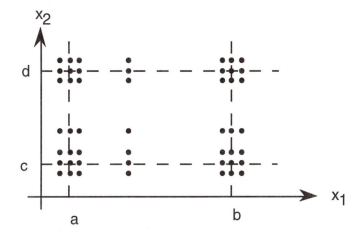

Figure 5.5   Robust Worst Case Test Cases for a Function of Two Variables

Despite all the apparent negatives, special value testing can be very useful. In the next section, you will find test cases generated by the methods we just discussed for our three unit level examples (not the ATM system). If you look carefully at these, especially for the NextDate function, you find that none is very satisfactory. If an interested tester defined special value test cases for NextDate, we would see several test cases involving February 28, February 29, and leap years. Even though special value testing is highly subjective, it often results in a set of test cases which is more effective in revealing faults than the test sets generated by the other methods we have studied— testimony to the craft of software testing.

5.5 EXAMPLES

Each of the three continuing examples is a function of three variables. Printing all the test cases from all the methods for each problem is very space consuming, so we'll just have selected examples.

5.5.1 TEST CASES FOR THE TRIANGLE PROBLEM

In the problem statement, there are no conditions on the triangle sides, other than being integers. Obviously, the lower bounds of the ranges are all 1. We arbitrarily take 200 as an upper bound. Table 1 contains boundary value test cases and Table 2 contains worst case test cases using these ranges.

Table 1   Boundary Value Analysis Test Cases

Case	a	b	c	Expected Output
1	100	100	1	Isosceles
2	100	100	2	Isosceles
3	100	100	100	Equilateral
4	100	100	199	Isosceles
5	100	100	200	Not a Triangle
6	100	1	100	Isosceles
7	100	2	100	Isosceles
8	100	100	100	Equilateral
9	100	199	100	Isosceles
10	100	200	100	Not a Triangle
11	1	100	100	Isosceles
12	2	100	100	Isosceles
13	100	100	100	Equilateral
14	199	100	100	Isosceles
15	200	100	100	Not a Triangle

Table 2   Worst Case Test Cases

Case	a	b	c	Expected Output
1	1	1	1	Equilateral
2	1	1	2	Not a Triangle
3	1	1	100	Not a Triangle
4	1	1	199	Not a Triangle
5	1	1	200	Not a Triangle
6	1	2	1	Not a Triangle
7	1	2	2	Isosceles
8	1	2	100	Not a Triangle
9	1	2	199	Not a Triangle
10	1	2	200	Not a Triangle
11	1	100	1	Not a Triangle
12	1	100	2	Not a Triangle
13	1	100	100	Isosceles
14	1	100	199	Not a Triangle
15	1	100	200	Not a Triangle
16	1	199	1	Not a Triangle
17	1	199	2	Not a Triangle
18	1	199	100	Not a Triangle
19	1	199	199	Isosceles
20	1	199	200	Not a Triangle
21	1	200	1	Not a Triangle
22	1	200	2	Not a Triangle
23	1	200	100	Not a Triangle
24	1	200	199	Not a Triangle
25	1	200	200	Isosceles

Case	a	b	c	Expected Output
26	2	1	1	Not a Triangle
27	2	1	2	Isosceles
28	2	1	100	Not a Triangle
29	2	1	199	Not a Triangle
30	2	1	200	Not a Triangle
31	2	2	1	Isosceles
32	2	2	2	Equilateral
33	2	2	100	Not a Triangle
34	2	2	199	Not a Triangle
35	2	2	200	Not a Triangle
36	2	100	1	Not a Triangle
37	2	100	2	Not a Triangle
38	2	100	100	Isosceles
39	2	100	199	Not a Triangle
40	2	100	200	Not a Triangle
41	2	199	1	Not a Triangle
42	2	199	2	Not a Triangle
43	2	199	100	Not a Triangle
44	2	199	199	Isosceles
45	2	199	200	Scalene
46	2	200	1	Not a Triangle
47	2	200	2	Not a Triangle
48	2	200	100	Not a Triangle
49	2	200	199	Scalene
50	2	200	200	Isosceles
51	100	1	1	Not a Triangle
52	100	1	2	Not a Triangle
53	100	1	100	Isosceles
54	100	1	199	Not a Triangle
55	100	1	200	Not a Triangle
56	100	2	1	Not a Triangle
57	100	2	2	Not a Triangle
58	100	2	100	Isosceles
59	100	2	199	Not a Triangle
60	100	2	200	Not a Triangle
61	100	100	1	Isosceles
62	100	100	2	Isosceles
63	100	100	100	Equilateral
64	100	100	199	Isosceles
65	100	100	200	Not a Triangle
66	100	199	1	Not a Triangle
67	100	199	2	Not a Triangle
68	100	199	100	Isosceles
69	100	199	199	Isosceles
70	100	199	200	Scalene
71	100	200	1	Not a Triangle
72	100	200	2	Not a Triangle
73	100	200	100	Not a Triangle
74	100	200	199	Scalene
75	100	200	200	Isosceles

Case	a	b	c	Expected Output
76	199	1	1	Not a Triangle
77	199	1	2	Not a Triangle
78	199	1	100	Not a Triangle
79	199	1	199	Scalene
80	199	1	200	Not a Triangle
81	199	2	1	Not a Triangle
82	199	2	2	Not a Triangle
83	199	2	100	Not a Triangle
84	199	2	199	Isosceles
85	199	2	200	Scalene
86	199	100	1	Not a Triangle
87	199	100	2	Not a Triangle
88	199	100	100	Isosceles
89	199	100	199	Isosceles
90	199	100	200	Scalene
91	199	199	1	Isosceles
92	199	199	2	Isosceles
93	199	199	100	Isosceles
94	199	199	199	Equilateral
95	199	199	200	Isosceles
96	199	200	1	Not a Triangle
97	199	200	2	Scalene
98	199	200	100	Scalene
99	199	200	199	Isosceles
100	199	200	200	Isosceles
101	200	1	1	Not a Triangle
102	200	1	2	Not a Triangle
103	200	1	100	Not a Triangle
104	200	1	199	Not a Triangle
105	200	1	200	Isosceles
106	200	2	1	Not a Triangle
107	200	2	2	Not a Triangle
108	200	2	100	Not a Triangle
109	200	2	199	Scalene
110	200	2	200	Isosceles
111	200	100	1	Not a Triangle
112	200	100	2	Not a Triangle
113	200	100	100	Not a Triangle
114	200	100	199	Scalene
115	200	100	200	Isosceles
116	200	199	1	Not a Triangle
117	200	199	2	Scalene
118	200	199	100	Scalene
119	200	199	199	Isosceles
120	200	199	200	Isosceles
121	200	200	1	Isosceles
122	200	200	2	Isosceles
123	200	200	100	Isosceles
124	200	200	199	Isosceles
125	200	200	200	Equilateral

5.5.2 TEST CASES FOR THE NEXTDATE PROBLEM

Table 3   Worst Case Test Cases

Case	month	day	year	expected output
1	1	1	1812	January 2, 1812
2	1	1	1813	January 2, 1813
3	1	1	1912	January 2, 1912
4	1	1	2011	January 2, 2011
5	1	1	2012	January 2, 2012
6	1	2	1812	January 3, 1812
7	1	2	1813	January 3, 1813
8	1	2	1912	January 3, 1912
9	1	2	2011	January 3, 2011
10	1	2	2012	January 3, 2012
11	1	15	1812	January 16, 1812
12	1	15	1813	January 16, 1813
13	1	15	1912	January 16, 1912
14	1	15	2011	January 16, 2011
15	1	15	2012	January 16, 2012
16	1	30	1812	January 31, 1812
17	1	30	1813	January 31, 1813
18	1	30	1912	January 31, 1912
19	1	30	2011	January 31, 2011
20	1	30	2012	January 31, 2012
21	1	31	1812	February 1, 1812
22	1	31	1813	February 1, 1813
23	1	31	1912	February 1, 1912
24	1	31	2011	February 1, 2011
25	1	31	2012	February 1, 2012

Case	month	day	year	expected output
26	2	1	1812	February 2, 1812
27	2	1	1813	February 2, 1813
28	2	1	1912	February 2, 1912
29	2	1	2011	February 2, 2011
30	2	1	2012	February 2, 2012
31	2	2	1812	February 3, 1812
32	2	2	1813	February 3, 1813
33	2	2	1912	February 3, 1912
34	2	2	2011	February 3, 2011
35	2	2	2012	February 3, 2012
36	2	15	1812	February 16, 1812
37	2	15	1813	February 16, 1813
38	2	15	1912	February 16, 1912
39	2	15	2011	February 16, 2011
40	2	15	2012	February 16, 2012
41	2	30	1812	error
42	2	30	1813	error
43	2	30	1912	error
44	2	30	2011	error
45	2	30	2012	error
46	2	31	1812	error
47	2	31	1813	error
48	2	31	1912	error
49	2	31	2011	error
50	2	31	2012	error

Case	month	day	year	expected output
51	6	1	1812	June 1, 1812
52	6	1	1813	June 1, 1813
53	6	1	1912	June 2, 1912
54	6	1	2011	June 2, 2011
55	6	1	2012	June 2, 2012
56	6	2	1812	June 3, 1812
57	6	2	1813	June 3, 1813
58	6	2	1912	June 3, 1912
59	6	2	2011	June 3, 2011
60	6	2	2012	June 3, 2012
61	6	15	1812	June 16, 1812
62	6	15	1813	June 16, 1813
63	6	15	1912	June 16, 1912
64	6	15	2011	June 16, 2011
65	6	15	2012	June 16, 2012
66	6	30	1812	July 31, 1812
67	6	30	1813	July 31, 1813
68	6	30	1912	July 31, 1912
69	6	30	2011	July 31, 2011
70	6	30	2012	July 31, 2012
71	6	31	1812	error
72	6	31	1813	error
73	6	31	1912	error
74	6	31	2011	error
75	6	31	2012	error
76	11	1	1812	November 2, 1812
77	11	1	1813	November 2, 1813
78	11	1	1912	November 2, 1912
79	11	1	2011	November 2, 2011
80	11	1	2012	November 2, 2012
81	11	2	1812	November 3, 1812
82	11	2	1813	November 3, 1813
83	11	2	1912	November 3, 1912
84	11	2	2011	November 3, 2011
85	11	2	2012	November 3, 2012
86	11	15	1812	November 16, 1812
87	11	15	1813	November 16, 1813
88	11	15	1912	November 16, 1912
89	11	15	2011	November 16, 2011
90	11	15	2012	November 16, 2012
91	11	30	1812	December 1, 1812
92	11	30	1813	December 1, 1813
93	11	30	1912	December 1, 1912
94	11	30	2011	December 1, 2011
95	11	30	2012	December 1, 2012
96	11	31	1812	error
97	11	31	1813	error
98	11	31	1912	error
99	11	31	2011	error
100	11	31	2012	error

Case	month	day	year	expected output
101	12	1	1812	December 2, 1812
102	12	1	1813	December 2, 1813
103	12	1	1912	December 2, 1912
104	12	1	2011	December 2, 2011
105	12	1	2012	December 2, 2012
106	12	2	1812	December 3, 1812
107	12	2	1813	December 3, 1813
108	12	2	1912	December 3, 1912
109	12	2	2011	December 3, 2011
110	12	2	2012	December 3, 2012
111	12	15	1812	December 16, 1812
112	12	15	1813	December 16, 1813
113	12	15	1912	December 16, 1912
114	12	15	2011	December 16, 2011
115	12	15	2012	December 16, 2012
116	12	30	1812	December 31, 1812
117	12	30	1813	December 31, 1813
118	12	30	1912	December 31, 1912
119	12	30	2011	December 31, 2011
120	12	30	2012	December 31, 2012
121	12	31	1812	January 1, 1813
122	12	31	1813	January 1, 1814
123	12	31	1912	January 1, 1913
124	12	31	2011	January 1, 2012
125	12	31	2012	January 1, 2013

5.5.3 TEST CASES FOR THE COMMISSION PROBLEM

Rather than go through 125 boring test cases again, we'll look at some more interesting test cases for the commission problem. This time we'll look at boundary values for the output range, especially near the threshold points of $1000 and $1800. The output space of the commission is shown in Figure 5.6. The intercepts of these threshold planes with the axes are shown.

The volume below the lower plane corresponds to sales below the $1000 threshold. The volume between the two planes is the 15% commission range. Part of the reason for using the output range to determine test cases is that cases from the input range are almost all in the 20% zone. We want to find input variable combinations that stress the boundary values: $100, $1000, $1800, and $7800. These test cases were developed with a spreadsheet, which saves a lot of calculator pecking. The minimum and maximum were easy, and the numbers happen to work out so that the border points are easy to generate. Here's where it gets interesting. Test case 9 is the $1000 border point. If we tweak the input variables we get values just below and just above the border (cases 6 - 8 and 10 - 12). If we wanted to, we could pick values near the intercepts like (22, 1, 1) and (21, 1, 1). As we continue in this way, we have a sense that we are "exercising" interesting parts of the code. We might claim that this is really a form of special value testing, because we used our mathematical insight to generate test cases.

5.6   GUIDELINES FOR BOUNDARY VALUE TESTING

With the exception of special value testing, the test methods based on the boundary values of a function (program) are the most rudimentary of all functional testing methods. They share the common assumption that the input variables are truly independent, and when this assumption is not warranted, the methods generate unsatisfactory test cases (such as February 31, 1912 for NextDate). These methods have two other distinctions: normal versus robust values, and the single fault versus the multiple fault assumption. Just using these distinctions carefully will result in better testing. Each of these methods can be applied to the output range of a program, as we did for the commission problem.

Another useful form of output-based test cases is for systems that generate error messages. The tester should devise test cases to check that error messages are generated when they are appropriate, and are not falsely generated. Boundary value analysis can also be used for internal variables, such as loop control variables, indices, and pointers. Strictly speaking, these are not input variables, but errors in the use of these variables are quite common. Robustness testing is a good choice for testing internal variables.

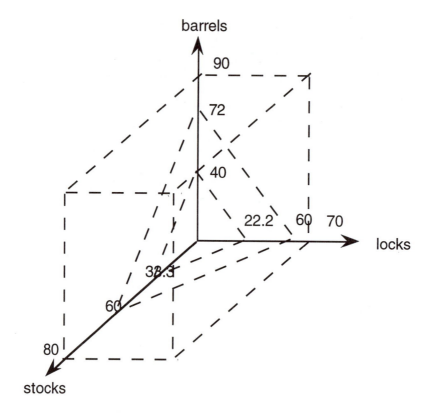

Figure 5.6 Input Space of the Commission Problem

Table 4   Output Boundary Value Analysis Test Cases

Case	locks	stocks	barrels	sales	comm	Comment
1	1	1	1	100	10	output minimum
2	1	1	2	125	12.5	output minimum +
3	1	2	1	130	13	output minimum +
4	2	1	1	145	14.5	output minimum +
5	5	5	5	500	50	midpoint
6	10	10	9	975	97.5	border point -
7	10	9	10	970	97	border point -
8	9	10	10	955	95.5	border point -
9	10	10	10	1000	100	border point
10	10	10	11	1025	103.75	border point +
11	10	11	10	1030	104.5	border point +
12	11	10	10	1045	106.75	border point +
13	14	14	14	1400	160	midpoint
14	18	18	17	1775	216.25	border point -
15	18	17	18	1770	215.5	border point -
16	17	18	18	1755	213.25	border point -
17	18	18	18	1800	220	border point
18	18	18	19	1825	225	border point +
19	18	19	18	1830	226	border point +
20	19	18	18	1845	229	border point +
21	48	48	48	4800	820	midpoint
22	70	80	89	7775	1415	output maximum -
23	70	79	90	7770	1414	output maximum -
24	69	80	90	7755	1411	output maximum -
25	70	80	90	7800	1420	output maximum

Table 5   Output Special Value Test Cases

Case	locks	stocks	barrels	sales	comm	Comment
1	10	11	9	1005	100.75	border point +
2	18	17	19	1795	219.25	border point -
3	18	19	17	1805	221	border point +

EXERCISES

1. Develop a formula for the number of robustness test cases for a function of n variables.
2. Develop a formula for the number of robust worst case test cases for a function of n variables.
3. Make a Venn diagram showing the relationships among test cases form boundary value analysis, robustness testing, worst case testing, and robust worst case testing.
4. What happens if we try to do output range robustness testing? Use the commission problem as an example.

Chapter

Equivalence Class Testing

The use of equivalence classes as the basis for functional testing has two motivations: we would like to have a sense of complete testing, and at the same time, we would hope that we are avoiding redundancy. Most of the standard testing texts [Myers 79], [Mosley 93] discuss a simple form of equivalence class testing; here we extend the notion to consider what we shall call weak and strong equivalence class testing.

6.1 EQUIVALENCE CLASSES

In Chapter 3, we noted that the important aspect of equivalence classes is that they form a partition of a set, where partition refers to a collection of mutually disjoint subsets whose union is the entire set. This has two important implications for testing: the fact that the entire set is represented provides a form of completeness, and the disjointness assures a form of non-redundancy. Because the subsets are determined by an equivalence relation, the elements of a subset have something in common. The idea of equivalence class testing is to identify test cases by using one element from each equivalence class. If the equivalence classes are chosen wisely, this greatly reduces the potential redundancy among test cases. In the Triangle Problem, for example, we would certainly have a test case for an equilateral triangle, and we might pick the triple (5, 5, 5) as inputs for a test case. If we did this, we would not expect to learn much from test cases such as (6, 6, 6) and (100, 100, 100). Our intuition tells us that these would be "treated the same" as the first test case, thus they would be redundant. When we consider structural testing in Part III, we shall see that "treated the same" maps onto "traversing the same execution path".

The key (and the craft!) of equivalence class testing is the choice of the equivalence relation that determines the classes. Very often, we make this choice by "second guessing" the likely implementation, and thinking about the functional manipulations that must somehow be present in the implementation. We will illustrate this with our continuing examples, but first, we need to make a distinction between weak and strong equivalence class testing. After that, we will compare these to the traditional form of equivalence class testing.

Suppose our program is a function of three variables, a, b, and c, and the input domain consists of sets A, B, and C. Now, suppose we choose an "appropriate" equivalence relation, which induces the following partition:

$$A = A1 \cup A2 \cup A3$$
$$B = B1 \cup B2 \cup B3 \cup B4$$
$$C = C1 \cup C2$$

Finally, we denote elements of the partitions as follows:

$$a1 \in A1$$
$$b3 \in B3$$
$$c2 \in C2$$

6.1.1 WEAK EQUIVALENCE CLASS TESTING

With the notation as given above, weak equivalence class testing is accomplished by using one variable from each equivalence class in a test case. For the above example, we would end up with the following weak equivalence class test cases:

Test Case	a	b	c
WE1	a1	b1	c1
WE2	a2	b2	c2
WE3	a3	b3	c1
WE4	a1	b4	c2

This set of test cases uses one value from each equivalence class. We identify these in a systematic way, hence the apparent pattern. In fact, we will always have the same number of weak equivalence class test cases as there are classes in the partition with the largest number of subsets.

6.1.2 STRONG EQUIVALENCE CLASS TESTING

Strong equivalence class testing is based on the Cartesian Product of the partition subsets. Continuing with this example, the Cartesian Product $A \times B \times C$ will have 3 x 4 x 2 = 24 elements, resulting in the test cases in the table below:

Test Case	a	b	c
SE1	a1	b1	c1
SE2	a1	b1	c2
SE3	a1	b2	c1
SE4	a1	b2	c2
SE5	a1	b3	c1
SE6	a1	b3	c2
SE7	a1	b4	c1
SE8	a1	b4	c2
SE9	a2	b1	c1
SE10	a2	b1	c2
SE11	a2	b2	c1
SE12	a2	b2	c2
SE13	a2	b3	c1
SE14	a2	b3	c2
SE15	a2	b4	c1
SE16	a2	b4	c2
SE17	a3	b1	c1
SE18	a3	b1	c2
SE19	a3	b2	c1
SE20	a3	b2	c2
SE21	a3	b3	c1
SE22	a3	b3	c2
SE23	a3	b4	c1
SE24	a3	b4	c2

Notice the similarity between the pattern of these test cases and the construction of a truth table in propositional logic. The Cartesian Product guarantees that we have a notion of "completeness" in two senses: we cover all the equivalence classes, and we have one of each possible combination of inputs.

As we shall see from our continuing examples, the key to "good" equivalence class testing is the selection of the equivalence relation. Watch for the notion of inputs being "treated the same". Most of the time, equivalence class testing defines classes of the input domain. There is no reason why we could not define equivalence relations on the output range of the program function being tested, in fact, this is the simplest approach for the Triangle Problem.

6.1.3 TRADITIONAL EQUIVALENCE CLASS TESTING

The traditional view of equivalence class testing defines equivalence classes in terms of validity. For each input variable, there are valid and invalid values; in the traditional approach, these are identified and numbered, and then incorporated into test cases in the weak sense discussed in section 6.1.1. As a brief example, consider the valid ranges defined for the variables in the Commission problem:

$$1 \leq lock \leq 70$$
$$1 \leq stock \leq 80$$
$$1 \leq barrel \leq 90$$

The corresponding invalid ranges are:

$$lock < 1$$
$$lock > 70$$
$$stock < 1$$
$$stock > 80$$
$$barrel < 1$$
$$barrel > 90$$

Given these valid and invalid sets of inputs, the traditional equivalence testing strategy identifies test cases as follows:

1. For valid inputs, use one value from each valid class (as in what we have called weak equivalence class testing. (Note that each input in these test cases will be valid.)
2. For invalid inputs, a test case will have one invalid value and the remaining values will all be valid. (Thus a "single failure" should cause the test case to fail.)

If the input variables have defined ranges (as we had in the various boundary value examples), then the test cases from traditional equivalence class testing will always be a subset of those that would be generated by robustness testing.

There are two problems with traditional equivalence testing. The first is that, very often, the specification does not define what the expected output for an invalid test case should be. (We could argue that this is a deficiency of the specification, but that doesn't get us anywhere.) Thus testers spend a lot of time defining expected outputs for these cases. The second problem is that strongly typed languages eliminate the need for the consideration of invalid inputs. Traditional equivalence testing is a product of the time when languages such as FORTRAN and COBOL were dominant, hence this type of error was common. In fact, it was the high incidence of such errors that led to the implementation of strongly typed languages.

6.2 EQUIVALENCE CLASS TEST CASES FOR THE TRIANGLE PROBLEM

In the problem statement, we note that there are four possible outputs: Not a Triangle, Scalene, Isosceles, and Equilateral. We can use these to identify output (range) equivalence classes as follows.

$$R1 = \{<a, b, c> : \text{the triangle with sides } a, b, \text{ and } c \text{ is equilateral}\}$$
$$R2 = \{<a, b, c> : \text{the triangle with sides } a, b, \text{ and } c \text{ is isosceles}\}$$
$$R3 = \{<a, b, c> : \text{the triangle with sides } a, b, \text{ and } c \text{ is scalene}\}$$
$$R4 = \{<a, b, c> : \text{sides } a, b, \text{ and } c \text{ do not form a triangle}\}$$

These classes yield a simple set of test cases:

Test Case	a	b	c	Expected Output
OE1	5	5	5	Equilateral
OE2	2	2	3	Isosceles
OE3	3	4	5	Scalene
OE4	4	1	2	Not a Triangle

If we base equivalence classes on the input domain, we obtain a richer set of test cases. What are some of the possibilities for the three integers, a, b, and c? They can all be equal, exactly one pair can be equal (this can happen three ways), or none can be equal.

$$D1 = \{<a, b, c> : a = b = c\}$$
$$D2 = \{<a, b, c> : a = b, a \neq c\}$$
$$D3 = \{<a, b, c> : a = c, a \neq b\}$$
$$D4 = \{<a, b, c> : b = c, a \neq b\}$$
$$D5 = \{<a, b, c> : a \neq b, a \neq c, b \neq c\}$$

As a separate question, we can apply the triangle property to see if they even constitute a triangle. (For example, the triplet <1, 4, 1> has exactly one pair of equal sides, but these sides do not form a triangle.)

$$D6 = \{<a, b, c> : a \geq b + c\}$$
$$D7 = \{<a, b, c> : b \geq a + c\}$$
$$D8 = \{<a, b, c> : c \geq a + b\}$$

If we wanted to be still more thorough, we could separate the "less than or equal to" into the two distinct cases, thus the set D6 would become

$$D6' = \{<a, b, c> : a = b + c\}$$
$$D6'' = \{<a, b, c> : a > b + c\}$$

and similarly for D7 and D8.

We need to make one more observation. Notice that we have not taken any form of Cartesian Product. This is because all of our equivalence classes were already defined in terms of triplets <a, b, c>. Had we followed the dictates of traditional equivalence testing, we would have equivalence classes of integers greater than zero and integers less than or equal to zero. There would lead to a boring, unsatisfactory set of test cases.

6.3 EQUIVALENCE CLASS TEST CASES FOR THE NEXTDATE FUNCTION

The NextDate Function illustrates very well the craft of choosing the underlying equivalence relation. It is also a good example on which to compare traditional, weak, and strong forms of equivalence class testing. NextDate is a function of three variables, month, day, and year, and these have ranges defined as follows:

$$1 \leq month \leq 12$$
$$1 \leq day \leq 31$$
$$1812 \leq year \leq 2012$$

Traditional Test Cases
The valid equivalence classes are

$$M1 = \{ month : 1 \leq month \leq 12 \}$$
$$D1 = \{ day : 1 \leq day \leq 31 \}$$
$$Y1 = \{ year : 1812 \leq year \leq 2012 \}$$

The invalid equivalence classes are

$$M2 = \{ month : month < 1 \}$$
$$M3 = \{ month : month > 12 \}$$
$$D2 = \{ day : day < 1 \}$$
$$D3 = \{ day : day > 31 \}$$
$$Y2 = \{ year : year < 1812 \}$$
$$Y3 = \{ year : year > 2012 \}$$

These classes yield the following test cases, where the valid inputs are mechanically selected from the approximate middle of the valid range:

Case ID	Month	Day	Year	Expected Output
TE1	6	15	1912	6/16/1912
TE2	-1	15	1912	invalid input
TE3	13	15	1912	invalid input
TE4	6	-1	1912	invalid input
TE5	6	32	1912	invalid input
TE6	6	15	1811	invalid input
TE7	6	15	2013	invalid input

If we more carefully choose the equivalence relation, the resulting equivalence classes will be more useful. Recall we said earlier that the gist of the equivalence relation is that elements in a class are "treated the same way". One way to see the deficiency of the traditional approach is that the "treatment" is at the valid/invalid level. We next reduce the granularity by focusing on more specific treatment.

What must be done to an input date? If it is not the last day of a month, the NextDate function will simply increment the day value. At the end of a month, the next day is 1 and the month is incremented. At the end of a year, both the day and the month are reset to 1, and the year is incremented. Finally, the problem of leap year makes determining the last day of a month interesting. With all this in mind, we might postulate the following equivalence classes:

$$M1 = \{ \text{month: month has 30 days}\}$$
$$M2 = \{ \text{month: month has 31 days}\}$$
$$M3 = \{ \text{month: month is February}\}$$
$$D1 = \{\text{day: } 1 \leq \text{day} \leq 28\}$$
$$D2 = \{\text{day: day} = 29 \}$$
$$D3 = \{\text{day: day} = 30 \}$$
$$D4 = \{\text{day: day} = 31 \}$$
$$Y1 = \{\text{year: year} = 1900\}$$
$$Y2 = \{\text{year: } 1812 \leq \text{year} \leq 2012 \text{ AND (year} \neq 1900) \text{ AND (year} = 0 \bmod 4)\}$$
$$Y3 = \{\text{year : } (1812 \leq \text{year} \leq 2012 \text{ AND year} \neq 0 \bmod 4)\}$$

By choosing separate classes for 30 and 31 day months, we simplify the last day of the month question. By taking February as a separate class, we can give more attention to leap year questions. We also give special attention to day values: days in D1 are (nearly) always incremented, while days in D4 only have meaning for months in M2. Finally, we have three classes of years, the special case of the year 1900, leap years, and common years. This isn't a perfect set of equivalence classes, but its use will reveal many potential errors.

Weak Equivalence Class Test Cases

These classes yield the following weak equivalence class test cases. As before, the inputs are mechanically selected from the approximate middle of the corresponding class:

Case ID	Month	Day	Year	Expected Output
WE1	6	14	1900	6/15/1900
WE2	7	29	1912	7/30/1912
WE3	2	30	1913	invalid input
WE4	6	31	1900	invalid input

Notice that following a simple pattern yields test cases that are not particularly reassuring. This is worth remembering, because any tool that attempts to automate this process will rely on some fairly simple value selection criterion.

Strong Equivalence Class Test Cases

Using the same equivalence classes, we find the strong equivalence class test cases shown in the table below. The same value selection criterion is used. We still don't have a "perfect" set of test cases, but I think any tester would be a lot happier with the 36 strong equivalence class test cases. To illustrate the sensitivity to the choice of classes, notice that, among these 36 test cases, we never get a Feb. 28. If we had chosen five day classes, where D1' would be days 1 - 27, D1" would be 28, and the other three would stay the same. We would have a set of 45 test cases, and among these, there would be better coverage of Feb. 28 considerations.

Case ID	Month	Day	Year	Expected Output
SE1	6	14	1900	6/15/1900
SE2	6	14	1912	6/15/1912
SE3	6	14	1913	6/15/1913
SE4	6	29	1900	6/30/1900
SE5	6	29	1912	6/30/1912
SE6	6	29	1913	6/30/1913
SE7	6	30	1900	7/1/1900
SE8	6	30	1912	7/1/1912
SE9	6	30	1913	7/1/1913
SE10	6	31	1900	ERROR
SE11	6	31	1912	ERROR
SE12	6	31	1913	ERROR
SE13	7	14	1900	7/15/1900
SE14	7	14	1912	7/15/1912
SE15	7	14	1913	7/15/1913
SE16	7	29	1900	7/30/1900
SE17	7	29	1912	7/30/1912
SE18	7	29	1913	7/30/1913
SE19	7	30	1900	7/31/1900
SE20	7	30	1912	7/31/1912
SE21	7	30	1913	7/31/1913
SE22	7	31	1900	8/1/1900
SE23	7	31	1912	8/1/1912
SE24	7	31	1913	8/1/1913
SE25	2	14	1900	2/15/1900
SE26	2	14	1912	2/15/1912
SE27	2	14	1913	2/15/1913
SE28	2	29	1900	ERROR
SE29	2	29	1912	3/1/1912
SE30	2	29	1913	ERROR
SE31	2	30	1900	ERROR
SE32	2	30	1912	ERROR
SE33	2	30	1913	ERROR
SE34	2	31	1900	ERROR
SE35	2	31	1912	ERROR
SE36	2	31	1913	ERROR

We could also streamline our set of test cases by taking a closer look at the year classes. If we merge Y1 and Y3, and call the result the set of common years, our 36 test cases would drop down to 24. This change suppresses special attention to considerations in the year 1900, and it also adds some complexity to the determination of which years are leap years. Balance this against how much might be learned from the present test cases. Take a look at the test cases in which Y1 is used (SE1, SE4, SE7, ...). We don't really learn much from these, so not much would be lost by skipping them. The only thing really interesting about the year 1900 is test case SE28, and a related test case that was not generated by the set of equivalence classes, Feb. 28, 1900.

6.4 EQUIVALENCE CLASS TEST CASES FOR THE COMMISSION PROBLEM

The Input domain of the Commission Problem is "naturally" partitioned by the limits on locks, stocks, and barrels. These equivalence classes are exactly those that would also be identified by traditional equivalence class testing. The first class is the valid input, the other two are invalid. The input domain equivalence classes lead to very unsatisfactory sets of test cases. We'll do a little better with equivalence classes defined on the output range of the commission function.

Variable   Input Domain Equivalence Classes

Lock   L1 = { lock: $1 \leq lock \leq 70$ }
        L2 = { lock: $lock < 1$ }
        L3 = { lock: $lock > 70$ }

Stock   S1 = { stock: $1 \leq stock \leq 80$ }
         S2 = { stock: $stock < 1$ }
         S3 = { stock: $stock > 80$ }

Barrel   B1 = { barrel: $1 \leq barrel \leq 90$ }
          B2 = { barrel: $barrel < 1$ }
          B3 = { barrel: $barrel > 90$ }

Weak Input Domain Equivalence Class Test Cases

These classes yield the following weak equivalence class test cases. As with the other examples, the inputs are mechanically selected.

Test Case	locks	stocks	barrels	sales	commission
WE1	35	40	45	500	50
WE2	0	0	0	ERROR	ERROR
WE3	71	81	91	ERROR	ERROR

Traditional Input Domain Equivalence Class Test Cases

The same classes yield the following traditional equivalence class test cases. As with the other examples, the inputs are mechanically selected.

Test Case	locks	stocks	barrels	sales	commission
SE1	35	40	45	500	50
SE2	35	40	0	ERROR	ERROR
SE3	35	40	91	ERROR	ERROR
SE4	35	0	45	ERROR	ERROR
SE5	35	0	0	ERROR	ERROR
SE6	35	0	91	ERROR	ERROR
SE7	35	81	45	ERROR	ERROR
SE8	35	81	0	ERROR	ERROR
SE9	35	81	91	ERROR	ERROR
SE10	0	40	45	ERROR	ERROR
SE11	0	40	0	ERROR	ERROR
SE12	0	40	91	ERROR	ERROR
SE13	0	0	45	ERROR	ERROR
SE14	0	0	0	ERROR	ERROR
SE15	0	0	91	ERROR	ERROR
SE16	0	81	45	ERROR	ERROR
SE17	0	81	0	ERROR	ERROR
SE18	0	81	91	ERROR	ERROR
SE19	71	40	45	ERROR	ERROR
SE20	71	40	0	ERROR	ERROR
SE21	71	40	91	ERROR	ERROR
SE22	71	0	45	ERROR	ERROR
SE23	71	0	0	ERROR	ERROR
SE24	71	0	91	ERROR	ERROR
SE25	71	81	45	ERROR	ERROR
SE26	71	81	0	ERROR	ERROR
SE27	71	81	91	ERROR	ERROR

Output Range Equivalence Class Test Cases

Notice that, of 27 test cases, only one is a legitimate input. If we were really worried about error cases, this might be a good set of test cases. It can hardly give us a sense of confidence about the calculation portion of the problem, however. We can get some help by considering equivalence classes defined on the output range. Recall that sales is a function of the number of locks, stocks and barrels sold:

$$\text{sales} = 45 \text{ x locks} + 30 \text{ x stocks} + 25 \text{ x barrels}$$
$$L1 = \{ <\text{lock, stock, barrel}> : \text{sales} < 1000 \}$$
$$L2 = \{ <\text{lock, stock, barrel}> : 1000 \leq \text{sales} \leq 1800 \}$$
$$L3 = \{ <\text{lock, stock, barrel}> : \text{sales} > 1800 \}$$

Figure 5.6 helps us get a better "feel" for the input space. Elements of L1 are points with integer coordinates in the pyramid near the origin. Elements of L2 are points in the "triangular slice" between the pyramid and the rest of the input space. Finally, elements of L3 are all those points in the rectangular volume that are not in L1 or in L2. All the error cases found by the strong equivalence classes of the input domain are outside of the rectangular space shown in Figure 5.6.

As was the case with the Triangle Problem, the fact that our input is a triplet means that we no longer take test cases from a Cartesian Product.

Output Range Equivalence Class Test Cases:

Test Case	locks	stocks	barrels	sales	commission
OR1	5	5	5	500	50
OR2	15	15	15	1500	175
OR3	25	25	25	2500	360

These test cases give us some sense that we are exercising important parts of the problem.

6.5 GUIDELINES AND OBSERVATIONS

Now that we have gone through three examples, we conclude with some observations about, and guidelines for equivalence class testing.

1. The traditional form of equivalence class testing is generally not as thorough as weak equivalence class testing, which in turn, is not as thorough as the strong form of equivalence class testing.
2. The only time it makes sense to use the traditional approach is when the implementation language is not strongly typed.
3. If error conditions are a high priority, we could extend strong equivalence class testing to include invalid classes.
4. Equivalence class testing is appropriate when input data is defined in terms of ranges and sets of discrete values. This is certainly the case when system malfunctions can occur for out-of-limit variable values.
5. Equivalence class testing is strengthened by a hybrid approach with boundary value testing. (We can "reuse" the effort made in defining the equivalence classes.)
6. Equivalence class testing is indicated when the program function is complex. In such cases, the complexity of the function can help identify useful equivalence classes, as in the NextDate function.
7. Strong equivalence class testing makes a presumption that the variables are independent when the Cartesian Product is taken. If there are any dependencies, these will often generate "error" test cases, as they did in the NextDate function. (The decision table technique in Chapter 7 resolves this problem.)
8. Several tries may be needed before "the right" equivalence relation is discovered, as we saw in the NextDate example. In other cases, there is an "obvious" or "natural" equivalence relation. When in doubt, the best bet is to try to second guess aspects of any reasonable implementation.

EXERCISES

1. Starting with the 36 strong equivalence class test cases for the NextDate function, revise the day classes as discussed, and then find the other nine test cases.
2. If you use a compiler for a strongly typed language, discuss how it would react to traditional equivalence class test cases.
3. Revise the set of equivalence classes for the extended Triangle Problem that considers right triangles.
4. Discuss how well the three forms of equivalence class testing deal with the multiple fault assumption.
5. The Spring and Fall changes between Standard and Daylight Savings time create an interesting problem for telephone bills. Develop equivalence classes for a long distance telephone service that bills calls at a flat rate of $0.05 per minute. Assume that the chargeable time of a call begins when the called party answers, and ends when the calling party disconnects.

Chapter 7

Decision Table Based Testing

Of all the functional testing methods, those based on decision tables are the most rigorous, because decision tables themselves enforce logical rigor. There are two closely related methods, Cause-Effect graphing [Elmendorf 73], {Myers 79} and the decision tableau method [Mosley 93]. These are more cumbersome to use, and are fully redundant with decision tables, so we will not discuss them here. Both are covered in [Mosley 93].

7.1 DECISION TABLES

Decision tables have been used to represent and analyze complex logical relationships since the early 1960s. They are ideal for describing situations in which a number of combinations of actions are taken under varying sets of conditions. Some of the basic decision table terms are illustrated in Figure 7.1

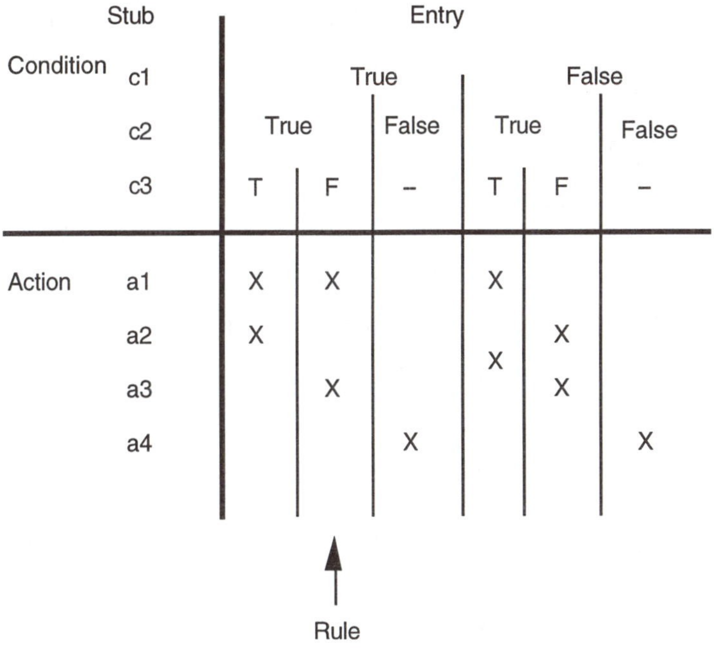

	Stub	Entry					
Condition	c1	True			False		
	c2	True		False	True		False
	c3	T	F	–	T	F	–
Action	a1	X	X		X		
	a2	X			X	X	
	a3		X			X	
	a4			X			X

↑
Rule

Figure 7.1 Decision Table Terminology

There are four portions of a decision table: the part to the left of the bold vertical line is the stub portion, to the right is the entry portion. The part above the bold line is the condition portion, below is the action portion. Thus we can refer to the condition stub, the condition entries, the action stub, and the action entries. A column in the entry portion is a rule. Rules indicate which actions are taken for the conditional circumstances indicated in the condition portion of the rule. In the decision table in Figure 7.1, when conditions c1, c2, and c3 are all true, actions a1 and a2 occur. When c1 and c2 are both true, and c3 is false, then actions a1 and a3 occur. The entry for c3 in the rule where c1 is true and c2 is false is called a "Don't Care" entry. The Don't Care entry has two major interpretations: the condition is irrelevant, or the condition does not apply. Sometimes people will enter the "n/a" symbol for this latter interpretation.

When we have binary conditions (True/False, Yes/No, 0/1), the condition portion of a decision table is a truth table (from propositional logic) that has been rotated 90°. This structure guarantees that we consider every possible combination of condition values. When we use decision tables for test case identification, this completeness property of a decision table will guarantee a form of complete testing. Decision tables in which all the conditions are binary are called Limited Entry Decision Tables. If conditions are allowed to have several values, the resulting tables are called Extended Entry Decision Tables. We will see examples of both types for the NextDate problem.

Decision tables are somewhat declarative (as opposed to imperative): there is no particular order implied by the conditions, and selected actions do not occur in any particular order.

7.1.2 TECHNIQUE

To identify test cases with decision tables, we interpret conditions as inputs, and actions as outputs. Sometimes, conditions end up referring to equivalence classes of inputs, and actions refer to major functional processing portions of the item being tested. The rules are then interpreted as test cases. Because the decision table can mechanically be forced to be complete, we know we have a comprehensive set of test cases. There are several techniques that produce decision tables that are more useful to testers. One helpful style is to add an action to show when a rule is logically impossible.

c1: a, b, c are a triangle?	N				Y				
c2: a = b?	--		Y				N		
c3: a = c?	--	Y		N		Y		N	
c4: b = c?	--	Y	N	Y	N	Y	N	Y	N
a1: not a triangle	X								
a2: Scalene									X
a3: Isosceles					X		X	X	
a4: Equilateral		X							
a5: Imposible			X	X		X			

Figure 7.2 Decision Table for the Triangle Problem

In the decision table in Figure 7.2, we see examples of Don't Care entries and impossible rule usage. If the integers a, b, and c do not constitute a triangle, we don't even care about possible equalities, as indicated in the first rule. In rules 3, 4, and 6, if two pairs of integers are equal, by transitivity, the third pair must be equal, thus the negative entry makes the rule(s) impossible.

The decision table in Figure 7.3 illustrates another consideration related to technique: the choice of conditions can greatly expand the size of a decision table. Here, we expanded the old condition (c1: a, b, c are a triangle?) to a more detailed view of the three inequalities of the triangle property. If any one of these fails, the three integers do not constitute sides of a triangle. We could expand this still further, because there are two ways an inequality could fail: one side could equal the sum of the other two, or it could be strictly greater. The rule entry portion of this decision table is as in Figure 7.3, except that each condition entry is explicitly shown. This is a matter of style, not content. I think the style in Figure 7.2 is more readable.

conditions											
c1: a<b+c?	F	T	T	T	T	T	T	T	T	T	T
c2: b<a+c?	-	F	T	T	T	T	T	T	T	T	T
c3: c<a+b?	-	-	F	T	T	T	T	T	T	T	T
c4: a = b?	-	-	-	T	T	T	T	F	F	F	F
c5: a = c?	-	-	-	T	T	F	F	T	T	F	F
c6: b = c?	-	-	-	T	F	T	F	T	F	T	F
a1: Not a triangle	X	X	X								
a2: Scalene											X
a3: Isosceles							X		X	X	
a4: Equilateral				X							
a5: Impossible					X	X		X			

Figure 7.3 Refined Decision Table for the Triangle Problem

When conditions refer to equivalence classes, decision tables have a characteristic appearance. Conditions in the decision table in Figure 7.4 are from the NextDate problem; they refer to the mutually exclusive possibilities for the month variable. Since a month is in exactly one equivalence class, we cannot ever have a rule in which two entries are true. The Don't Care entries (—) really mean "must be false". Some decision table aficionados use the notation F! to make this point.

conditions	R1	R2	R3
c1: month in M1	T	--	--
c2: month in M2	--	T	--
c3: month in M3	--	--	T
a1			
a2			
a3			

Figure 7.4 Decision Table with Mutually Exclusive Conditions

Use of Don't Care entries has a subtle effect on the way in which complete decision tables are recognized. For limited entry decision tables, if there are n conditions, there must be 2^n rules. When Don't Care entries really indicate that the condition is irrelevant, we can develop a rule count as follows. Rules in which no Don't Care entries occur count as one rule. Each Don't Care entry in a rule doubles the count of that rule. The rule counts for the decision table in Figure 7.3 are shown below. Notice that the sum of the rule counts is 64 (as it should be).

conditions											
c1: a<b+c?	F	T	T	T	T	T	T	T	T	T	T
c2: b<a+c?	-	F	T	T	T	T	T	T	T	T	T
c3: c<a+b?	-	-	F	T	T	T	T	T	T	T	T
c4: a = b?	-	-	-	T	T	T	T	F	F	F	F
c5: a = c?	-	-	-	T	T	F	F	T	T	F	F
c6: b = c?	-	-	-	T	F	T	F	T	F	T	F
Rule Count	32	16	8	1	1	1	1	1	1	1	1
a1: Not a triangle	X	X	X								
a2: Scalene											X
a3: Isosceles							X		X	X	
a4: Equilateral				X							
a5: Impossible					X	X		X			

If we applied this simplistic algorithm to the decision table in Figure 7.4, we get the rule counts shown below:

conditions	R1	R2	R3
c1: month in M1	T	–	–
c2: month in M2	–	T	–
c3: month in M3	–	–	T
Rule Count	4	4	4
a1			

Since we should only have eight rules, we clearly have a problem. To see where the problem lies, we expand each of the three rules, replacing the — entries with the T and F possibilities.

conditions	1.1	1.2	1.3	1.4	2.1	2.2	2.3	2.4	3.1	3.2	3.3	3.4
c1: mo. in M1	T	T	T	T	T	T	F	F	T	T	F	F
c2: mo. in M2	T	T	F	F	T	T	T	T	T	F	T	F
c3: mo. in M3	T	F	T	F	T	F	T	F	T	T	T	T
Rule Count	1	1	1	1	1	1	1	1	1	1	1	1
a1												

Notice that we have three rules in which all entries are T: rules 1.1, 2.1, and 3.1. We also have two rules with T, T, F entries: rules 1.2 and 2.2. Similarly, rules 1.3 and 3.2 are identical; so are rules 2.3 and 3.3. If we delete the repetitions, we end up with seven rules; the missing rule is the one in which all conditions are false. The result of this process in shown in Figure 7.5. The impossible rules are also shown.

conditions	1.1	1.2	1.3	1.4	2.3	2.4	3.4	
c1: mo. in M1	T	T	T	T	F	F	F	F
c2: mo. in M2	T	T	F	F	T	T	F	F
c3: mo. in M3	T	F	T	F	T	F	T	F
Rule Count	1	1	1	1	1	1	1	1
a1: Impossible	X	X	X		X			X
a2								
a3								

Figure 7.5 Mutually Exclusive Conditions with Impossible Rules

The ability to recognize (and develop) complete decision tables puts us in a powerful position with respect to redundancy and inconsistency. The decision table in Figure 7.6 is redundant — there are three conditions and nine rules. (Rule 9 is identical to rule 4.)

conditions	1-4	5	6	7	8	9
c1	T	F	F	F	F	T
c2	--	T	T	F	F	F
c3	--	T	F	T	F	F
a1	X	X	X	--	--	X
a2	--	X	X	X	--	--
a3	X	--	X	X	X	X

Figure 7.6 A Redundant Decision Table

Notice that the action entries in rule 9 are identical to those in rules 1 - 4. As long as the actions in a redundant rule are identical to the corresponding part of the decision table, there isn't much of a problem. If the action entries are different, as they are in Figure 7.7, we have a bigger problem.

conditions	1-4	5	6	7	8	9
c1	T	F	F	F	F	T
c2	--	T	T	F	F	F
c3	--	T	F	T	F	F
a1	X	X	X	--	--	--
a2	--	X	X	X	--	X
a3	X	--	X	X	X	--

Figure 7.7 An Inconsistent Decision Table

If the decision table in Figure 7.7 were to process a transaction in which c1 is true and both c2 and c3 are false, both rules 4 and 9 apply. We can make two observations:

1. Rules 4 and 9 are inconsistent.
2. The decision table is non-deterministic.

Rules 4 and 9 are inconsistent because the action sets are different. The whole table is non-deterministic because there is no way to decide whether to apply rule 4 or rule 9. The bottom line for testers is that care should be taken when Don't Care entries are used in a decision table.

7.2 TEST CASES FOR THE TRIANGLE PROBLEM

Using the decision table in Figure 7.3, we obtain eleven functional test cases: three impossible cases, three ways to fail the triangle property, one way to get an equilateral triangle, one way to get a scalene triangle, and three ways to get an isosceles triangle. If we extended the decision table to show both ways to fail an inequality, we would pick up three more test cases (where one side is exactly the sum of the other two). Some judgment is required in this because of the exponential growth of rules. In this case, we would end up with many more don't care entries, and more impossible rules.

Case ID	a	b	c	Expected Output
DT1	4	1	2	Not a Triangle
DT2	1	4	2	Not a Triangle
DT3	1	2	4	Not a Triangle
DT4	5	5	5	Equilateral
DT5	?	?	?	Impossible
DT6	?	?	?	Impossible
DT7	2	2	3	Isosceles
DT8	?	?	?	Impossible
DT9	2	3	2	Isosceles
DT10	3	2	2	Isosceles
DT11	3	4	5	Scalene

7.3 TEST CASES FOR THE NEXTDATE FUNCTION

The NextDate function was chosen because it illustrates the problem of dependencies in the input domain. This makes it a perfect example for decision table based testing, because decision tables can highlight such dependencies. Recall that, in chapter 6, we identified equivalence classes in the input domain of the NextDate function. One of the limitations we found in Chapter 6 was that indiscriminate selection of input values from the equivalence classes resulted in "strange" test cases, such as finding the next date to June 31, 1812. The problem stems from the presumption that the variables are independent. If they are, a Cartesian Product of the classes makes sense. When there are logical dependencies among variables in the input domain, these dependencies are lost (suppressed is better) in a Cartesian Product. The decision table format lets us emphasize such dependencies using the notion of the "impossible action" to denote impossible combinations of conditions. In this section, we will make three tries at a decision table formulation of the NextDate function.

First Try

Identifying appropriate conditions and actions presents an opportunity for craftsmanship. Suppose we start with a set of equivalence classes close to the one we used in Chapter 6.

Variable   Equivalence Classes

Month   M1 = { month : month has 30 days}
         M2 = { month : month has 31 days}
         M3 = { month : month is February}

Day   D1 = {day : 1 ≤ day ≤ 28}
       D2 = {day : day = 29 }
       D3 = {day : day = 30 }
       D4 = {day : day = 31 }

Year   Y1 = {year : year is a leap year}
        Y2 = {year : year is a common year}

If we wish to highlight impossible combinations, we could make a Limited Entry Decision Table with the following conditions and actions. (Note that the equivalence classes for the year variable collapse into one condition.)

conditions												
c1: month in M1?	T											
c2: month in M2?		T										
c3: month in M3?			T									
c4: day in D1?												
c5: day in D2?												
c6: day in D3?												
c7: day in D4?												
c8: year in Y1?												
a1: impossible												
a2: next date												

This decision table will have 256 rules, many of which will be impossible. If we wanted to show why these rules were impossible, we might revise our actions to the following:

Actions

  a1: Too many days in a month
  a2: Cannot happen in a common year
  a3: Compute the next date

Second Try

If we focus on the leap year aspect of the NextDate function, we could use the set of equivalence classes as they were in Chapter 6. These classes have a Cartesian Product that contains 36 triples, with several being impossible.

To illustrate another decision table technique, this time we'll develop an Extended Entry Decision Table, and we'll take a closer look at the action stub. In making an Extended Entry Decision Table, we must ensure that the equivalence classes form a true partition of the input domain. (Recall from Chapter 3 that a partition is a set of disjoint subsets whose union is the entire set.) If there were any "overlap" among the rule entries, we would have a redundant case in which more than one rule could be satisfied. Here, Y2 is the set of years between 1812 and 2012 evenly divisible by four excluding the year 1900.

Variable   Equivalence Classes

Month   M1 = { month: month has 30 days}
         M2 = { month: month has 31 days}
         M3 = { month: month is February}

Day   D1 = {day: $1 \leq day \leq 28$}
         D2 = {day: day = 29 }
         D3 = {day: day = 30 }
         D4 = {day: day = 31 }

Year   Y1 = {year: year = 1900}
         Y2 = {year: $1812 \leq year \leq 2012$ AND (year $\neq$ 1900) AND (year = 0 mod 4)}
         Y3 = {year: ($1812 \leq year \leq 2012$ AND year $\neq$ 0 mod 4)}

In a sense, we could argue that we have a "gray box" technique, because we take a closer look at the NextDate function. In order to produce the next date of a given date, there are only five possible manipulations: incrementing and resetting the day and month, and incrementing the year, (we won't let time go backwards by resetting the year).

conditions	1	2	3	4	5	6	7	8
c1: month in	M1	M1	M1	M1	M2	M2	M2	M2
c2: day in	D1	D2	D3	D4	D1	D2	D3	D4
c3: year in	-	-	-	-	-	-	-	-
Rule Count	3	3	3	3	3	3	3	3
actions								
a1: impossible				X				
a2: increment day	X	X			X	X	X	
a3: reset day			X					X
a4: increment month			X					?
a5: reset month								?
a6: increment year								?

conditions	9	10	11	12	13	14	15	16
c1: month in	M3	M3	M3	M3	M3	M3	M3	M3
c2: day in	D1	D1	D1	D2	D2	D2	D3	D3
c3: year in	Y1	Y2	Y3	Y1	Y2	Y3	-	-
Rule Count	1	1	1	1	1	1	3	3
actions								
a1: impossible				X		X	X	X
a2: increment day		X						
a3: reset day	X		X		X			
a4: increment month	X		X		X			
a5: reset month								
a6: increment year								

This decision table has 36 rules, and corresponds to the Cartesian Product of the equivalence classes. We still have the problem with logically impossible rules, but this formulation helps us identify the expected outputs of a test case. If you develop this table, you will find some cumbersome problems with December (in rule 8). We fix these next.

Third Try

We can clear up the end of year considerations with a third set of equivalence classes. This time, we are very specific about days and months, and we revert to the simpler leap-year or common year condition of the first try, so the year 1900 gets no special attention. (We could do a fourth try, showing year equivalence classes as in the second try, but by now, you get the point.)

Revised NextDate Domain Equivalence Classes

Month: M1 = {month: month has 30 days}
          M2 = {month: month has 31 days except Dec.}
          M3 = {month: month is December}
          M4 = {month: month is February}

Day: D1 = {day: $1 \leq$ day ≤ 27}
          D2 = {day: day = 28 }
          D3 = {day: day = 29 }
          D4 = {day: day = 30 }
          D5 = {day: day = 31 }

Year: Y1 = {year: year is a leap year}
          Y2 = {year: year isa common year}

The Cartesian product of these contains 40 elements. The full decision table is given in Figure 7.8; it has 22 rules, compared to the 36 of the second try. Recall from Chapter 1 the question of whether a large set of test cases is necessarily better than a smaller set. Here we have a 22 rule decision table that gives a clearer picture of the NextDate function than does the 36 rule decision table. The first five rules deal with 30 day months; notice that the leap year considerations are irrelevant. The next two sets of rules (6 - 10 and 11 - 15) deal with 31 day months, where the first five deal with months other than December, and the second five deal with December. There are no impossible rules in this portion of the decision table, though there is some redundancy that an efficient tester might question. Eight of the ten rules simply increment the day. Would we really require eight separate test cases for this subfunction? Probably not, but note the insights we can get from the decision table. Finally, the last seven rules focus on February and leap year.

The decision table in Figure 7.8 is the basis for the source code for the NextDate function in Chapter 2. As an aside, this example shows how good testing can improve programming. All of the decision table analysis could have been done during the detailed design of the NextDate function.

conditions	1	2	3	4	5	6	7	8	9	10
c1: month in	M1	M1	M1	M1	M1	M2	M2	M2	M2	M2
c2: day in	D1	D2	D3	D4	D5	D1	D2	D3	D4	D5
c3: year in	-	-	-	-	-	-	-	-	-	-
actions										
a1: impossible					X					
a2: increment day	X	X	X			X	X	X	X	
a3: reset day				X						X
a4: increment month				X						X
a5: reset month										
a6: increment year										

conditions	11	12	13	14	15	16	17	18	19	20	21	22
c1: month in	M3	M3	M3	M3	M3	M4	M4	M4	M4	M4	M4	M4
c2: day in	D1	D2	D3	D4	D5	D1	D2	D2	D3	D3	D4	D5
c3: year in	-	-	-	-	-	-	Y1	Y2	Y1	Y2	-	-
actions												
a1: impossible										X	X	X
a2: incr. day	X	X	X	X		X	X					
a3: reset day					X			X	X			
a4: incr. month								X	X			
a5: reset month					X							
a6: incr. year					X							

Figure 7.8 Decision Table for the NextDate Function

Corresponding Test Cases:

Case ID	Month	Day	Year	Expected Output
1	April	15	1993	April 16, 1993
2	April	28	1993	April 29, 1993
3	April	29	1993	April 30, 1993
4	April	30	1993	May 1, 1993
5	April	31	1993	Impossible
6	Jan.	15	1993	Jan. 16, 1993
7	Jan.	28	1993	Jan. 29, 1993
8	Jan.	29	1993	Jan. 30, 1993
9	Jan.	30	1993	Jan. 31, 1993
10	Jan.	31	1993	Feb. 1, 1993
11	Dec.	15	1993	Dec. 16, 1993
12	Dec.	28	1993	Dec. 29, 1993
13	Dec.	29	1993	Dec. 30, 1993
14	Dec.	30	1993	Dec. 31, 1993
15	Dec.	31	1993	Jan. 1, 1994
16	Feb.	15	1993	Feb. 16, 1993
17	Feb.	28	1992	Feb. 29, 1992
18	Feb.	28	1993	Mar. 1, 1993
19	Feb.	29	1992	Mar. 1, 1992
20	Feb.	29	1993	Impossible
21	Feb.	30	1993	Impossible
22	Feb.	31	1993	Impossible

7.4 TEST CASES FOR THE COMMISSION PROBLEM

As we will see in this section, the Commission Problem is not well-served by a decision table analysis. Not surprising, because there is very little decisional logic in the problem. What we can do is see how decision tables can help to improve an under-specified problem (the Commission Problem is a good example of this all too common situation).

To get started, recall that the Commission Problem is a portion of the larger Lock, Stock, and Barrel example, in which telegrams representing orders are sent to a central point. The functional view of the entire problem is that the salesperson's commission is a function of the telegrams:

$$F(telegrams) = commission$$

This decomposes naturally into three subfunctions:

$$F1(telegrams) = (locks, stocks, barrels)$$
$$F2(locks, stocks, barrels) = sales$$
$$F3(sales) = commission$$

The Commission Problem is just the composition of F2 and F3. As we saw in Chapter 6, the input domain is partitioned by the limits on locks, stocks, and barrels.

Variable   Equivalence Classes for F2

Lock $L1 = \{lock: lock < 1\}$
            $L2 = \{lock: 1 \leq lock \leq 70\}$
            $L3 = \{lock: lock > 70\}$

Stock   S1 = {stock: stock < 1 }
                    S2 = {stock: 1 ≤ stock ≤ 80 }
                    S3 = {stock: stock > 80 }

Barrel   B1 = {barrel: barrel < 1 }
                    B2 = {barrel: 1 ≤ barrel ≤ 90 }
                    B3 = {barrel: barrel > 90 }

These equivalence classes lead directly to a possible set of conditions for a decision table:

c_1: lock < 1
c_2: 1 ≤ lock ≤ 70
c_3: lock > 70
c_4: stock < 1
c_5: 1 ≤ stock ≤ 80
c_6: stock > 80
c_7: barrel < 1
c_8: 1 ≤ barrel ≤ 90
c_9: barrel > 90

So far, so good. Now, what actions shall we postulate? The original problem statement only addresses the cases where c_2, c_5, and c_8 are all true. There is no information for what should happen if any of the remaining conditions are true. This is an error of omission at specification time. A tester might use decision tables as the skeleton of an interview to determine, from the user/customer, just what actions should be taken in these circumstances. (The specifier could also have done this!) We might end up with actions such as the following:

a_1: Error: must sell at least one rifle lock.
a_2: Error: cannot sell more than 70 rifle locks.
a_3: Error: must sell at least one rifle stock.
a_4: Error: cannot sell more than 80 rifle stocks.
a_5: Error: must sell at least one rifle barrel.
a_6: Error: cannot sell more than 90 rifle barrels.

An analysis such as this raises follow-up questions. For example, what if a negative number were entered as the value of one of the variables? Would that indicate returned items? If so, the company would likely wish to reduce the salesperson's commission. Now, what if such a reduction moved the commission to a less favorable level, such as from the 20% level to the 10% level?

We get into similar questions when the sales limits are exceeded. How should excess sales be treated? Are they simply carried over to the next month? The company might prefer this, because it would likely reduce the commission level; obviously, the salesperson would prefer excess sales to contribute to the higher commission levels.

This discussion ties back to the Chapter 1 discussion on specified, programmed, and tested behaviors. The examples in which limits are violated are good examples of test cases that are "outside" the sets of specified and programmed behaviors. (We might have added a fourth circle, that refers to what the customer really wants.)

We can do a little more for the F3 subfunction. Since there are three commission levels, there will clearly be three equivalence classes.

Variable   Equivalence Classes for F3

Sales   L1 = {sales: sales < 1000 }
                    L2 = {sales: 1000 ≤ sales ≤ 1800 }
                    L3 = {sales: sales > 1800 }

These equivalence classes lead to the simple decision table in Figure 7.9:

c1: sales < 1000	T	-	-
c2: 1000 ≤ sales ≤ 1800	-	T	-
c3: sales > 1800	-	-	T
a1: compute 10% commission	X	-	-
a2: compute 15% commission	-	X	-
a3: compute 20% commission	-	-	X

Figure 7.9 Decision Table for F3 of the Commission Problem

Our last step is to identify actual test cases for the Commission Problem. Note that we cannot simply provide values of sales that would give us test cases for the subfunction F3. Now you will see how arithmetically contrived this problem really is.

Test Cases for the Commission Problem:

Test Case	locks	stocks	barrels	sales	commission
DT1	5	5	5	500	50
DT2	15	15	15	1500	175
DT3	25	25	25	2500	360

7.5 GUIDELINES AND OBSERVATIONS

As with the other testing techniques, decision table based testing works well for some applications (like NextDate) and is not worth the trouble for others (like the Commission Problem). Not surprisingly, the situations in which it works well are those where there is a lot of decision making (like the Triangle Problem), and those in which there are important logical relationships among input variables (like the NextDate function).

1. The decision table technique is indicated for applications characterized by any of the following:
   prominent If-Then-Else logic
   logical relationships among input variables
   calculations involving subsets of the input variables
   cause and effect relationships between inputs and outputs
   high cyclomatic (McCabe) complexity (see Chapter 9)
2. Decision tables don't scale up very well (a limited entry table with n conditions has 2^n rules). There are several ways to deal with this: use extended entry decision tables, algebraically simplify tables, "factor" large tables into smaller ones, and look for repeating patterns of condition entries. For more on these techniques, see [Topper 93].
3. As with other techniques, iteration helps. The first set of conditions and actions you identify may be unsatisfactory. Use it as a stepping stone, and gradually improve on it until you are satisfied with a decision table.

EXERCISES

1. Develop a decision table and additional test cases for the right triangle addition to the Triangle Problem (see Chapter 2 exercises). Note that there can be isosceles right triangles, but not with integer sides.
2. Develop a decision table for the "second try" at the NextDate function. At the end of a 31-day month, the day is always reset to 1. For all non-December months, the month is incriminated, and for December, the month is reset to January, and the year is incremented.
3. Develop a decision table for the YesterDate function (see Chapter 2 exercises).
4. Expand the Commission Problem to consider "violations" of the sales limits. Develop the corresponding decision tables and test cases for a "company friendly" version and a "salesperson friendly" version.
5. Discuss how well decision table testing deals with the multiple fault assumption.
6. Develop decision table test cases for the time change problem (Chapter 6, problem 5.)

8

Retrospective on Functional Testing

In the preceding three chapters, we studied as many types of functional testing. The common thread among these is that all view a program as a mathematical function that maps its inputs onto its outputs. With the boundary-based approaches, test cases are identified in terms of the boundaries of the ranges of the input variables, and variations give us four techniques: boundary value analysis, robustness testing, worst case testing, and robust worst case testing. We next took a closer look at the input variables, defining equivalence classes in terms of values that should receive "similar treatment" from the program being tested. There are three forms of equivalence class testing: traditional, weak, and strong. The goal of examining similar treatment is to reduce the sheer number of test cases generated by the boundary based techniques. We pushed this a step further when we used decision tables to analyze the logical dependencies imposed by the function of the program. Whenever we have a choice among alternatives, we naturally want to know which is preferred, or at least, how to make an informed choice. In this chapter we will look at questions about testing effort, testing efficiency, and then try to get a handle on test effectiveness. For convenient reference, selected sets of test cases for the continuing examples are repeated here.

8.1 SELECTED TEST CASES

In the following subsections, test cases are organized first by problem, and then by method. Rather than print all the test cases from the input domain methods, a representative sample is reprinted here. In the case of the triangle problem, Tables 1, 2, and 3 contain test cases generated by, respectively, boundary value analysis, equivalence class testing, and decision table testing. (For the triangle problem, weak and strong equivalence classes collapsed onto one set.) Tables 4, 5, and 6 contain test cases for the NextDate problem generated by worst case analysis, strong equivalence classes, and decision tables. Finally, Tables 7, 8, and 9 contain test cases for the commission problem generated by output based boundary value analysis, traditional equivalence class testing, and decision table testing.

8.1.1 TRIANGLE PROGRAM TEST CASES

The difference between the equivalence class test cases and the decision table test cases is due to the choice of ≤ in the decision table conditions. The equivalence classes were identified explicitly for one side strictly greater than the sum of the other two (cases 6, 8, and 10) and also for one side equal to the sum of the other two (cases 7, 9, and 11). Using similar conditions in the decision table would have generated three more test cases. The eleven equivalence class test cases correspond exactly to the eleven feasible paths in the FORTRAN-like version of the triangle problem. The impossible test cases generated by the decision table are due to the logical dependencies among the conditions about equal sides. (If a = b, and b = c, we must have a = c, so attempting to make it false is impossible.) These cases are indicated by the question mark entries in the decision table test cases.

Table 1   Boundary Value Functional Test Cases

Case	a	b	c	expected output
1	100	100	1	Isosceles
2	100	100	2	Isosceles
3	100	100	100	Equilateral
4	100	100	199	Isosceles
5	100	100	200	Not a Triangle
6	100	1	100	Isosceles
7	100	2	100	Isosceles
8	100	199	100	Isosceles
9	100	200	100	Not a Triangle
10	1	100	100	Isosceles
11	2	100	100	Isosceles
12	199	100	100	Isosceles
13	200	100	100	Not a Triangle

Table 2   Equivalence Class Functional Test Cases

Case	a	b	c	expected output
1	5	5	5	Equilateral
2	5	5	3	Isosceles
3	5	3	5	Isosceles
4	3	5	5	Isosceles
5	3	4	5	Scalene
6	8	3	4	Not a Triangle
7	7	3	4	Not a Triangle
8	3	8	4	Not a Triangle
9	3	7	4	Not a Triangle
10	3	4	8	Not a Triangle
11	3	4	7	Not a Triangle

Table 3   Decision Table Functional Test Cases

Case	a	b	c	expected output
1	4	1	2	Not a Triangle
2	1	4	2	Not a Triangle
3	1	2	4	Not a Triangle
4	5	5	5	Equilateral
5	?	?	?	Impossible
6	?	?	?	Impossible
7	2	2	3	Isosceles
8	?	?	?	Impossible
9	2	3	2	Isosceles
10	3	2	2	Isosceles
11	3	4	5	Scalene

8.1.2 NEXTDATE PROBLEM TEST CASES

Table 4   Worst Case Functional Test Cases

Case	month	day	year	expected output
1	1	1	1812	January 2, 1812
2	1	1	1813	January 2, 1813
3	1	1	1912	January 2, 1912
4	1	1	2011	January 2, 2011
5	1	1	2012	January 2, 2012
6	1	2	1812	January 3, 1812
7	1	2	1813	January 3, 1813
8	1	2	1912	January 3, 1912
9	1	2	2011	January 3, 2011
10	1	2	2012	January 3, 2012
11	1	15	1812	January 16, 1812
12	1	15	1813	January 16, 1813
13	1	15	1912	January 16, 1912
14	1	15	2011	January 16, 2011
15	1	15	2012	January 16, 2012
16	1	30	1812	January 31, 1812
17	1	30	1813	January 31, 1813
18	1	30	1912	January 31, 1912
19	1	30	2011	January 31, 2011
20	1	30	2012	January 31, 2012
21	1	31	1812	February 1, 1812
22	1	31	1813	February 1, 1813
23	1	31	1912	February 1, 1912
24	1	31	2011	February 1, 2011
25	1	31	2012	February 1, 2012
26	2	1	1812	February 2, 1812
27	2	1	1813	February 2, 1813
28	2	1	1912	February 2, 1912
29	2	1	2011	February 2, 2011
30	2	1	2012	February 2, 2012
31	2	2	1812	February 3, 1812
32	2	2	1813	February 3, 1813
33	2	2	1912	February 3, 1912
34	2	2	2011	February 3, 2011
35	2	2	2012	February 3, 2012
36	2	15	1812	February 16, 1812
37	2	15	1813	February 16, 1813
38	2	15	1912	February 16, 1912
39	2	15	2011	February 16, 2011
40	2	15	2012	February 16, 2012
41	2	30	1812	impossible
42	2	30	1813	impossible
43	2	30	1912	impossible
44	2	30	2011	impossible
45	2	30	2012	impossible
46	2	31	1812	impossible
47	2	31	1813	impossible

48	2	31	1912	impossible
49	2	31	2011	impossible
50	2	31	2012	impossible
51	6	1	1812	June 1 1812
52	6	1	1813	June 1 1813
53	6	1	1912	June 2, 1912
54	6	1	2011	June 2, 2011
55	6	1	2012	June 2, 2012
56	6	2	1812	June 3, 1812
57	6	2	1813	June 3, 1813
58	6	2	1912	June 3, 1912
59	6	2	2011	June 3, 2011
60	6	2	2012	June 3, 2012
61	6	15	1812	June 16, 1812
62	6	15	1813	June 16, 1813
63	6	15	1912	June 16, 1912
64	6	15	2011	June 16, 2011
65	6	15	2012	June 16, 2012
66	6	30	1812	July 1, 1812
67	6	30	1813	July 1, 1813
68	6	30	1912	July 1, 1912
69	6	30	2011	July 1, 2011
70	6	30	2012	July 1, 2012
71	6	31	1812	impossible
72	6	31	1813	impossible
73	6	31	1912	impossible
74	6	31	2011	impossible
75	6	31	2012	impossible
76	11	1	1812	November 2, 1812
77	11	1	1813	November 2, 1813
78	11	1	1912	November 2, 1912
79	11	1	2011	November 2, 2011
80	11	1	2012	November 2, 2012
81	11	2	1812	November 3, 1812
82	11	2	1813	November 3, 1813
83	11	2	1912	November 3, 1912
84	11	2	2011	November 3, 2011
85	11	2	2012	November 3, 2012
86	11	15	1812	November 16, 1812
87	11	15	1813	November 16, 1813
88	11	15	1912	November 16, 1912
89	11	15	2011	November 16, 2011
90	11	15	2012	November 16, 2012
91	11	30	1812	December 1, 1812
92	11	30	1813	December 1, 1813
93	11	30	1912	December 1, 1912
94	11	30	2011	December 1, 2011
95	11	30	2012	December 1, 2012
96	11	31	1812	impossible
97	11	31	1813	impossible
98	11	31	1912	impossible
99	11	31	2011	impossible
100	11	31	2012	impossible

101	12	1	1812	December 2, 1812
102	12	1	1813	December 2, 1813
103	12	1	1912	December 2, 1912
104	12	1	2011	December 2, 2011
105	12	1	2012	December 2, 2012
106	12	2	1812	December 3, 1812
107	12	2	1813	December 3, 1813
108	12	2	1912	December 3, 1912
109	12	2	2011	December 3, 2011
110	12	2	2012	December 3, 2012
111	12	15	1812	December 16, 1812
112	12	15	1813	December 16, 1813
113	12	15	1912	December 16, 1912
114	12	15	2011	December 16, 2011
115	12	15	2012	December 16, 2012
116	12	30	1812	December 31, 1812
117	12	30	1813	December 31, 1813
118	12	30	1912	December 31, 1912
119	12	30	2011	December 31, 2011
120	12	30	2012	December 31, 2012
121	12	31	1812	January 1, 1813
122	12	31	1813	January 1, 1814
123	12	31	1912	January 1, 1913
124	12	31	2011	January 1, 2012
125	12	31	2012	January 1, 2013

Table 5   Strong Equivalence Class Functional Test Cases

Case	Month	Day	Year	Expected Output
1	6	14	1900	June 15, 1900
2	6	14	1912	June 15, 1912
3	6	14	1913	June 15, 1913
4	6	29	1900	June 30, 1900
5	6	29	1912	June 30, 1912
6	6	29	1913	June 30, 1913
7	6	30	1900	July 1, 1900
8	6	30	1912	July 1, 1912
9	6	30	1913	July 1, 1913
10	6	31	1900	impossible
11	6	31	1912	impossible
12	6	31	1913	impossible
13	7	14	1900	July 15, 1900
14	7	14	1912	July 15, 1912
15	7	14	1913	July 15, 1913
16	7	29	1900	July 30, 1900
17	7	29	1912	July 30, 1912
18	7	29	1913	July 30, 1913
19	7	30	1900	July 31, 1900
20	7	30	1912	July 31, 1912
21	7	30	1913	July 31, 1913

Table 5   Continued

22	7	31	1900	August 1, 1900
23	7	31	1912	August 1, 1912
24	7	31	1913	August 1, 1913
25	2	14	1900	February 15, 1900
26	2	14	1912	February 15, 1912
27	2	14	1913	February 15, 1913
28	2	29	1900	impossible
29	2	29	1912	March 1, 1912
30	2	29	1913	impossible
31	2	30	1900	impossible
32	2	30	1912	impossible
33	2	30	1913	impossible
34	2	31	1900	impossible
35	2	31	1912	impossible
36	2	31	1913	impossible

Table 6   Decision Table Functional Test Cases

Case	Month	Day	Year	Expected Output
1	Apr.	15	1993	April 16, 1993
2	Apr.	28	1993	April 29, 1993
3	Apr.	29	1993	April 30, 1993
4	Apr.	30	1993	May 1, 1993
5	Apr.	31	1993	Impossible
6	Jan.	15	1993	January 16, 1993
7	Jan.	28	1993	January 29, 1993
8	Jan.	29	1993	January 30, 1993
9	Jan.	30	1993	January 31, 1993
10	Jan.	31	1993	February 1, 1993
11	Dec.	15	1993	December 16, 1993
12	Dec.	28	1993	December 29, 1993
13	Dec.	29	1993	December 30, 1993
14	Dec.	30	1993	December 31, 1993
15	Dec.	31	1993	January 1, 1994
16	Feb.	15	1993	February 16, 1993
17	Feb.	28	1992	February 29, 1992
18	Feb.	28	1993	March 1, 1993
19	Feb.	29	1992	March 1, 1992
20	Feb.	29	1993	Impossible
21	Feb.	30	1993	Impossible
22	Feb.	31	1993	Impossible

8.1.3 COMMISSION PROBLEM TEST CASES

Table 7   Output Boundary Value Functional Test Cases

Case	locks	stocks	barrels	sales	commission
1	1	1	1	100	10
2	1	1	2	125	12.5
3	1	2	1	130	13
4	2	1	1	145	14.5
5	10	10	9	975	97.5
6	10	9	10	970	97
7	9	10	10	955	95.5
8	5	5	5	500	50
9	10	10	10	1000	100
10	10	10	11	1025	103.75
11	10	11	10	1030	104.5
12	11	10	10	1045	106.75
13	14	14	14	1400	160
14	18	18	17	1775	216.25
15	18	17	18	1770	215.5
16	17	18	18	1755	213.25
17	18	18	18	1800	220
18	18	18	19	1825	225
19	18	19	18	1830	226
20	19	18	18	1845	229
21	48	48	48	4800	820
22	70	80	89	7775	1415
23	70	79	90	7770	1414
24	69	80	90	7755	1411
25	70	80	90	7800	1420

Table 8   Traditional Equivalence Class Functional Test Cases

Case	locks	stocks	barrels	sales	commission
1	35	40	45	500	50
2	35	40	0	error	error
3	35	40	91	error	error
4	35	0	45	error	error
5	35	0	45	error	error
6	0	40	45	error	error
7	71	40	45	error	error

Table 9   Decision Table Functional Test Cases

Case	locks	stocks	barrels	sales	commission
1	5	5	5	500	50
2	15	15	15	1500	175
3	25	25	25	2500	360

8.2 TESTING EFFORT

Let's return to our craftsperson metaphor for a minute. We usually think of such people as knowing their craft so well that their time is spent very effectively. Even if it takes a little longer, we like to think that the time is well spent. We are finally in a position to see a hint of this as far as testing techniques are concerned. The functional methods we have studied vary both in terms of the number of test cases generated and the effort to develop these test cases. Figures 8.1 and 8.2 show the general trends, but the sophistication axis needs some explanation.

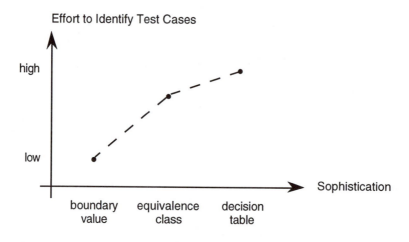

Figure 8.1 Trendline of Test Cases per Testing Method

The boundary based techniques have no recognition of data or logical dependencies; they are very mechanical in the way they generate test cases. Because of this, they are also easy to automate. The equivalence class techniques pay attention to data dependencies and to the function itself. More thought is required to use these techniques — also more judgment, or craft. The thinking goes into the identification of the equivalence classes; after that, the process is also mechanical. The decision table technique is the most sophisticated, because it requires the tester to consider both data and logical dependencies. As we saw in our examples, you might not get the conditions of a decision table right on the first try, but once you have a good set of conditions, the resulting test cases are both complete and, in some sense, minimal.

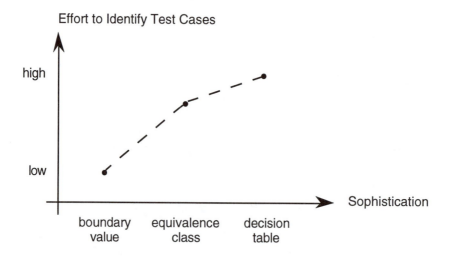

Figure 8.2 Trendline of Test Case Identification Effort per Testing Method

The end result is a satisfying trade-off between test identification effort and test execution effort: methods that are easy to use generate numerous test cases, which in turn, are more time consuming to execute. If we shift our effort toward more sophisticated testing methods, we are repaid with less test execution time. This is particularly important, since typically tests are executed several times. We might also note that judging testing quality in terms of the sheer number of test cases has drawbacks similar to judging programming productivity in terms of Lines Of Code.

Our examples bear out the trends of Figures 8.1 and 8.2. The following three graphs (Figures 8.2 - 8.5) are taken from a spreadsheet that summarized the number of test cases for each of our examples in terms of the various methods. The boundary based numbers are identical, reflecting both the mechanical nature of the techniques and the formulas that describe the number of test cases generated by each method. The main differences are seen in strong equivalence class testing and decision table testing. Both of these reflect the logical complexity of the problems, so we would expect to see differences here. When we study structural testing (Chapters 9 and 10), we will see that these distinctions have an important implication for testing. The three graphs are superimposed on each other in Figure 8.6. The robust worst case method (with its 343 test cases) is deleted so that the rest of the graph would be clearer.

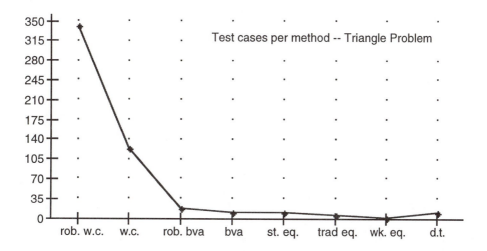

Figure 8.3   Test Case Trendline for the Triangle Problem

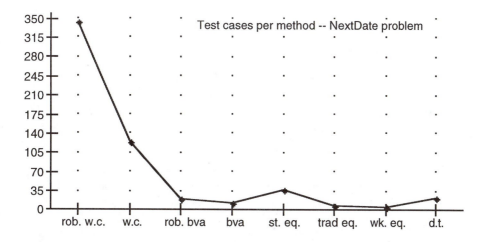

Figure 8.4   Test Case Trendline for the NextDate Problem

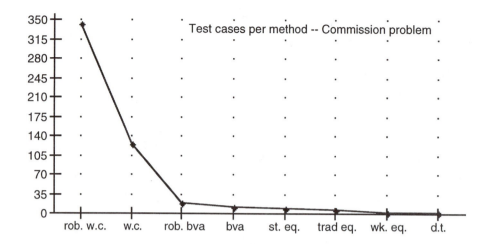

Figure 8.5 Test Case Trendline for the Commission Problem

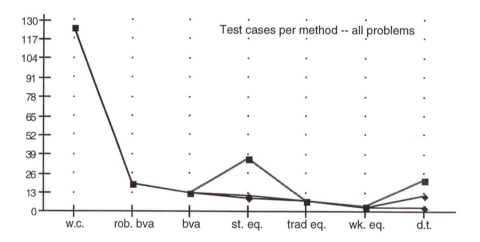

Figure 8.6 Test Case Trendline for All Three Problems

8.3 TESTING EFFICIENCY

If you look closely at these sets of test cases, you can get a feel for the fundamental limitation of functional testing: the twin possibilities of gaps of untested functionality and redundant tests. Consider the NextDate problem, for example. The decision table (that took three tries to get it right) yields 22 test cases. We have confidence that these test cases are complete (in some sense) because the decision table is complete. On the other hand, worst case boundary value analysis yielded 125 test cases. When we look closely at these, they aren't very satisfactory: what do we expect to learn from cases 1 - 5? These test cases check the NextDate function for January 1 in five different years. Since the year has nothing to do with this part of the calendar, we would expect that one of these would suffice. If we roughly estimate a "times five" redundancy, we might expect a reduction to 25 test cases, quite compatible with the 22 from the decision table approach. Looking closer, we find a few February cases, but none happen to hit February 28 or 29, and there is no interesting connection with leap years. Not only do we have a times five redundancy, we also have some severe gaps around the end of February and leap years.

The strong equivalence class test cases move in the right direction: 36 test cases, of which 11 are impossible. Once again, the impossible test cases result from the presumed independence among the equivalence classes. All but six of the decision table test cases (cases 2, 7, 12, 15, 17, and 18 of Table 6) map to corresponding strong equivalence class test cases (Table 5). Half of these deal with the twenty-eighth day of non-February months, so they aren't very interesting. The remaining three are useful test cases, especially because they test possibilities that are missed by the strong equivalence class test cases. All of this supports two conclusions: there are gaps in the functional test cases, and these are reduced by using more sophisticated techniques.

Can we push this a little further by trying to quantify what we mean by testing efficiency? The intuitive notion is that a set of test cases is "just right", that is, no gaps and no redundancy. We can develop various ratios of total number of test cases generated by method A to those generated by method B, or even ratios on a test case basis. This is usually more trouble than it is worth, but sometimes management demands numbers even when they have little real meaning. We will revisit this in Chapter 11, after we complete our study of structural testing. The structural approaches support interesting (and useful) metrics, and these will provide a much better quantification of testing efficiency. Meanwhile, we can help recognize redundancy by annotating test cases with a brief purpose comment. When we see several test cases with the same purpose, we (correctly) sense redundancy. Detecting gaps is harder: if we are can only use functional testing, the best we can do is compare the test cases that result from two methods. In general, the more sophisticated methods will help us recognize gaps, but there are no guarantees. We could develop excellent strong equivalence classes for a program, and then produce a klutzy decision table.

8.4 TESTING EFFECTIVENESS

What we would really like to know about a set of test cases is how effective they are, but we need to clarify what "effective" means. The easy choice is to be dogmatic: mandate a method, use it to generate test cases, and then run the test cases. This is absolute, and conformity is measurable, so it can be used as a basis for contractual compliance. We can improve on this by relaxing a dogmatic mandate, and require that testers choose "appropriate methods", using the guidelines given at the ends of various chapters here. We can gain another incremental improvement by devising appropriate hybrid methods, as we did with the commission problem in Chapter 5.

Structured testing techniques yield a second choice for test effectiveness. In Chapter 9 we will discuss the notion of program execution paths, which provide a good formulation of test effectiveness. We will be able to examine a set of test cases in terms of the execution paths traversed. When a particular path is traversed more than once, we might question the redundancy. Sometimes such redundancy can have a purpose, as we shall see in Chapter 10.

The best interpretation for testing effectiveness is (no great surprise) the most difficult. We would really like to know how effective a set of test cases is for finding faults present in a program. This is problematic for two reasons: first, it presumes we know all the faults in a program. Quite a circularity: if we did, we'd take care of them. Since we don't know all the faults in a program, we could never know if the test cases from a given method revealed them. The second reason is more theoretical: proving that a program is fault free is equivalent to the famous halting problem of computer science, which is known to be impossible. The best we can do is to work backwards from fault types. Given a particular kind of fault, we can choose testing methods (functional and structural) that are likely to reveal faults of that type. If we couple this with knowledge of the most likely kinds of faults, we end up with a pragmatic approach to testing effectiveness. This is improved if we track the kinds (and frequencies) of faults in the software we develop.

8.5 GUIDELINES

One of my favorite testing stories is about an inebriated man who was crawling around on the sidewalk beneath a street light. When a policeman asked him what he was doing, he replied that he was looking for his car keys. "Did you lose them here?" the policeman asked. "No, I lost them in the parking lot, but the light is better here."

This little story contains an important message for testers: there is no point testing for faults that are not likely to be present. It is far more effective to have a good idea of the kinds of faults that are most likely (or most damaging) and then to select testing methods that are likely to reveal these faults.

Many times, we don't even have a feeling for the kinds of faults that may be prevalent. What then? The best we can do is use known attributes of the program to select methods that deal with the attributes, sort of a "punishment fits the crime" view. The attributes that are most helpful in choosing functional testing methods are:

- whether the variables represent physical or logical quantities
- whether or not there are dependencies among the variables
- whether single or multiple faults are assumed
- whether exception handling is prominent

Here is the beginning of an "expert system" on functional testing technique selection.

1. If the variables refer to physical quantities, boundary testing and equivalence class testing are indicated.
2. If the variables are independent, boundary testing and equivalence class testing are indicated.
3. If the variables are dependent, decision table testing is indicated.
4. If the single-fault assumption is warranted, boundary value analysis and robustness testing are indicated.
5. If the multiple-fault assumption is warranted, worst case testing, robust worst case testing, and decision table testing are indicated.
6. If the program contains significant exception handling, robustness testing and decision table testing are indicated.
7. If the variables refer to logical quantities, equivalence class testing and decision table testing are indicated.

Since combinations of these may occur, the guidelines are summarized in decision table form below

c1.	variables are	physical					logical				
c2.	independent variables?	Y				N	Y				N
c3.	fault assumption is	S		M		-	S		M		-
c4.	exception handling?	Y	N	Y	N	-	Y	N	Y	N	-
a1.	boundary value analysis		X								
a2.	robustness testing	X									
a3.	worst case testing				X						
a4.	robust worst case			X							
a5.	trad. equiv. class	X		X			X		X		
a6.	weak equiv. class	X	X				X	X			
a7.	strong equiv. class			X	X	X			X	X	X
a8.	decision table					X					X

Part III

Structural Testing

Chapter 9

Path Testing

The distinguishing characteristic of structural testing methods is that they are all based on the source code of the program being tested, and not on the definition. Because of this absolute basis, structural testing methods are very amenable to rigorous definitions, mathematical analysis, and precise measurement. In this chapter, we will examine the two most common forms of path testing. The technology behind these has been available since the mid-1970s, and the originators of these methods now have companies that market very successful tools that implement the techniques. Both techniques start with the program graph; we repeat the improved definition from Chapter 4 here.

Definition
Given a program written in an imperative programming language, its ***program graph*** is a directed graph in which nodes are either entire statements or fragments of a statement, and edges represent flow of control.

If i and j are nodes in the program graph, there is an edge from node i to node j iff the statement (fragment) corresponding to node j can be executed immediately after the statement (fragment) corresponding to node i.

Constructing a program graph from a given program is an easy process. It's illustrated here with the Pascal implementation of the Triangle program from Chapter 2. Line numbers refer to statements and statement fragments. There is an element of judgment here: sometimes it is convenient to keep a fragment (like a BEGIN) as a separate node, as at line 4. Other times is seems better to include this with another portion of a statement: the BEGIN at line 13 could really be merged with the THEN on line 12. We will see that this latitude collapses onto a unique DD-Path graph, so the differences introduced by differing judgments are moot. (A mathematician would make the point that, for a given program, there might be several distinct program graphs, all of which reduce to a unique DD-Path graph.) We also need to decide whether to associate nodes with non-executable statements such as variable and type declarations: here we do not.

A program graph of this program is given in Figure 9.1. Examine it closely to find (sub)graphs of the structured programming constructs we discussed in Chapter 4.

Nodes 4 through 7 are a sequence, nodes 8 through 11 are an IF-THEN-ELSE construct (that terminates on an IF clause), and nodes 14 through 16 are an IF-THEN construct. Nodes 4 and 22 are the program source and sink nodes, corresponding to the single entry, single exit criteria.. There are no loops, so this is a directed acyclic graph.

The importance of the program graph is that program executions correspond to paths from the source to the sink nodes. Since test cases force the execution of some such program path, we now have a very explicit description of the relationship between a test case and the part of the program it exercises. We also have an elegant, theoretically respectable way to deal with the potentially large number of execution paths in a program. Figure 9.2 is a graph of a simple program; it is typical of the kind of example used to show the impossibility of completely testing even simple programs [Schach 93].

In this program, there are 5 paths from node B to node F in the interior of the loop. If the loop may have up to 18 repetitions, there are some 4.77 trillion distinct program execution paths.

108

```
1.  program triangle (input,output);
2.  VAR a, b, c        : integer;
3.      IsATriangle    : boolean;
4.  BEGIN
5.  writeln('Enter three integers which are sides of a triangle:');
6.  readln(a,b,c);
7.  writeln('Side A is ',a,'Side B is ',b,'Side C is ',c);
8.  IF (a < b + c) AND (b < a + c) AND (c < a + b)
9.      THEN IsATriangle := TRUE
10.      ELSE IsATriangle := FALSE ;
11. IF IsATriangle
12.      THEN
13.      BEGIN
14.      IF (a = b) XOR (a = c) XOR (b = c) AND NOT((a=b) AND (a=c))
15.          THEN Writeln ('Triangle is Isosceles');
16.      IF (a = b) AND (b = c)
17.          THEN Writeln ('Triangle is Equilateral');
18.      IF (a <> b) AND (a <> c) AND (b <> c)
19.          THEN Writeln ('Triangle is Scalene');
20.      END
21.      ELSE WRITELN('Not a Triangle');
22. END.
```

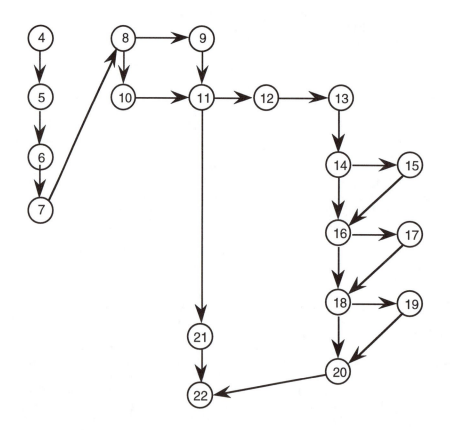

Figure 9.1 Program Graph of the Pascal Triangle Program

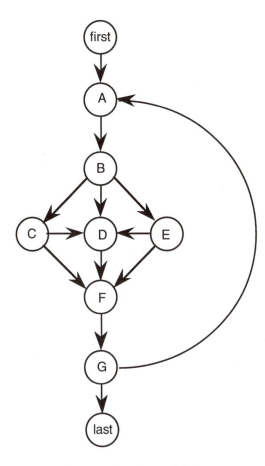

Figure 9.2 Trillions of Paths

9.1 DD-PATHS

The best known form of structural testing is based on a construct known as a decision-to-decision path (DD-Path) [Miller 77]. The name refers to a sequence of statements that, in Miller's words, begins with the "outway" of a decision statement and ends with the "inway" of the next decision statement. There are no internal branches in such a sequence, so the corresponding code is like a row of dominoes lined up so that when the first falls, all the rest in the sequence fall. Miller's original definition works well for second generation languages like FORTRAN II, because decision making statements (such as arithmetic IFs and DO loops) use statement labels to refer to target statements. With block structured languages (Pascal, Ada, C), the notion of statement fragments resolves the difficulty of applying Miller's original definition—otherwise, we end up with program graphs in which some statements are members of more than one DD-Path.

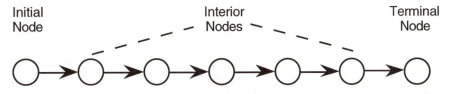

Initial
Node

Interior
Nodes

Terminal
Node

Figure 9.3 A Chain Of Nodes In A Directed Graph

We will define DD-Paths in terms of paths of nodes in a directed graph. We might call these paths chains, where a *chain* is a path in which the initial and terminal nodes are distinct, and every interior node has indegree = 1 and outdegree = 1. Notice that the initial node is 2-connected to every other node in the chain, and there are no instances of 1- or 3-connected nodes, as shown in Figure 9.3. The length (number of edges) of the chain in Figure 9.3 is 6. We can have a degenerate case of a chain that is of length 0, that is, a chain consisting of exactly one node and no edges.

Definition

A **DD-Path** is a chain in a program graph such that

Case 1: it consists of a single node with indeg = 0,
Case 2: it consists of a single node with outdeg = 0,
Case 3: it consists of a single node with indeg ≥ 2 or outdeg ≥ 2,
Case 4: it consists of a single node with indeg = 1 and outdeg = 1,
Case 5: it is a maximal chain of length ≥ 1.

Cases 1 and 2 establish the unique source and sink nodes of the program graph of a structured program as initial and final DD-Paths. Case 3 deals with complex nodes; it assures that no node is contained in more than one DD-Path. Case 4 is needed for "short branches"; it also preserves the one fragment, one DD-Path principle. Case 5 is the "normal case", in which a DD-Path is a single entry, single exit sequence of nodes (a chain). The "maximal" part of the case 5 definition is used to determine the final node of a normal (non–trivial) chain.

Table 1: Types of DD-Paths in Figure 9.1

Program Graph Nodes	DD-Path Name	Case of Definition
4	first	1
5 - 8	A	5
9	B	4
10	C	4
11	D	3
12 - 14	E	5
15	F	4
16	G	3
17	H	4
18	I	3
19	J	4
20	K	3
21	L	4
22	last	2

This is a complex definition, so we'll apply it to the program graph in Figure 9.1. Node 4 is a Case 1 DD-Path, we'll call it "first"; similarly, node 22 is a Case 2 DD-Path, and we'll call it "last". Nodes 5 through 8 are a Case 5 DD-Path. We know that node 8 is the last node in this DD-Path because it is the last node that preserves the 2-connectedness property of the chain. If we went beyond node 8 to include nodes 9 and 10, these would both be 2-connected to the rest of the chain, but they are only 1-connected to each other. If we stopped at node 7, we would violate the "maximal" criterion. Node 11 is a Case 3 DD-Path, which forces nodes 9 and 10 to be individual DD-Paths by case 4. Nodes 12 through 14 are a case 5 DD-Path by the same reasoning as for nodes 5 - 8. Nodes 14 through 20 correspond to a sequence of IF-THEN statements. Nodes 16 and 18 are both Case 3 DD-Paths, and this forces nodes 15, 17, and 19 to be Case 4 DD-Paths. Node 20 is a Case 3 DD-Path, and node 21 is a Case 4 DD-Path. All of this is summarized in Table 1, where the DD-Path names correspond to the DD-Path graph in Figure 9.4.

Part of the confusion with this example is that the triangle problem is logic intensive and computationally sparse. This combination yields many short DD-Paths. If the THEN and ELSE clauses contained BEGIN .. END blocks of computational statements, we would have longer DD-Paths, as we do in the commission problem.

We can now define the DD-Path graph of a program.

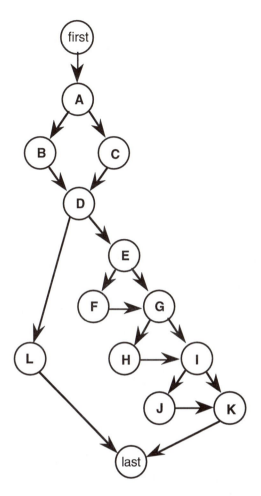

Figure 9.4   DD-Path Graph for the Triangle Program

Definition

Given a program written in an imperative language, its ***DD-Path graph*** is the directed graph in which nodes are DD-Paths of its program graph, and edges represent control flow between successor DD-Paths.

In effect, the DD-Path graph is a form of condensation graph (see Chapter 4); in this condensation, 2-connected components are collapsed into individual nodes that correspond to Case 5 DD-Paths. The single node DD-Paths (corresponding to Cases 1 - 4) are required to preserve the convention that a statement (or statement fragment) is in exactly one DD-Path. Without this convention, we end up with rather clumsy DD-Path graphs, in which some statement (fragments) are in several DD-Paths.

Testers shouldn't be intimidated by this process — there are high quality commercial tools that generate the DD-Path graph of a given program. The vendors make sure that their products work for a wide variety of programming languages. In practice, it's reasonable to make DD-Path graphs for programs up to about 100 source lines. Beyond that, most testers look for a tool.

9.2 TEST COVERAGE METRICS

The *raison d'être* of DD-Paths is that they enable very precise descriptions of test coverage. Recall (from Chapter 8) that one of the fundamental limitations of functional testing is that it is impossible to know either the extent of redundancy or the possibility of gaps corresponding to the way a set of functional test cases exercises a program. Back in Chapter 1, we had a Venn diagram showing relationships among specified, programmed, and tested behaviors. Test coverage metrics are a device to measure the extent to which a set of test cases covers (or exercises) a program.

There are several widely accepted test coverage metrics; most of those in Table 2 are due to the early work of E. F. Miller [Miller 77]. Having an organized view of the extent to which a program is tested makes it possible to sensibly manage the testing process. Most quality organizations now expect the C_1 metric (DD-Path coverage) as the minimum acceptable level of test coverage. The statement coverage metric (C_0) is still widely accepted: it is mandated by ANSI Standard 187B, and has been used successfully throughout IBM since the mid-1970s.

Table 2   Structural Test Coverage Metrics

Metric	Description of Coverage
C_0	Every statement
C_1	Every DD-Path (predicate outcome)
C_1p	Every predicate to each outcome
C_2	C_1 coverage + loop coverage
C_d	C_1 coverage + every dependent pair of DD-Paths
C_{MCC}	Multiple condition coverage
C_ik	Every program path that contains up to k repetitions of a loop (usually $k = 2$)
C_{stat}	"Statistically significant" fraction of paths
C_∞	All possible execution paths

These coverage metrics form a lattice (see Chapter 10) in which some are equivalent, and some are implied by others. The importance of the lattice is that there are always fault types that can be revealed at one level, and can escape detection by inferior levels of testing. E. F. Miller observes that when DD-Path coverage is attained by a set of test cases, roughly 85% of all faults are revealed [Miller 91].

9.2.1 METRIC BASED TESTING

The test coverage metrics in Table 2 tell us what to test, but not how to test it. In this section, we take a closer look at techniques that exercise source code in terms of the metrics in Table 2. We must keep an important distinction in mind: Miller's test coverage metrics are based on program graphs in which nodes are full statements, whereas our formulation allows statement fragments to be nodes. For the remainder of this section, the statement fragment formulation is "in effect".

Statement and Predicate Testing

Because our formulation allows statement fragments to be individual nodes, the statement and predicate levels (C_0 and C_1) to collapse into one consideration. In our triangle example (see Figure 9.1), nodes 8, 9, and 10 are a complete Pascal IF-THEN-ELSE statement. If we required nodes to correspond to full statements, we could execute just one of the decision alternatives and satisfy the statement coverage criterion. Because we allow statement fragments, it is "natural" to divide such a statement into three nodes. Doing so results in predicate outcome coverage. Whether or not our convention is followed, these coverage metrics require that we find a set of test cases such that, when executed, every node of the program graph is traversed at least once.

DD-Path Testing

When every DD-Path is traversed (the C_1 metric), we know that each predicate outcome has been executed; this amounts to traversing every edge in the DD-Path graph (or program graph), as opposed to just every node. For IF-THEN and IF-THEN-ELSE statements, this means that both the true and the false branches are covered (C_1p coverage). For CASE statements, each clause is covered. Beyond this, it is useful to ask what else we might do to test a DD-Path. Longer DD-Paths generally represent complex computations, which we can rightly consider as individual functions. For such DD-Paths, it may be appropriate to apply a number of functional tests, especially those for boundary and special values.

Dependent Pairs of DD-Paths

The C_d metric foreshadows the topic of Chapter 10 — dataflow testing. The most common dependency among pairs of DD-Paths is the define/reference relationship, in which a variable is defined (receives a value) in one DD-Path and is referenced in another DD-Path. The importance of these dependencies is that they are closely related to the problem of infeasible paths. We have good examples of dependent pairs of DD-Paths: in Figure 9.4, B and D are such a pair, so are DD-Paths C and L. Simple DD-Path coverage might not exercise these dependencies, thus a deeper class of faults would not be revealed.

Multiple Condition Coverage

Look closely at the compound conditions in DD-Paths A and E. Rather than simply traversing such predicates to their TRUE and FALSE outcomes, we should investigate the different ways that each outcome can occur. One possibility is to make a truth table; a compound condition of three simple conditions would have eight rows, yielding eight test cases. Another possibility is to reprogram compound predicates into nested simple IF-THEN-ELSE logic, which will result in more DD-Paths to cover. We see an interesting trade-off: statement complexity versus path complexity. Multiple condition coverage assures that this complexity isn't swept under the DD-Path coverage rug.

Loop Coverage

The condensation graphs we studied in Chapter 4 provide us with an elegant resolution to the problems of testing loops. Loop testing has been studied extensively, and with good reason — loops are a highly fault prone portion of source code. To start, there is an amusing taxonomy of loops in [Beizer 83]: concatenated, nested, and horrible, shown in Figure 9.5.

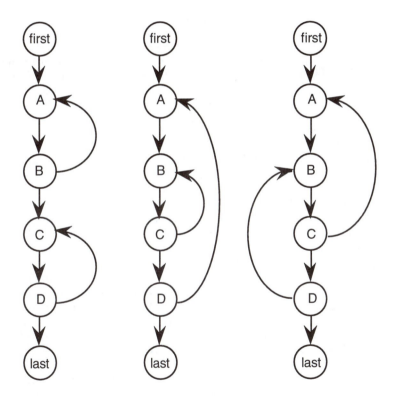

Figure 9.5 Concatenated, Nested, and Knotted Loops

Concatenated loops are simply a sequence of disjoint loops, while nested loops are such that one is contained inside another. Horrible loops cannot occur when the structured programming precepts are followed. When it is possible to branch into (or out from) the middle of a loop, and these branches are internal to other loops, the result is Beizer's horrible loop. (Other sources define this as a knot—how appropriate.) The simple view of loop testing is that every loop involves a decision, and we need to test both outcomes of the decision: one is to traverse the loop, and the other is to exit (or not enter) the loop.

This is carefully proved in [Huang 79]. We can also take a modified boundary value approach, where the loop index is given its minimum, nominal, and maximum values (see Chapter 5). We can push this further, to full boundary value testing and even robustness testing. If the body of a simple loop is a DD-Path that performs a complex calculation, this should also be tested, as discussed above. Once a loop has been tested, the tester condenses it into a single node. If loops are nested, this process is repeated starting with the innermost loop and working outward. This results in the same multiplicity of test cases we found with boundary value analysis, which makes sense, because each loop index variable acts like an input variable. If loops are knotted, it will be necessary to carefully analyze them in terms of the dataflow methods discussed in Chapter 10. As a preview, consider the infinite loop that could occur if one loop tampers with the value of the other loop's index.

9.2.2. TEST COVERAGE ANALYZERS

Coverage analyzers are a class of test tools that offer automated support for this approach to testing management. With a coverage analyzer, the tester runs a set of test cases on a program that has been "instrumented" by the coverage analyzer. The analyzer then uses information produced by the instrumentation code to generate a coverage report. In the common case of DD-Path coverage, for example, the instrumentation identifies and labels all DD-Paths in an original program. When the instrumented program is executed with test cases, the analyzer tabulates the DD-Paths traversed by each test case. In this way, the tester can experiment with different sets of test cases to determine the coverage of each set.

9.3 BASIS PATH TESTING

The mathematical notion of a "basis" has attractive possibilities for structural testing. Certain sets can have a basis, and when they do, the basis has very important properties with respect to the entire set. Mathematicians usually define a basis in terms of a structure called a "vector space", which is a set of elements (called vectors) and which has operations that correspond to multiplication and addition defined for the vectors. If a half dozen other criteria apply, the structure is said to be a vector space, and all vector spaces have a basis (in fact they may have several bases). The basis of a vector space is a set of vectors such that the vectors are independent of each other and they "span" the entire vector space in the sense that any other vector in the space can be expressed in terms of the basis vectors. Thus a set of basis vectors somehow represents "the essence" of the full vector space: everything else in the space can be expressed in terms of the basis, and if one basis element is deleted, this spanning property is lost. The potential for testing is that, if we can view a program as a vector space, then the basis for such a space would be a very interesting set of elements to test. If the basis is "OK", we could hope that everything that can be expressed in terms of the basis is also "OK". In this section, we examine the early work of Thomas McCabe, who recognized this possibility in the mid-1970s.

9.3.1 McCABE'S BASIS PATH METHOD

Figure 9.6 is taken from [McCabe 82]; it is a directed graph which we might take to be the program graph (or the DD-Path graph) of some program. For the convenience of readers who have encountered this example elsewhere ([McCabe 87], [Perry 87]), the original notation for nodes and edges is repeated here. (Notice that this is not a graph derived from a structured program: nodes B and C are a loop with two exits, and the edge from B to E is a branch into the IF-THEN statement in nodes D, E, and F. The program does have a single entry (A) and a single exit (G).) McCabe based his view of testing on a major result from graph theory, which states that the cyclomatic number (see Chapter 4) of a strongly connected graph is the number of linearly independent circuits in the graph. (A circuit is similar to a chain: no internal loops or decisions, but the initial node is the terminal node. A circuit is a set of 3-connected nodes.)

We can always create a strongly connected graph by adding an edge from the (every) sink node to the (every) source node. (Notice that, if the single entry, single exit precept is violated, we greatly increase the cyclomatic number, because we need to add edges from each sink node to each source node.) Figure 9.7 shows the result of doing this; it also contains edge labels that are used in the discussion that follows.

There is some confusion in the literature about the correct formula for cyclomatic complexity. Some sources give the formula as $V(G) = e - n + p$, while others use the formula $V(G) = e - n + 2p$; everyone agrees that e is the number of edges, n is the number of nodes, and p is the number of connected regions.

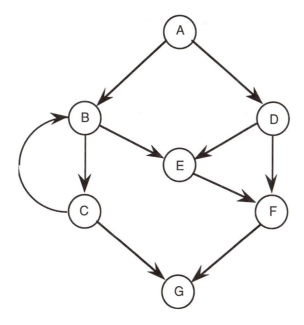

Figure 9.6 McCabe's Control Graph

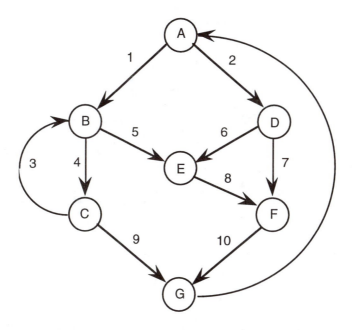

Figure 9.7 McCabe's Derived Strongly Connected Graph

The confusion apparently comes from the transformation of an arbitrary directed graph (such as the one in Figure 9.6) to a strongly connected directed graph obtained by adding one edge from the sink to the source node (as in Figure 9.7). Adding an edge clearly affects value computed by the formula, but it shouldn't affect the number of circuits. Here's a way to resolve the apparent inconsistency: The number of linearly independent paths from the source node to the sink node in Figure 9.6 is

$$V(G) = e - n + 2p$$
$$= 10 - 7 + 2(1) = 5,$$

and the number of linearly independent circuits in the graph in Figure 9.7 is

$$V(G) = e - n + p$$
$$= 11 - 7 + 1 = 5.$$

The cyclomatic complexity of the strongly connected graph in Figure 9.7 is 5, thus there are five linearly independent circuits. If we now delete the added edge form node G to node A, these five circuits become five linearly independent paths from node A to node G. In small graphs, we can visually identify independent paths. Here we identify paths as sequences of nodes:

  p1: A, B, C, G
  p2: A, B, C, B, C, G
  p3: A, B, E, F, G
  p4: A, D, E, F, G
  p5: A, D, F, G

We can force this beginning to look like a vector space by defining notions of addition and scalar multiplication: path addition is simply one path followed by another path, and multiplication corresponds to repetitions of a path. With this formulation, McCabe arrives at a vector space of program paths. His illustration of the basis part of this framework is that the path A, B, C, B, E, F, G is the basis sum p2 + p3 - p1, and the path A, B, C, B, C, B, C, G is the linear combination 2p2 - p1. It is easier to see this addition with an incidence matrix (see Chapter 4) in which rows correspond to paths, and columns correspond to edges, as in Table 3. The entries in this table are obtained by following a path and noting which edges are traversed. Path p1, for example, traverses edges 1, 4, and 9; while path p2 traverses the following edge sequence: 1, 4, 3, 4, 9. Since edge 4 is traversed twice by path p2, that is the entry for the edge 4 column.

Table 3 Path/Edge Traversal

path \ edges traversed	1	2	3	4	5	6	7	8	9	10
p1: A, B, C, G	1	0	0	1	0	0	0	0	1	0
p2: A, B, C, B, C, G	1	0	1	2	0	0	0	0	1	0
p3: A, B, E, F, G	1	0	0	0	1	0	0	1	0	1
p4: A, D, E, F, G	0	1	0	0	0	1	0	1	0	1
p5: A, D, F, G	0	1	0	0	0	0	1	0	0	1
ex1: A, B, C, B, E, F, G	1	0	1	1	1	0	0	1	0	1
ex2: A, B, C, B, C, B, C, G	1	0	2	3	0	0	0	0	1	0

We can check the independence of paths p1 - p5 by examining the first five rows of this incidence matrix. The bold entries show edges that appear in exactly one path, so paths p2 - p5 must be independent. Path p1 is independent of all of these, because any attempt to express p1 in terms of the others introduces unwanted edges. None can be deleted, and these five paths span the set of all paths from node A to node G. At this point, you should check the linear combinations of the two example paths. The addition and multiplication are performed on the column entries.

McCabe next develops an algorithmic procedure (called the "baseline method") to determine a set of basis paths. The method begins with the selection of a "baseline" path, which should correspond to some "normal case" program execution. This can be somewhat arbitrary; McCabe advises choosing a path with as many decision nodes as possible. Next the baseline path is retraced, and in turn each decision is "flipped", that is when a node of outdegree ≥ 2 is reached, a different edge must be taken. Here we follow McCabe's example, in which he first postulates the path through nodes A, B, C, B, E, F, G as the baseline. (This was expressed in terms of paths p1 - p5 earlier.) The first decision node (outdegree ≥ 2) in this path is node A, so for the next basis path, we traverse edge 2 instead of edge 1. We get the path A, D, E, F, G, where we retrace nodes E, F, G in path 1 to be as minimally different as possible. For the next path, we can follow the second path, and take the other decision outcome of node D, which gives us the path A, D, F, G. Now only decision nodes B and C have not been flipped; doing so yields the last two basis paths, A, B, E, F, G and A, B, C, G. Notice that this set of basis paths is distinct from the one in Table 3: this is not problematic, because there is no requirement that a basis be unique.

9.3.2 OBSERVATIONS ON McCABE'S BASIS PATH METHOD

If you had trouble following some of the discussion on basis paths and sums and products of these, you may have felt a haunting skepticism, something along the lines of "Here's another academic oversimplification of a real-world problem". Rightly so, because there are two major soft spots in the McCabe view: one is that testing the set of basis paths is sufficient (it's not), and the other has to do with the yoga-like contortions we went through to make program paths look like a vector space. McCabe's example that the path A, B, C, B, C, B, C, G is the linear combination 2p2 - p1 is very unsatisfactory. What does the 2p2 part mean? Execute path p2 twice? (Yes, according to the math.) Even worse, what does the - p1 part mean? Execute path p1 backwards? Undo the most recent execution of p1? Don't do p1 next time? Mathematical sophistries like this are a real turn-off to practitioners looking for solutions to their very real problems. To get a better understanding of these problems, we'll go back to the triangle program example.

Start with the DD-Path graph of the triangle program in Figure 9.4. We begin with a baseline path that corresponds to a scalene triangle, say with sides 3, 4, 5. This test case will traverse the path p1. Now if we flip the decision at node A, we get path p2. Continuing the procedure, we flip the decision at node D, which yields the path p3. Now we continue to flip decision nodes in the baseline path p1; the next node with outdegree = 2 is node E. When we flip node E, we get the path p4. Next we flip node G to get p5. Finally, (we know we're done, because there are only 6 basis paths) we flip node I to get p6. This procedure yields the following basis paths:

p1:	A-B-D-E-G-I-J-K-Last.
p2:	A-C-D-E-G-I-J-K-Last
p3:	A-B-D-L-Last
p4:	A-B-D-E-F-G-I-J-K-Last
p5:	A-B-D-E-F-G-H-I-J-K-Last
p6:	A-B-D-E-F-G-H-I-K-Last

Time for a reality check: if you follow paths p2, p3, p4, p5, and p6, you find that they are all infeasible. Path p2 is infeasible, because passing through node C means the sides are not a triangle, so none of the sequel decisions can be taken. Similarly, in p3, passing through node B means the sides do form a triangle, so node L cannot be traversed. The others are all infeasible because they involve cases where a triangle is of two types (e.g., isosceles and equilateral). The problem here is that there are several inherent dependencies in the triangle problem. One is that if three integers constitute sides of a triangle, they must be one of the three possibilities: equilateral, isosceles, or scalene. A second dependency is that the three possibilities are mutually exclusive: if one is true, the other two must be false.

Recall that dependencies in the input data domain caused difficulties for boundary value testing, and that we resolved these by going to decision table based functional testing, where we addressed data dependencies in the decision table. Here we are dealing with code level dependencies, and these are absolutely incompatible with the latent assumption that basis paths are independent. McCabe's procedure successfully identifies basis paths that are topologically independent, but when these contradict semantic dependencies, topologically possible paths are seen to be logically infeasible. One solution to this problem is to always require that flipping a decision results in a semantically feasible path. Another is to reason about logical dependencies. If we think about this problem we can identify several rules:

If node B is traversed, then we must traverse nodes D and E.
If node C is traversed, then we must traverse nodes D and L.
If node E is traversed, then we must traverse one of nodes F, H, and J.
If node F is traversed, then we cannot traverse nodes H and J.
If node H is traversed, then we cannot traverse nodes F and J.
If node J is traversed, then we cannot traverse nodes F and I.

Taken together, these rules, in conjunction with McCabe's baseline method, will yield the following feasible basis path set:

fp1: A-C-D-L-Last	(Not a triangle)
fp2: A-B-D-E-F-G-I-K-Last	(Isosceles)
fp3: A-B-D-E-G-H-I-K-Last	(Equilateral)
fp4: A-B-D-E-G-I-J-K-Last	(Scalene)

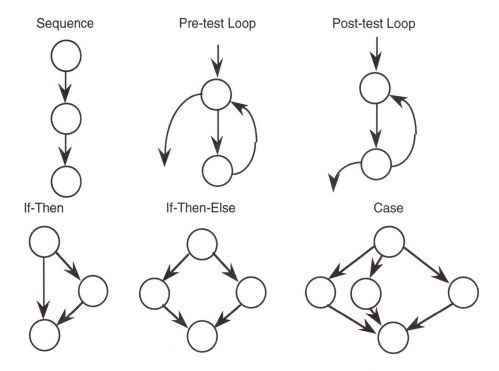

Figure 9.8 Structured Programming Constructs

The triangle problem is atypical in that there are no loops. The program has only 18 topologically possible paths, and of these, only the four basis paths listed above are feasible. Thus for this special case, we arrive at the same test cases as we did with special value testing and output range testing.

For a more positive observation, basis path coverage guarantees DD-Path coverage: the process of flipping decisions guarantees that every decision outcome is traversed, which is the same as DD-Path coverage. We see this by example from the incidence matrix description of basis paths, and in our triangle program feasible basis paths. We could push this a step further and observe that the set of DD-Paths acts like a basis, because any program path can be expressed as a linear combination of DD-Paths..

9.3.3 ESSENTIAL COMPLEXITY
Part of McCabe's work on cyclomatic complexity does more to improve programming than testing. In this section we take a quick look at this elegant blend of graph theory, structured programming, and the implications these have for testing. This whole package centers on the notion of essential complexity [McCabe 82], which is just the cyclomatic complexity of yet another form of condensation graph. Recall that condensation graphs are a way of simplifying an existing graph; so far our simplifications have been based on removing either strong components or DD-Paths. Here, we condense around the structured programming constructs, which are repeated as Figure 9.8.

The basic idea is to look for the graph of one of the structured programming constructs, collapse it into a single node, and repeat until no more structured programming constructs can be found. This process is followed in Figure 9.9, which starts with the DD-Path graph of the Pascal triangle program. The IF-THEN-ELSE construct involving nodes A, B, C, and D is condensed into node a, and then the three IF-THEN constructs are condensed onto nodes b, c, and d. The remaining IF-THEN-ELSE (which corresponds to the IF IsATriangle statement) is condensed into node e, resulting in a condensed graph with cyclomatic complexity $V(G) = 1$. In general, when a program is well structured (i.e., is composed solely of the structured programming constructs), it can always be reduced to a graph with one path.

The graph in Figure 9.6 cannot be reduced in this way (try it!). The loop with nodes B and C cannot be condensed because of edge from B to E. Similarly, nodes D, E, and F look like an IF-THEN construct, but the edge from B to E violates the structure. McCabe went on to find elemental "unstructures" that violate the precepts of structured programming [McCabe 76]. These are shown in Figure 9.10.

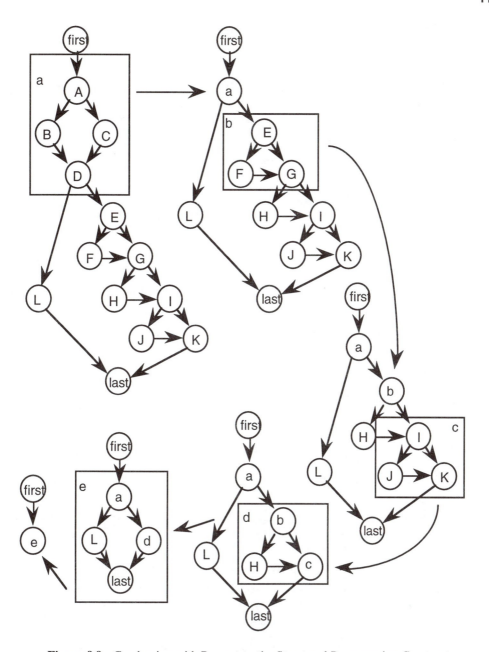

Figure 9.9 Condensing with Respect to the Structured Programming Constructs

Each of these "unstructures" contains three distinct paths, as opposed to the two paths present in the corresponding structured programming constructs, so one conclusion is that such violations increase cyclomatic complexity. The *piece d' resistance* of McCabe's analysis is that these unstructures cannot occur by themselves: if there is one in a program, there must be at least one more, so a program cannot be just slightly unstructured. Since these increase cyclomatic complexity, the minimum number of test cases is thereby increased. In the next chapter, we will see that the unstructures have interesting implications for dataflow testing.

The bottom line for testers is this: programs with high cyclomatic complexity require more testing. Of the organizations that use the cyclomatic complexity metric, most set some guideline for maximum acceptable complexity; $V(G) = 10$ is a common choice. What happens if a unit has a higher complexity? Two possibilities: either simplify the unit or plan to do more testing. If the unit is well structured, its

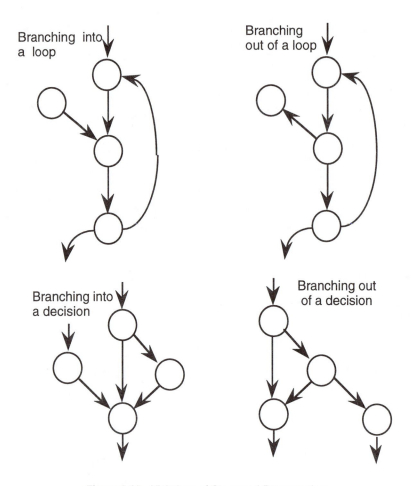

Figure 9.10 Violations of Structured Programming

essential complexity is 1, so it can be simplified easily. If the unit has an essential complexity that exceeds the guidelines, often the best choice is to eliminate the unstructures.

9.4 GUIDELINES AND OBSERVATIONS

In our study of functional testing, we observed that gaps and redundancies can both exist, and at the same time, cannot be recognized. The problem was that functional testing removes us "too far" from the code. The path testing approaches to structural testing represent the case where the pendulum has swung too far the other way: moving from code to directed graph representations and program path formulations obscures important information that is present in the code, in particular the distinction between feasible and infeasible paths. In the next chapter, we look at dataflow based testing. These techniques move closer to the code, so the pendulum will swing back from the path analysis extreme.

McCabe was partly right when he observed: "It is important to understand that these are purely criteria that measure the quality of testing, and not a procedure to identify test cases" [McCabe 82]. He was referring to the DD-Path coverage metric (which is equivalent to the predicate outcome metric) and the cyclomatic complexity metric that requires at least the cyclomatic number of distinct program paths must be traversed. Basis path testing therefore gives us a lower bound on how much testing is necessary.

Path based testing also provides us with a set of metrics that act as cross checks on functional testing. We can use these metrics to resolve the gaps and redundancies question. When we find that the same program path is traversed by several functional test cases, we suspect that this redundancy is not revealing new faults. When we fail to attain DD-Path coverage, we know that there are gaps in the functional test cases. As an example, suppose we have a program that contains extensive error handling, and we test it with boundary value test cases (min, mi n+, nom, max-, and max). Because these are all permissible values, DD-Paths corresponding to the error handling code will not be traversed. If we add test cases derived from robustness testing or traditional equivalence class testing, the DD-Path coverage will improve. Beyond this rather obvious use of coverage metrics, there is an opportunity for real testing craftsmanship. The coverage metrics in Table 2 can operate in two ways: as a blanket mandated standard (e.g., all units shall be tested to attain full DD-Path coverage) or as a mechanism to selectively test portions of code more rigorously than others. We might choose multiple condition coverage for modules with complex logic, while those with extensive iteration might be tested in terms of the loop coverage techniques. This is probably the best view of structural testing: use the properties of the source code to identify appropriate coverage metrics, and then use these as a cross check on functional test cases. When the desired coverage is not attained, follow interesting paths to identify additional (special value) test cases.

This is a good place to revisit the Venn diagram view of testing that we used in Chapter 1. Figure 9.11 shows the relationship between specified behaviors (set S), programmed behaviors (set P), and topologically feasible paths in a program (set T). As usual, region 1 is the most desirable — it contains specified behaviors that are implemented by feasible paths. By definition, every feasible path is topologically possible, so the shaded portion (regions 2 and 6) of the set P must be empty. Region 3 contains feasible paths that correspond to unspecified behaviors. Such extra functionality needs to be examined: if useful, the specification should be changed, otherwise these feasible paths should be removed. Regions 4 and 7 contain the infeasible paths; of these, region 4 is problematic. Region 4 refers to specified behaviors that have almost been implemented: topologically possible yet infeasible program paths. This region very likely corresponds to coding errors, where changes are needed to make the paths feasible. Region 5 still corresponds to specified behaviors that have not been implemented. Path based testing will never recognize this region. Finally, region 7 is a curiosity: unspecified, infeasible, yet topologically possible paths. Strictly speaking, there is no problem here, because infeasible paths cannot execute. If the corresponding code is incorrectly changed by a maintenance action (maybe by a programmer who doesn't fully understand the code), these could become feasible paths, as in region 3.

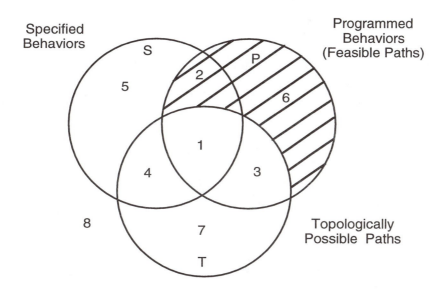

Figure 9.11 Feasible and Topologically Possible Paths

EXERCISES

1. Find the cyclomatic complexity of the graph in Figure 9.2.
2. Identify a set of basis paths for the graph in Figure 9.2.
3. Discuss McCabe's concept of "flipping" for nodes with outdegree ≥ 3.

4. Suppose we take Figure 9.2 as the DD-Path graph of some program. Develop sets of paths (which would be test cases) for the C_0, C_1, and C_2 metrics.

5. Develop multiple condition coverage test cases for the Pascal triangle program. Pay attention to the dependency between statement fragments 14 and 16 with the expression (a = b) AND (c = d). Rewrite the program segment 14 - 21 such that the compound conditions are replaced by nested IF-THEN-ELSE statements. Compare the cyclomatic complexity of your program with that of the existing version.

6. For a set V to be a vector space, two operations (addition and scalar multiplication) must be defined for elements in the set. In addition, the following criteria must hold for all vectors x, y, and z $\in$ V, and for all scalars k, l, 0, and 1:

   i. if x, y $\in$ V, the vector x + y $\in$ V.

   ii. x + y = y + x.

  iii. (x + y) + z = x + (y + z).

  iv. there is a vector 0 $\in$ V such that x + 0 = x.

   v. for any x $\in$ V, there is a vector -x such that x + (-x) = 0.

  vi. for any x $\in$ V, the vector kx $\in$ V.

 vii. k(x + y) = kx + ky.

viii. (k + l)x = kx + lx.

  ix. k(lx) = (kl)x.

   x. 1x = x.

How many of these ten criteria hold for the "vector space" of paths in a program?

Chapter 10

Data Flow Testing

Data flow testing is an unfortunate term, because most software developers immediately think about some connection with dataflow diagrams. Data flow testing refers to forms of structural testing that focus on the points at which variables receive values and the points at which these values are used (or referenced). We will see that data flow testing serves as a "reality check" on path testing; indeed, many of the data flow testing proponents (and researchers) see this approach as a form of path testing. We will look at two mainline forms of data flow testing: one provides a set of basic definitions and a unifying structure of test coverage metrics, while the second is based on a concept called a "program slice". Both of these formalize intuitive behaviors (and analyses) of testers, and although they both start with a program graph, both move back in the direction of functional testing.

Most programs deliver functionality in terms of data. Variables that represent data somehow receive values, and these values are used to compute values for other variables. Since the early 1960s, programmers have analyzed source code in terms of the points (statements) at which variables receive values and points at which these values are used. Many times, their analyses were based on concordances that list statement numbers in which variable names occur. Concordances were popular features of second generation language compilers (they are still popular with COBOL programmers). Early "data flow" analyses often centered on a set of faults that are now known as define/reference anomalies:

- a variable that is defined but never used (referenced)
- a variable that is used but never defined
- a variable that is defined twice before it is used

Each of these anomalies can be recognized from the concordance of a program. Since the concordance information is compiler generated, these anomalies can be discovered by what is known as "static analysis": finding faults in source code without executing it.

10.1 DEFINE/USE TESTING

Much of the formalization of define/use testing was done in the early 1980s [Rapps 85]; the definitions in this section are compatible with those in [Clarke 89], an article which summarizes most of define/use testing theory. This body of research is very compatible with the formulation we developed in chapters 4 and 9. It presumes a program graph in which nodes are statement fragments (a fragment may be an entire statement), and programs that follow the structured programming precepts.

The following definitions refer to a program P that has a program graph G(P), and a set of program variables V. The program graph G(P) is constructed as in Chapter 4, with statement fragments as nodes, and edges that represent node sequences. G(P) has a single entry node, and a single exit node. We also disallow edges from a node to itself. Paths, subpaths, and cycles are as they were in Chapter 4.

Definition
Node $n \in G(P)$ is a *defining node* of the variable $v \in V$, written as DEF(v,n), iff the value of the variable v is defined at the statement fragment corresponding to node n.

Input statements, assignment statements, loop control statements, and procedure calls are all examples of statements that are defining nodes. When the code corresponding to such statements executes, the contents of the memory location(s) associated with the variables are changed.

Definition
Node n ∈ G(P) is a *usage node* of the variable v ∈ V, written as USE(v, n), iff the value of the variable v is used at the statement fragment corresponding to node n.

Output statements, assignment statements, conditional statements, loop control statements, and procedure calls are all examples of statements that are usage nodes. When the code corresponding to such statements executes, the contents of the memory location(s) associated with the variables remain unchanged.

Definition
A usage node USE(v, n) is a *predicate use* (denoted as P-use) iff the statement n is a predicate statement; otherwise USE(v, n) is a *computation use* , (denoted C-use).

The nodes corresponding to predicate uses always have an outdegree ≥ 2, and nodes corresponding to computation uses always have outdegree ≤ 1.

Definition
A *definition-use (sub)path* with respect to a variable v (denoted du-path) is a (sub)path in PATHS(P) such that, for some v ∈ V, there are define and usage nodes DEF(v, m) and USE(v, n) such that m and n are the initial and final nodes of the (sub)path.

Definition
A *definition-clear (sub)path* with respect to a variable v (denoted dc-path) is a definition-use (sub)path in PATHS(P) with initial and final nodes DEF (v, m) and USE (v, n) such that no other node in the (sub)path is a defining node of v.

Testers should notice how these definitions capture the essence of computing with stored data values. Du-paths and dc-paths describe the flow of data across source statements from points at which the values are defined to points at which the values are used. Du-paths that are not definition-clear are potential trouble spots.

10.1.1 EXAMPLE
We will use the Commission Problem and its program graph to illustrate these definitions. The numbered source code is given next, followed by a program graph constructed according to the procedures we discussed in Chapter 4. This program computes the commission on the sales of four salespersons, hence the outer For-loop that repeats four times. During each repetition, a salesperson's name is read from the input device, and the input from that person is read to compute the total numbers of locks, stocks, and barrels sold by the person. The While-loop is a classical sentinel controlled loop in which a value of -1 for locks signifies the end of that person's data. The totals are accumulated as the data lines are read in the While-loop. After printing this preliminary information, the sales value is computed, using the constant item prices defined at the beginning of the program. The sales value is then used to compute the commission in the conditional portion of the program.

```
1      program lock_stock_and_barrel
2      const
3            lock_price    = 45.0;
4            stock_price   = 30.0;
5            barrel_price = 25.0;
6      type
7            STRING_30 = string[30];    {Salesman's Name}
8      var
9             locks,  stocks,  barrels,  num_locks,  num_stocks,
10            num_barrels,  salesman_index,  order_index  :    INTEGER;
11           sales,  commission  :  REAL;
12           salesman  :  STRING_30;
13
14      BEGIN  {program  lock_stock_and_barrel}
```

```
15          FOR   salesman_index := 1 TO 4 DO
16            BEGIN
17               READLN(salesman);
18               WRITELN ('Salesman is ',  salesman);
19               num_locks := 0;
20               num_stocks := 0;
21               num_barrels := 0;
22               READ(locks);
23               WHILE locks <> -1 DO
24                 BEGIN
25                    READLN(stocks, barrels);
26                    num_locks := num_locks + locks;
27                    num_stocks := num_stocks + stocks;
28                    num_barrels := num_barrels + barrels;
29                    READ(locks);
30                 END; {WHILE locks}
31               READLN;
32               WRITELN('Sales for ',salesman);
33               WRITELN('Locks sold: ', num_locks);
34               WRITELN('Stocks sold: ', num_stocks);
35               WRITELN('Barrels sold: ', num_barrels);
36               sales := lock_price*num_locks + stock_price*num_stocks
                               + barrel_price*num_barrels;
37               WRITELN('Total sales: ', sales:8:2);
38               WRITELN;
39               IF (sales > 1800.0) THEN
40                 BEGIN
41                    commission := 0.10 * 1000.0;
42                    commission := commission + 0.15 * 800.0;
43                    commission := commission + 0.20 * (sales-1800.0);
44                 END;
45               ELSE IF (sales > 1000.0) THEN
46                 BEGIN
47                    commission := 0.10 * 1000.0;
48                    commission := commission + 0.15*(sales - 1000.0);
49                 END
50               ELSE commission := 0.10 * sales;
51               WRITELN('Commission is $',commission:6:2);
52            END; {FOR salesman}
53       END. {program lock_stock_and_barrel}
```

The DD-Paths in this program are given in Table 1, and the DD-Path graph is shown in Figure 10.2. Tables 2 and 3 list the define and usage nodes for five variables in the commission problem. We use this information in conjunction with the program graph in Figure 10.1 to identify various definition-use and definition-clear paths. It's a judgment call whether or not non-executable statements such as constant (CONST) and variable (VAR) declaration statements should be considered as defining nodes. Technically, these only define memory space (the CONST declaration creates a compiler-produced initial value). Such nodes aren't very interesting when we follow what happens along their du-paths, but if there is something wrong, it's usually helpful to include them. Take your pick. We will refer to the various paths as sequences of node numbers.

First, let's look at the du-paths for the variable stocks. We have DEF(stocks, 25) and USE(stocks, 27), so the path <25, 27> is a du-path wrt (with respect to) stocks. Since there are no other defining nodes for stocks, this path is also definition-clear.

Two defining and two usage nodes make the locks variable more interesting: we have DEF(locks, 22), DEF(locks, 29), USE(locks, 23), and USE(locks, 26). These yield four du-paths:

    p1 = <22, 23>
    p2 = <22, 23, 24, 25, 26>
    p3 = <29, 30, 23>
    p4 = <29, 30, 23, 24, 25, 26>

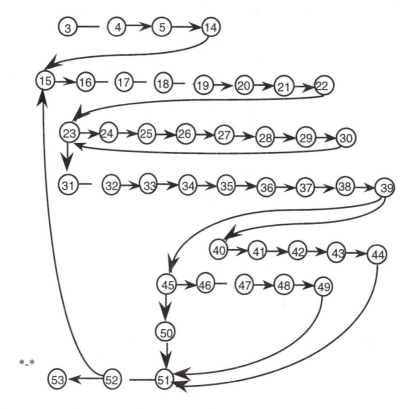

Figure 10.1 Program Graph of the Commission Program

Table 1   DD-Paths in Figure 10.1

DD-Path	Nodes
1	14
2	15 - 22
3	23
4	24 - 30
5	31 - 39
6	40 - 44
7	45
8	46 - 49
9	50
10	51, 52
11	53

Du-paths p1 and p2 refer to the priming value of locks which is read at node 22: locks has a predicate use in the While statement (node 23), and if the condition is true (as in path p2), a computation use at statement 26. The other two du-paths start near the end of the While loop and occur when the loop repeats. If we "extended" paths p1 and p3 to include node 31,

p1' = <22, 23, 31>
p3' = <29, 30, 23, 31>

then the paths p1', p2, p3', and p4 form a very complete set of test cases for the While-loop: bypass the loop, begin the loop, repeat the loop, and exit the loop. All of these du-paths are definition-clear.

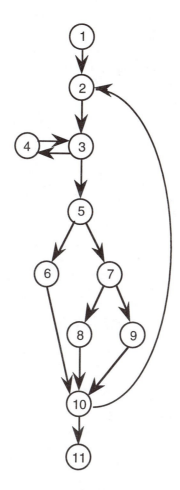

Figure 10.2 DD-Path Graph of the Commission Program

Table 2: Define/Use Information for locks, stocks, and num_locks

Variable	Defined at	Used at	Comment
locks	9		(to compiler)
locks	22		READ
locks		23	predicate use
locks		26	computation use
locks	29		READ
stocks	9		(to compiler)
stocks	25		READ
stocks		27	computation use
num_locks	9		(to compiler)
num_locks	19		assignment
num_locks	26		assignment
num_locks		26	computation use
num_locks		33	WRITE
num_locks		36	computation use

Table 3: Define/Use Information for Sales and Commission

Variable	Defined at	Used at	Comment
sales	11		(to compiler)
sales	36		assignment
sales		37	WRITE
sales		39	predicate use
sales		43	computation use
sales		45	predicate use
sales		48	computation use
sales		50	computation use
commission	11		(to compiler)
commission	41		assignment
commission	42		assignment
commission		42	computation use
commission	43		assignment
commission		43	computation use
commission	47		assignment
commission	48		assignment
commission		48	computation use
commission	50		assignment
commission		51	WRITE

The du-paths for num_locks will lead us to typical test cases for computations. With two defining nodes (DEF(num_locks, 19) and DEF(num_locks, 26)) and three usage nodes (USE(num_locks, 26), USE(num_locks, 33), USE(num_locks, 36)), we might expect six du-paths. Let's take a closer look.

Path p5 = <19, 20, 21, 22, 23, 24, 25, 26> is a du-path in which the initial value (0) has a computation use. This path is definition-clear. The next path is problematic:

p6 = <19, 20, 21, 22, 23, 24, 25, 26, 27, 28, 29, 30, 31, 32, 33>

We have ignored the possible repetition of the While-loop. We could highlight this by noting that the subpath <26, 27, 28, 29, 30, 22, 23, 24, 25> might be traversed several times. Ignoring this for now, we still have a du-path that fails to be definition-clear. If there is a problem with the value of num_locks at node 33 (the WRITE statement), we should look at the intervening DEF(num_locks, 26) node.

The next path contains p6; we can show this by using a path name in place of its corresponding node sequence:

p7 = <19, 20, 21, 22, 23, 24, 25, 26, 27, 28, 29, 30, 31, 32, 33, 34, 35, 36>
p7 = < p6, 34, 35, 36>

Du-path p7 is not definition-clear because it includes node 26.

Subpaths that begin with node 26 (an assignment statement) are interesting. The first, <26, 26>, seems degenerate. If we "expanded" it into machine code, we would be able to separate the define and usage portions. We will disallow these as du-paths. Technically, the usage on the right-hand side of the assignment refers to a value defined at node 19, (see path p5). The remaining two du-paths are both subpaths of p7:

p8 = <26, 27, 28, 29, 30, 31, 32, 33>
p9 = <26, 27, 28, 29, 30, 31, 32, 33, 34, 35, 36>

Both of these are definition-clear, and both have the loop iteration problem we discussed before.

Since there is only one defining node for sales, all the du-paths wrt sales must be definition-clear. They are interesting because they illustrate predicate and computation uses. The first three du-paths are easy:

p10 = <36, 37>
p11 = <36, 37, 38, 39>
p12 = <36, 37, 38, 39, 40, 41, 42, 43>

Notice that p12 is a definition-clear path with three usage nodes; it also contains paths p10 and p11. If we were testing with p12, we know we would also have covered the other two paths. We will revisit this toward the end of the chapter.

The IF, ELSE IF logic in statements 39 through 50 highlights an ambiguity in the original research. There are two choices for du-paths that begin with path p11: the static choice is the path <36, 37, 38, 39, 40, 41, 42, 43>, the dynamic choice is the path <36, 37, 38, 39, 45>. Here we will use the dynamic view, so the remaining du-paths for sales are

p13 = <36, 37, 38, 39, 45, 46, 47, 48>
p14 = <36, 37, 38, 39, 45, 50>

Note that the dynamic view is very compatible with the kind of thinking we used for DD-Paths in Chapter 9.

If you have followed this discussion carefully, you are probably dreading the stuff on du-paths wrt commission. You're right — it's time for a change of pace. In statements 39 through 51, the calculation of commission is controlled by ranges of the variable sales. Statements 41 to 43 build up the value of commission by using the memory location to hold intermediate values. This is a common programming practice, and it is desirable because it shows how the final value is computed. (We could replace these lines with the statement "commission := 220 + 0.20*(sales -1800)", where 220 is the value of 0.10*1000 + 0.15*800, but this would be hard for a maintainer to understand.) The "built-up" version uses intermediate values, and these will appear as define and usage nodes in the du-path analysis. Since we decided to disallow du-paths from assignment statements like 41 and 42, we'll just consider du-paths that begin with the three "real" defining nodes: DEF(commission, 43), DEF(commission, 48), and DEF(commission, 50). There is only one usage node, USE(commission, 51).

We have another ambiguity. The static view results in one du-path:

<43, 44, 45, 48, 50, 51>

This path contains the three definitions of commission, so it is not definition-clear. The dynamic view results in three paths:

p15 = <43, 51>
p16 = <48, 51>
p17 = <50, 51>

Again, the dynamic view is preferable; it also results in definition-clear paths. (A sharp tester might ask how we would ever execute the "path" <43, 44, 45, 48, 50, 51>. We cannot.) The full set of du-paths in the problem is given in Table 4 (they are renumbered).

10.1.2 DU-PATH TEST COVERAGE METRICS

The whole point of analyzing a program as in the previous section is to define a set of test coverage metrics known as the Rapps-Weyuker data flow metrics [Rapps 85]. The first three of these are equivalent to three of E. F. Miller's metrics in Chapter 9: All-Paths, All-Edges, and All-Nodes. The others presume that define and usage nodes have been identified for all program variables, and that du-paths have been identified with respect to each variable. In the following definitions, T is a set of (sub)paths in the program graph G(P) of a program P, with the set V of variables.

Definition
The set T satisfies the *All-Defs* criterion for the program P iff for every variable v ∈ V, T contains definition clear (sub)paths from every defining node of v to a use of v.

Definition
The set T satisfies the *All-Uses* criterion for the program P iff for every variable v ∈ V, T contains definition-clear (sub)paths from every defining node of v to every use of v, and to the successor node of each USE(v,n).

Definition
The set T satisfies the *All-P-Uses /Some C-Uses* criterion for the program P iff for every variable v ∈ V, T contains definition-clear (sub)paths from every defining node of v to every predicate use of v, and if a definition of v has no P-uses, there is a definition-clear path to at least one computation use.

Table 4: Du-Paths in Figure 10.1

Du-Path	Variable	Def Node	Use Node
1	locks	22	23
2	locks	22	26
3	locks	29	23
4	locks	29	26
5	stocks	25	27
6	barrels	25	28
7	num_locks	19	26
8	num_locks	19	33
9	num_locks	19	36
10	num_locks	26	33
11	num_locks	26	36
12	num_stocks	20	27
13	num_stocks	20	34
14	num_stocks	20	36
15	num_stocks	27	34
16	num_stocks	27	36
17	num_barrels	21	28
18	num_stocks	21	35
19	num_stocks	21	36
20	num_stocks	28	35
21	num_stocks	28	36
22	sales	36	37
23	sales	36	39
24	sales	36	43
25	sales	36	45
26	sales	36	48
27	sales	36	50
28	commission	41	42
29	commission	42	43
30	commission	43	51
31	commission	47	48
32	commission	48	51
33	commission	50	51

Definition

The set T satisfies the *All-C-Uses /Some P-Uses* criterion for the program P iff for every variable v ∈ V, T contains definition-clear (sub)paths from every defining node of v to every computation use of v, and if a definition of v has no C-uses, there is a definition-clear path to at least one predicate use.

Definition

The set T satisfies the *All-DU-paths* criterion for the program P iff for every variable v ∈ V, T contains definition-clear (sub)paths from every defining node of v to every use of v, and to the successor node of each USE(v,n), and that these paths are either single loop traversals, or they are cycle free.

These test coverage metrics have several set-theory based relationships, which are referred to as "subsumption" in [Rapps 85]. When one test coverage metric subsumes another, a set of test cases that attains coverage in terms of the first metric necessarily attains coverage with respect to the subsumed metric. These relationships are shown in Figure 10.3.

We now have a more refined view of structural testing possibilities between the extremes of the (typically unattainable) All-Paths metric, and the generally accepted minimum, All-Edges.

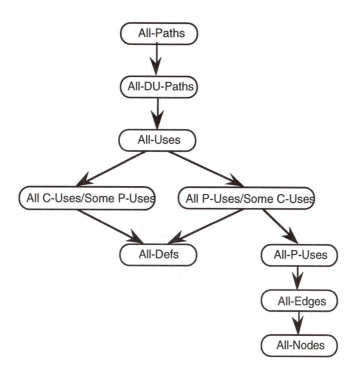

Figure 10.3 Rapps/Weyuker Hierarchy of Data Flow Coverage Metrics

Since several du-paths are present in a full program execution path (traversed by a test case), the higher forms of coverage metrics don't always imply significantly higher numbers of test cases. In our continuing example, the three decision table functional test cases cover all the DD-Paths (see Table 5) and most of the du-paths (see Table 6). The missing du-paths (8, 9, 14, 18, 19) are all traversed by a test case in which nothing is sold (i.e., the first value of locks is -1).

10.2 SLICE-BASED TESTING

Program slices have surfaced and submerged in software engineering literature since the early 1980s. They were originally proposed in [Weiser 85], used as an approach to software maintenance in [Gallagher 91], and most recently used to quantify functional cohesion in [Bieman 94]. Part of this versatility is due to the natural, intuitively clear intent of the program slice concept. Informally, a program slice is a set of program statements that contribute to, or affect a value for a variable at some point in the program. This notion of slice corresponds to other disciplines as well. We might study history in terms of slices: US history, European history, Russian history, Far East history, Roman history, and so on. The way such historical slices interact turns out to be very analogous to the way program slices interact.

Table 5   DD-Path Coverage of Decision Table Functional Test Cases

Case	locks	stocks	barrels	sales	commission	DD-Paths
1	5	5	5	500	50	1-5, 7, 9, 10, 11
2	15	15	15	1500	175	1-5, 7, 8, 10, 11
3	25	25	25	2500	360	1-5, 9, 10, 11

Table 6: Du-Path Coverage of Decision Table Functional Test Cases

Du-Path	Case 1	Case 2	Case 3
1	X	X	X
2	X	X	X
3	X	X	X
4	X	X	X
5	X	X	X
6	X	X	X
7	X	X	X
8			
9			
10	X	X	X
11	X	X	X
12	X	X	X
13	X	X	X
14			
15	X	X	X
16	X	X	X
17	X	X	X
18			
19			
20	X	X	X
21	X	X	X
22	X	X	X
23	X	X	X
24			X
25	X	X	
26		X	
27	X		
28			X
29			X
30			X
31		X	
32		X	
33	X		

We'll start by growing our working definition of a program slice. We continue with the notation we used for define-use paths: a program P that has a program graph G(P), and a set of program variables V. The first try refines the definition in [Gallagher 91] to allow nodes in P(G) to refer to statement fragments.

Definition
Given a program P, and a set V of variables in P, a *slice on the variable set V at statement n*, written S(V,n), is the set of all statements in P that contribute to the values of variables in V.

Listing elements of a slice S(V,n) will be cumbersome, because the elements are program statement fragments. Since it is much simpler to list fragment numbers in P(G), we make the following trivial change (it keeps the set theory purists happy):

Definition
Given a program P, and a program graph G(P) in which statements and statement fragments are numbered, and a set V of variables in P, the *slice on the variable set V at statement fragment n*, written S(V,n), is the set node numbers of all statement fragments in P prior to n that contribute to the values of variables in V at statement fragment n.

The idea of slices is to separate a program into components that have some useful meaning. First, we need to explain two parts of the definition. Here we mean "prior to" in the dynamic sense, so a slice captures the execution time behavior of a program with respect to the variable(s) in the slice. Eventually, we will develop a lattice (a directed, acyclic graph) of slices, in which nodes are slices, and edges correspond to the subset relationship.

The "contribute" part is more complex. In a sense, declarative statements (such as CONST and TYPE) have an effect on the value of a variable. A CONST definition sets a value that can never be changed by a definition node, and the difference between INTEGER and REAL variables can be a source of trouble. One resolution might be to simply exclude all non-executable statements. We will include CONST declarations in slices. The notion of contribution is partially clarified by the predicate (P-use) and computation (C-use) usage distinction of [Rapps 85], but we need to refine these forms of variable usage. Specifically, the USE relationship pertains to five forms of usage:

P-use	used in a predicate (decision)
C-use	used in computation
O-use	used for output
L-use	used for location (pointers, subscripts)
I-use	iteration (internal counters, loop indices)

While we're at it, we identify two forms of definition nodes:

I-def	defined by input
A-def	defined by assignment

For now, presume that the slice S(V, n) is a slice on one variable, that is, the set V consists of a single variable, v. If statement fragment n is a defining node for v, then n is included in the slice. If statement fragment n is a usage node for v, then n is not included in the slice. P-uses and C-uses of other variables (not the v in the slice set V) are included to the extent that their execution affects the value of the variable v. As a guideline, if the value of v is the same whether a statement fragment is included or excluded, exclude the statement fragment.

L-use and I-use variables are typically invisible outside their modules, but this hardly precludes the problems such variables often create. Another judgment call: here (with some peril) we choose to exclude these from the intent of "contribute". Thus O-use, L-use, and I-use nodes are excluded from slices..

10.2.1 EXAMPLE

The commission problem is used in this book because it contains interesting data flow properties, and these are not present in the Triangle problem (or in NextDate). Follow these examples while looking at the source code for the commission problem that we used to analyze in terms of define-use paths.

S_1: S(salesman, 17) = {17}
S_2: S(salesman, 18) = {17}
S_3: S(salesman, 32) = {17}

The salesman variable is the simplest case in the program. It has one defining node (an I-def at node 17). It also occurs at nodes 18 and 22, both times as an output variable (O-use), hence it is not included in slices S_2 and S_3. Both <17, 18> and <17, 32> are definition-clear du-paths.

Slices on the locks variable show why it is potentially fault-prone. It has a P-use at node 23 and a C-use at node 26, and has two definitions, the I-defs at nodes 22 and 24.

S_4: S(locks, 22) = {22}
S_5: S(locks, 23) = {22, 23, 24, 29, 30}
S_6: S(locks, 26) = {22, 23, 24, 29, 30}
S_7: S(locks, 29) = {29}

The slices for stocks and barrels are boring. Both are short, definition-clear paths contained entirely within a loop, so they are not affected by iterations of the loop. (Think of the loop body as a DD-Path.)

S_8: S(stocks, 25) = {22, 23, 24, 25, 29, 30}
S_9: S(stocks, 27) = {22, 23, 24, 25, 29, 30}
S_{10}: S(barrels, 25) = {22, 23, 24, 25, 29, 30}
S_{11}: S(barrels, 28) = {22, 23, 24, 25, 29, 30}

The next four slices illustrate how repetition appears in slices. Node 19 is an A-def for num_locks, and node 26 contains both an A-def and a C-use. The remaining nodes in S_{13} (22, 23, 24, 29, and 30) pertain to the While-loop controlled by locks. Slices S_{13}, S_{14}, and S_{15} are equal because nodes 33 and 36 are, respectively, an O-use and a C-use of num_locks.

S_{12}: S(num_locks, 19) = {19}
S_{13}: S(num_locks, 26) = {19, 22, 23, 24, 26, 29, 30}
S_{14}: S(num_locks, 33) = {19, 22, 23, 24, 26, 29, 30}
S_{15}: S(num_locks, 36) = {19, 22, 23, 24, 26, 29, 30}

The slices on num_stocks and num_barrels are quite similar. They are initialized by A-defs at nodes 20 and 21, and then are redefined by A-defs at nodes 27 and 28. Again, the remaining nodes (22, 23, 24, 29, and 30) pertain to the While-loop controlled by locks.

S_{16}: S(num_stocks, 20) = {20}
S_{17}: S(num_stocks, 27) = {20, 22, 23, 24, 25, 27, 29, 30}
S_{18}: S(num_stocks, 34) = {20, 22, 23, 24, 25, 27, 29, 30}
S_{19}: S(num_stocks, 36) = {20, 22, 23, 24, 25, 27, 29, 30}
S_{20}: S(num_barrels, 21) = {21}
S_{21}: S(num_barrels, 28) = {21, 22, 23, 24, 25, 28, 29, 30}
S_{22}: S(num_barrels, 35) = {21, 22, 23, 24, 25, 28, 29, 30}
S_{23}: S(num_barrels, 36) = {21, 22, 23, 24, 25, 28, 29, 30}

The next three slices demonstrate our convention regarding compiler-defined values.

S_{24}: S(lock_price, 36) = {3}
S_{25}: S(stock_price, 36) = {4}
S_{26}: S(barrel_price, 36) = {5}

The slices on sales and commission are the interesting ones. There is only one defining node for sales, the A-def at node 36. The remaining slices on sales show the P-uses, C-uses, and the O-use in definition-clear paths.

S_{27}: S(sales, 36) = {3, 4, 5, 19, 20, 21, 22, 23, 24, 25, 26, 27, 28, 29, 30, 36}
S_{28}: S(sales, 37) = {3, 4, 5, 19, 20, 21, 22, 23, 24, 25, 26, 27, 28, 29, 30, 36}
S_{29}: S(sales, 39) = {3, 4, 5, 19, 20, 21, 22, 23, 24, 25, 26, 27, 28, 29, 30, 36}
S_{30}: S(sales, 43) = {3, 4, 5, 19, 20, 21, 22, 23, 24, 25, 26, 27, 28, 29, 30, 36}
S_{31}: S(sales, 45) = {3, 4, 5, 19, 20, 21, 22, 23, 24, 25, 26, 27, 28, 29, 30, 36}
S_{32}: S(sales, 48) = {3, 4, 5, 19, 20, 21, 22, 23, 24, 25, 26, 27, 28, 29, 30, 36}
S_{33}: S(sales, 50) = {3, 4, 5, 19, 20, 21, 22, 23, 24, 25, 26, 27, 28, 29, 30, 36}

Think about slice S_{27} in terms of its "components", the slices on the C-use variables. We can write $S_{27} = S_{24} \cup S_{25} \cup S_{26} \cup S_{13} \cup S_{17} \cup S_{21}$, where the values of the six C-use variables at node 36 are defined by the six slices joined together by the union operation. Notice how the formalism corresponds to our intuition: if the value of sales is wrong, we first look at how it is computed, and if this is OK, we check how the components are computed.

Everything comes together (literally) with the slices on commission. There are six A-def nodes for commission (corresponding to the six du-paths we identified earlier). Three computations of commission are controlled by P-uses of sales in the IF, ELSE IF logic. This yields three "paths" of slices that compute commission. (See Figure 10.4.)

S_{34}: S(commission, 41) = {41}
S_{35}: S(commission, 42) = {41, 42}
S_{36}: S(commission, 43) = {3, 4, 5, 19, 20, 21, 22, 23, 24, 25, 26, 27, 28, 29, 30, 36, 41, 42, 43}
S_{37}: S(commission, 47) = {47}
S_{38}: S(commission, 48) = {3, 4, 5, 19, 20, 21, 22, 23, 24, 25, 26, 27, 28, 29, 30, 36, 47, 48}
S_{39}: S(commission, 50) = {3, 4, 5, 19, 20, 21, 22, 23, 24, 25, 26, 27, 28, 29, 30, 36, 50}

Whichever computation is taken, all come together in the last slice.

S_{40}: S(commission, 51) = {3, 4, 5, 19, 20, 21, 22, 23, 24, 25, 26, 27, 28, 29, 30, 36, 41, 42, 43, 47, 48, 50}

The slice information improves our insight. Look at the lattice in Figure 10.4; it is a directed acyclic graph in which slices are nodes, and an edge represents the proper subset relationship.

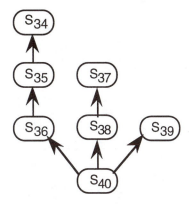

Figure 10.4   Lattice of Slices on Commission

This lattice is drawn so that the position of the slice nodes roughly corresponds with their position in the source code. The definition-clear paths <43, 51>, <48, 51>, and <50,51> correspond to the edges that show slices S_{36}, S_{38}, and S_{39} are subsets of slice S_{40}. Figure 10.5 shows a lattice of slices for the entire program. Some slices (those that are identical to others) have been deleted for clarity. All are listed in Table 7, along with slice-specific test objectives that are appropriate.

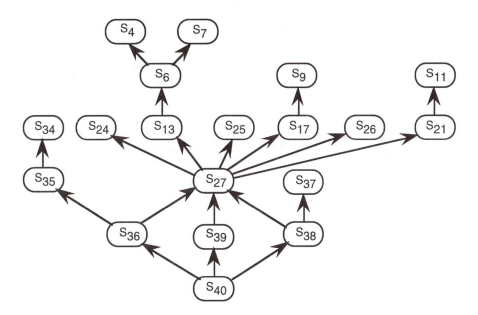

Figure 10.5   Lattice of Slices in the Commission Program

There is a natural hybrid between slice-based testing and functional testing. Since slices are defined with respect to variables, slices correspond to a functional decomposition of a program. Because the sub-functions are smaller, corresponding sets of functional test cases will be more reasonable.

10.2.2 STYLE AND TECHNIQUE
When we analyze a program in terms of "interesting" slices, we can focus on parts of interest while disregarding unrelated parts. We couldn't do this with du-paths — they are sequences that include

Table 7   Test Objectives for Slices in Figure 10.5

Equivalent Slices	Test Objective
1, 2, 3	salesman read and written correctly
4	locks read correctly
5, 6	locks sentinel correct
7	additional locks read correctly
8, 9 (10, 11)	iterative read of stocks correct
(8, 9) 10, 11	iterative read of barrels correct
12	num_locks initialized correctly
13, 14, 15	num_locks computed correctly
16	num_stocks initialized correctly
17, 18, 19	num_stocks computed correctly
20	num_barrels initialized correctly
21, 22, 23	num_barrels computed correctly
24	lock_price constant definition correct
25	stock_price constant definition correct
26	barrel_price constant definition correct
27, 28, 29, 30, 31, 32, 33	sales computed correctly
34	commission on first 1000 correct for sales >1800
35	commission on next 800 correct for sales >1800
36	commission on excess over 1800 correct for sales >1800
37	commission on first 1000 correct for 1000 <sales <1800
38	commission on excess over 1000 correct for 1000 <sales <1800
39	commission on sales < 1000 correct
40	commission written correctly

statements and variables that may not be of interest. Before discussing some analytic techniques, we'll first look at "good style". We could have built these stylistic precepts into the definitions, but then the definitions become even more cumbersome.

1. Never make a slice S(V, n) for which variables v of V do not appear in statement fragment n. This possibility is permitted by the definition of a slice, but it is bad practice. As an example, suppose we defined a slice on the locks variable at node 27. Defining such slices necessitates tracking the values of all variables at all points in the program.
2. Make slices on one variable. The set V in slice S(V,n) can contain several variables, and sometimes such slices are useful. The slice S(V, 36) where

$$V = \{ \text{num\_locks, num\_stocks, num\_barrels} \}$$

contains all the elements of the slice S({sales}, 36) except the CONST declarations and statement 36. Since these two slices are so similar, why define the one in terms of C-uses?
3. Make slices for all A-def nodes. When a variable is computed by an assignment statement, a slice on the variable at that statement will include (portions of) all du-paths of the variables used in the computation. Slice S({sales}, 36) is a good example of an A-def slice.

4. Make slices for P-use nodes. When a variable is used in a predicate, the slice on that variable at the decision statement shows how the predicate variable got its value. This is very useful in decision-intensive programs like the Triangle program and NextDate.

5. Slices on non-P-use usage nodes aren't very interesting. We discussed C-use slices in point 2, where we saw they were very redundant with the A-def slice. Slices on O-use variables can always be expressed as unions of slices on all the A-defs (and I-defs) of the O-use variable. Slices on I-use and O-use variables are useful during debugging, but if they are mandated for all testing, the test effort is dramatically increased.

6. Consider making slices compilable. Nothing in the definition of a slice requires that the set of statements is compilable, but if we make this choice, it means that a set of compiler directive and declarative statements is a subset of every slice. As an example, the slice S_5, which is S(locks, 23) = {22, 23, 24, 29, 30}, contains the statements

```
22        READ(locks);
23        WHILE locks <> -1 DO
24          BEGIN
29            READ(locks);
30          END; {WHILE locks}
```

If we add statements 1-14 and 53, we have the compilable slice shown here:

```
1    program lock_stock_and_barrel
2    const
3        lock_price = 45.0;
4        stock_price = 30.0;
5        barrel_price = 25.0;
6    type
7        STRING_30 = string[30]; {Salesman's Name}
8    var
9        locks, stocks, barrels, num_locks, num_stocks,
10       num_barrels, salesman_index, order_index : INTEGER;
11       sales, commission : REAL;
12       salesman : STRING_30;
13
14   BEGIN {program lock_stock_and_barrel}
22       READ(locks);
23       WHILE locks <> -1 DO
24         BEGIN
29           READ(locks);
30         END; {WHILE locks}
53   END. {program lock_stock_and_barrel}
```

If we added this same set of statements to all the slices we made for the commission program, our lattices remain undisturbed, but each slice is separately compilable (and therefore executable). In the first chapter, we suggested that good testing practices lead to better programming practices. Here we have a good example. Think about developing programs in terms of compilable slices. If we did this, we could code a slice and immediately test it. We can then code and test other slices, and them merge them (Gallagher calls this "slice splicing") into a pretty solid program. Try coding the commission program this way.

10.3 GUIDELINES AND OBSERVATIONS

Dataflow testing is clearly indicated for programs that are computationally intensive. As a corollary, in control intensive programs, if control variables are computed (P-uses), dataflow testing is also indicated. The definitions we made for define/use paths and slices give us very precise ways to describe parts of a program that we would like to test. There are academic tools that support these definitions, but they haven't migrated to the commercial marketplace. Some pieces are there; you can find programming language compilers that provide on-screen highlighting of slices, and most debugging tools let you "watch" certain variables as you step through a program execution. Here are some tidbits that may prove helpful to you, particularly when you have a difficult module to test.

1. Slices don't map nicely into test cases (because the other, non-related code is still in an executable path). On the other hand, they are a handy way to eliminate interaction among variables. Use the slice composition approach to re-develop difficult sections of code, and these slices before you splice (compose) them with other slices.

2. Relative complements of slices yield a "diagnostic" capability. The relative complement of a set B with respect to another set A is the set of all elements of A that are not elements of B. It is denoted as A - B. Consider the relative complement set S(commission, 48) - S(sales, 35):

    S(commission, 48) = {3, 4, 5,36,18,19, 20, 23, 24, 25, 26, 27, 34, 38, 39, 40, 44,45,47}
    S(sales, 35)   = {3, 4, 5, 36, 18, 19, 20, 23, 24, 25, 26, 27}
    S(commission, 48) - S(sales, 35) = {34, 38, 39, 40, 44,45,47}

    If there is a problem with commission at line 48, we can divide the program into two parts, the computation of sales at line 34, and the computation of commission between lines 35 and 48. If sales is OK at line 34, the problem must lie in the relative complement; if not, the problem may be in either portion.

3. There is a many-to-many relationship between slices and DD-Paths: statements in one slice may be in several DD-Paths, and statements in one DD-Path may be in several slices. Well-chosen relative complements of slices can be identical to DD-Paths. For example, consider S(commission, 40) - S(commission, 37).

4. If you develop a lattice of slices, it's convenient to postulate a slice on the very first statement. This way, the lattice of slices always terminates in one root node. Show equal slices with a two-way arrow.

5. Slices exhibit define/reference information. Consider the following slices on num_locks:

    S(num_locks, 17) = ∅
    S(num_locks, 24) = {17, 20, 27?}
    S(num_locks, 31) = {17, 20, 24, 27}
    S(num_locks, 34) = {17, 20, 24, 27}
    S(num_locks, 17) is the first definition of num_locks.
    S(num_locks, 24) - S(num_locks, 17) is a definition-clear, define reference path.

When slices are equal, the corresponding paths are definition-clear.

EXERCISES

1. Think about the static versus dynamic ambiguity of du-paths in terms of DD-Paths. As a start, what DD-Paths are found in the du-paths p12, p13, and p14 for sales?

2. Try to merge some of the DD-Path based test coverage metrics into the Rapps/Weyuker hierarchy shown in Figure 10.2.

3. Express slice S_{40} as the union of other pertinent slices.

4. Find the following program slices:
    a. S(commission, 48)
    b. S(sales, 35)
    c. S(commission, 40), S(commission, 39), S(commission, 38)
    d. S(num_locks, 34)
    e. S(num_stocks, 34)
    f. S(num_barrels, 34)

5. Find the definition-clear paths (with respect to SALES) from line 35 to:
    36, 40, 42, 45, 47.

6. Make a lattice of "interesting" slices. As a minimum, include the ones from question 4.

11

Retrospective on Structural Testing

When should testing stop? Here are some possible answers:

1. When you run out of time.
2. When continued testing causes no new failures.
3. When continued testing reveals no new faults.
4. When you can't think of any new test cases.
5. When you reach a point of diminishing returns.
6. When mandated coverage has been attained.
7. When all faults have been removed.

Unfortunately, the first answer is all too common, and the seventh cannot be guaranteed. This leaves the testing craft person somewhere in the middle. Software reliability models provide answers that support the second and third choices; both of these have been used with success in industry. The fourth choice is curious: if you have followed the precepts and guidelines we have been discussing, this is probably a good answer. On the other hand, if the reason is due to a lack of motivation, this choice is as unfortunate as the first. The point of diminishing returns choice has some appeal: it suggests that serious testing has continued, and the discovery of new faults has slowed dramatically. Continued testing becomes very expensive, and may reveal no new faults. If the cost (or risk) of remaining faults can be determined, the trade-off is clear. (This is a big If.) We're left with the coverage answer, and it's a pretty good one. In this chapter, we'll see how using structural testing as a cross check on functional testing yields powerful results. First, we demonstrate (by example) the gaps and redundancies problem of functional testing. Next, we develop some metrics of testing efficiency. Since these metrics are expressed in terms of structural coverage, we have an obvious answer to the gaps and redundancies question. Then the question reduces to which coverage metric to use. The answer that is most common in industrial practice is DD-paths.

11.1 GAPS AND REDUNDANCIES

The gaps and redundancies problem of functional testing is very prominent in the Triangle problem. We use the (FORTRAN-like) traditional implementation here, mostly because it is the most frequently used in testing literature [Brown 75] and [Pressman 82]. Recall that this implementation has exactly eleven feasible paths. They given in Table 1. The path names will be used later; the node numbers are shown in Figure 11.1.

140

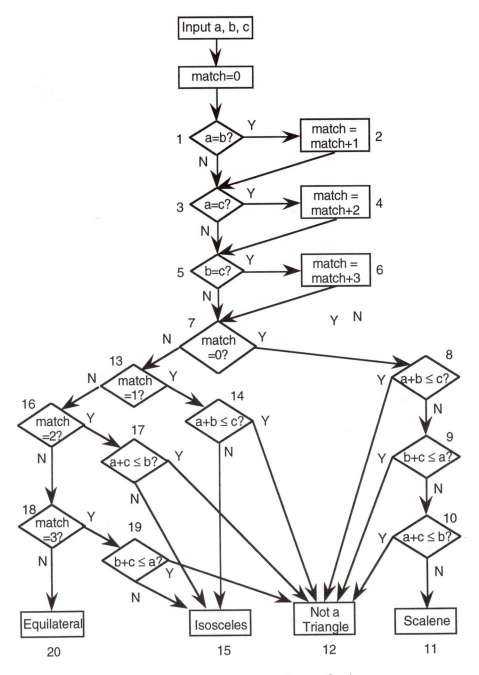

Figure 11.1 Traditional Triangle Program Graph

Table 1　　Paths in the Triangle Program

Path	Node Sequence	Description
p1	1-2-3-4-5-6-7-13-16-18-20	Equilateral
p2	1-3-5-6-7-13-16-18-19-15	Isosceles (b=c)
p3	1-3-5-6-7-13-16-18-19-12	Not a Triangle (b=c)
p4	1-3-4-5-7-13-16-17-15	Isosceles (a=c)
p5	1-3-4-5-7-13-16-17-12	Not a Triangle (a=c)
p6	1-2-3-5-7-13-14-15	Isosceles (a=b)
p7	1-2-3-5-7-13-14-12	Not a Triangle (a=b)
p8	1-3-5-7-8-12	Not a Triangle (a+b≤c)
p9	1-3-5-7-8-9-12	Not a Triangle (b+c≤a)
p10	1-3-5-7-8-9-10-12	Not a Triangle (a+c≤b)
p11	1-3-5-7-8-9-10-11	Scalene

Now, suppose we use boundary value testing to define test cases. We will do this for both the nominal and worst case formulations. Table 2 shows the test cases generated using the nominal boundary value form of functional testing. The last column shows the path (in Figure 11.1) taken by the test case.

Table 2　　Path Coverage of Nominal Values

Case	a	b	c	Expected Output	path
1	100	100	1	Isosceles	p6
2	100	100	2	Isosceles	p6
3	100	100	100	Equilateral	p1
4	100	100	199	Isosceles	p6
5	100	100	200	Not a Triangle	p7
6	100	1	100	Isosceles	p4
7	100	2	100	Isosceles	p4
8	100	100	100	Equilateral	p1
9	100	199	100	Isosceles	p4
10	100	200	100	Not a Triangle	p5
11	1	100	100	Isosceles	p2
12	2	100	100	Isosceles	p2
13	100	100	100	Equilateral	p1
14	199	100	100	Isosceles	p2
15	200	100	100	Not a Triangle	p3

The following paths are covered: p1, p2, p3, p4, p5, p6, p7, and paths p8, p9, p10, p11 are missed. Now, suppose we use a more powerful functional testing technique, worst case boundary value testing. We saw, in Chapter 5, that this yields 125 test cases; they are repeated here in Table 3 (in groups of 25) so you can see the extent of the redundant path coverage.

Table 3   Path Coverage of Worst Case Values

Case	a	b	c	Expected Output	path
1	1	1	1	Equilateral	p1
2	1	1	2	Not a Triangle	p7
3	1	1	100	Not a Triangle	p7
4	1	1	199	Not a Triangle	p7
5	1	1	200	Not a Triangle	p7
6	1	2	1	Not a Triangle	p5
7	1	2	2	Isosceles	p2
8	1	2	100	Not a Triangle	p8
9	1	2	199	Not a Triangle	p8
10	1	2	200	Not a Triangle	p8
11	1	100	1	Not a Triangle	p5
12	1	100	2	Not a Triangle	p10
13	1	100	100	Isosceles	p2
14	1	100	199	Not a Triangle	p8
15	1	100	200	Not a Triangle	p8
16	1	199	1	Not a Triangle	p5
17	1	199	2	Not a Triangle	p10
18	1	199	100	Not a Triangle	p10
19	1	199	199	Isosceles	p2
20	1	199	200	Not a Triangle	p8
21	1	200	1	Not a Triangle	p5
22	1	200	2	Not a Triangle	p10
23	1	200	100	Not a Triangle	p10
24	1	200	199	Not a Triangle	p10
25	1	200	200	Isosceles	p2

In test cases 1 through 25, the following paths were covered: p1, p2, p5, p7, p8, p10, and the following paths were missed: p3, p4, p6, p9, p11

Case	a	b	c	Expected Output	path
26	2	1	1	Not a Triangle	p3
27	2	1	2	Isosceles	p4
28	2	1	100	Not a Triangle	p8
29	2	1	199	Not a Triangle	p8
30	2	1	200	Not a Triangle	p8
31	2	2	1	Isosceles	p6
32	2	2	2	Equilateral	p1
33	2	2	100	Not a Triangle	p7
34	2	2	199	Not a Triangle	p7
35	2	2	200	Not a Triangle	p7
36	2	100	1	Not a Triangle	p10
37	2	100	2	Not a Triangle	p5
38	2	100	100	Isosceles	p2
39	2	100	199	Not a Triangle	p8
40	2	100	200	Not a Triangle	p8
41	2	199	1	Not a Triangle	p10
42	2	199	2	Not a Triangle	p10
43	2	199	100	Not a Triangle	p10

Table 3   Continued

44	2	199	199	Isosceles	p2
45	2	199	200	Scalene	p11
46	2	200	1	Not a Triangle	p10
47	2	200	2	Not a Triangle	p10
48	2	200	100	Not a Triangle	p10
49	2	200	199	Scalene	p11
50	2	200	200	Isosceles	p2

In test cases 26 through 50, the following paths were covered: p1, p2, p3, p4, p5, p6, p7, p8, p10, p11, and the following path was missed: p9.

Case	a	b	c	Expected Output	path
51	100	1	1	Not a Triangle	p3
52	100	1	2	Not a Triangle	p9
53	100	1	100	Isosceles	p4
54	100	1	199	Not a Triangle	p8
55	100	1	200	Not a Triangle	p8
56	100	2	1	Not a Triangle	p9
57	100	2	2	Not a Triangle	p3
58	100	2	100	Isosceles	p4
59	100	2	199	Not a Triangle	p8
60	100	2	200	Not a Triangle	p8
61	100	100	1	Isosceles	p6
62	100	100	2	Isosceles	p6
63	100	100	100	Equilateral	p1
64	100	100	199	Isosceles	p6
65	100	100	200	Not a Triangle	p8
66	100	199	1	Not a Triangle	p10
67	100	199	2	Not a Triangle	p10
68	100	199	100	Isosceles	p4
69	100	199	199	Isosceles	p2
70	100	199	200	Scalene	p11
71	100	200	1	Not a Triangle	p10
72	100	200	2	Not a Triangle	p10
73	100	200	100	Not a Triangle	p10
74	100	200	199	Scalene	p11
75	100	200	200	Isosceles	p2

In test cases 51 through 75, the following paths were covered: p1, p2, p3, p4, p6, p8, p9, p10, p11, and the following paths were missed: p5, p7.

Case	a	b	c	Expected Output	path
76	199	1	1	Not a Triangle	p3
77	199	1	2	Not a Triangle	p9
78	199	1	100	Not a Triangle	p9

Table 3   Continued

79	199	1	199	Scalene	p4
80	199	1	200	Not a Triangle	p8
81	199	2	1	Not a Triangle	p9
82	199	2	2	Not a Triangle	p3
83	199	2	100	Not a Triangle	p9
84	199	2	199	Isosceles	p4
85	199	2	200	Scalene	p11
86	199	100	1	Not a Triangle	p9
87	199	100	2	Not a Triangle	p9
88	199	100	100	Isosceles	p2
89	199	100	199	Isosceles	p4
90	199	100	200	Scalene	p11
91	199	199	1	Isosceles	p6
92	199	199	2	Isosceles	p6
93	199	199	100	Isosceles	p6
94	199	199	199	Equilateral	p1
95	199	199	200	Isosceles	p6
96	199	200	1	Not a Triangle	p10
97	199	200	2	Scalene	p11
98	199	200	100	Scalene	p11
99	199	200	199	Isosceles	p4
100	199	200	200	Isosceles	p2

In test cases 76 through 100, the following paths were covered: p1, p2, p3, p4, p6, p8, p9, p10, p11, and the following paths were missed: p5, p7.

Case	a	b	c	Expected Output	path
101	200	1	1	Not a Triangle	p3
102	200	1	2	Not a Triangle	p9
103	200	1	100	Not a Triangle	p9
104	200	1	199	Not a Triangle	p9
105	200	1	200	Isosceles	p4
106	200	2	1	Not a Triangle	p9
107	200	2	2	Not a Triangle	p9
108	200	2	100	Not a Triangle	p9
109	200	2	199	Scalene	p11
110	200	2	200	Isosceles	p5
111	200	100	1	Not a Triangle	p9
112	200	100	2	Not a Triangle	p9
113	200	100	100	Not a Triangle	p9
114	200	100	199	Scalene	p11
115	200	100	200	Isosceles	p4
116	200	199	1	Not a Triangle	p9
117	200	199	2	Scalene	p11
118	200	199	100	Scalene	p11
119	200	199	199	Isosceles	p2
120	200	199	200	Isosceles	p4
121	200	200	1	Isosceles	p6
122	200	200	2	Isosceles	p6

Table 3   Continued

123	200	200	100	Isosceles	p6
124	200	200	199	Isosceles	p6
125	200	200	200	Equilateral	p1

In test cases 101 through 125, the following paths were covered: p1, p2, p3, p4, p5, p6, p9, p11, and the following paths were missed: p7, p8, p10.

Taken together, the 125 test cases provide full path coverage, but the redundancy is onerous. Here are some comparisons of the paths traversed by the two techniques.

	p1	p2	p3	p4	p5	p6	p7	p8	p9	p10	p11
Nominal	3	3	1	3	1	3	1	0	0	0	0
Worst Case	5	12	6	11	6	12	7	17	18	19	12

11.2 METRICS FOR METHOD COMPARISON

Having convinced ourselves that the functional methods are indeed open to the twin problems of gaps and redundancies, we can develop some metrics that relate the effectiveness of a functional technique with the achievement of a structural metric. Functional testing techniques always result in a set of test cases, and the structural metric is always expressed in terms of something countable, like the number of program paths, the number of DD-Paths, or the number of slices. In the following definitions, we assume that a functional testing technique M generates m test cases, and that these test cases are tracked with respect to a structural metric S that identifies s coverage elements in the unit under test. When the m test cases are executed, they traverse n of the s structural coverage elements.

Definition
The *coverage of a methodology M with respect to a metric S* is defined by $C(M,S) = n/s$.

Definition
The *redundancy of a methodology M with respect to a metric S* is defined by $R(M,S) = m/s$.

Definition
The *net redundancy of a methodology M with respect to a metric S* is defined by $NR(M,S) = m/n$.

Notice that when full coverage is attained, $C(M,S) = 1$, which forces $R(M,S) = NR(M,S)$. We interpret these metrics as follows: the coverage metric, $C(M,S)$, deals with gaps. When it is less than 1, there are gaps in the coverage with respect to the metric. The redundancy metric is obvious — the bigger it is, the greater the redundancy. Net redundancy is more useful when full coverage cannot be attained; it refers to things actually traversed, not the total space of things to be traversed. Taken together, these three metrics provide a quantifiable way to evaluate the effectiveness of any functional testing method (except special value testing) with respect to any structural metric. This is only half the battle, however. What we really would like is to know how effective test cases are with respect to kinds of faults. Unfortunately, information such as this simply isn't available. We can come close by selecting structural metrics with respect to the kinds of faults we anticipate (or maybe faults we most fear). See the guidelines near the ends of Chapters 9 and 10 for specific advice.

11.2.1 COMPARING FUNCTIONAL TESTING METHODS
We apply these definitions to the data derived from the Triangle program example (in Section 11.1). We studied two functional methods, the nominal and the worst case boundary value methods, and the structural metric was program paths (there were eleven of these). The various quantities and the metric values are shown in Table 4.

Table 4   Metrics for the Triangle Program

Method	m	n	s	C(M, S)=n/s	R(M, S)=m/s	NR(M, S)=m/n
nominal	15	7	11	0.64	1.36	2.14
worst case	125	11	11	1.00	11.36	11.36

The data in Tables 5 and 6 describe DD-Path coverage of output boundary value analysis test cases and decision table test cases, respectively.

Table 5 DD-Path Coverage of Output Boundary Value Functional Test Cases

Case	locks	stocks	barrels	sales	commission	DD-Paths
1	1	1	1	100	10	1-5, 7, 9, 10, 11
2	1	1	2	125	12.5	1-5, 7, 9, 10, 11
3	1	2	1	130	13	1-5, 7, 9, 10, 11
4	2	1	1	145	14.5	1-5, 7, 9, 10, 11
5	10	10	9	975	97.5	1-5, 7, 9, 10, 11
6	10	9	10	970	97	1-5, 7, 9, 10, 11
7	9	10	10	955	95.5	1-5, 7, 9, 10, 11
8	5	5	5	500	50	1-5, 7, 9, 10, 11
9	10	10	10	1000	100	1-5, 7, 9, 10, 11
10	10	10	11	1025	103.75	1-5, 7, 8, 10, 11
11	10	11	10	1030	104.5	1-5, 7, 8, 10, 11
12	11	10	10	1045	106.75	1-5, 7, 8, 10, 11
13	14	14	14	1400	160	1-5, 7, 8, 10, 11
14	18	18	17	1775	216.25	1-5, 7, 8, 10, 11
15	18	17	18	1770	215.5	1-5, 7, 8, 10, 11
16	17	18	18	1755	213.25	1-5, 7, 8, 10, 11
17	18	18	18	1800	220	1-5, 7, 8, 10, 11
18	18	18	19	1825	225	1-5, 6, 10, 11
19	18	19	18	1830	226	1-5, 6, 10, 11
20	19	18	18	1845	229	1-5, 6, 10, 11
21	48	48	48	4800	820	1-5, 6, 10, 11
22	70	80	89	7775	1415	1-5, 6, 10, 11
23	70	79	90	7770	1414	1-5, 6, 10, 11
24	69	80	90	7755	1411	1-5, 6, 10, 11
25	70	80	90	7800	1420	1-5, 6, 10, 11

Table 6 DD-Path Coverage of Decision Table Functional Test Cases

Case	locks	stocks	barrels	sales	commission	DD-Paths
1	5	5	5	500	50	1-5, 7, 9, 10, 11
2	15	15	15	1500	175	1-5, 7, 8, 10, 11
3	25	25	25	2500	360	1-5, 6, 10, 11

Since both functional testing methods attained complete DD-Path coverage, the net redundancy metric is omitted from Table 7.

Table 7 Comparison of Two Functional Testing Methods

Method	m	n	s	C(M, S)=n/s	R(M, S)=m/s
Output bva	25	11	11	1	2.27
Decision table	3	11	11	1	0.27

This bears out the comparisons made earlier (in Chapter 8); a more sophisticated functional technique reduces the redundancy, and therefore improves the testing efficiency.

11.2.2 COMPARING STRUCTURAL TESTING METRICS

We can also use these metrics to analyze the effectiveness of a functional technique with respect to several structural metrics. Tables 5 and 8 relate output boundary value analysis test cases to two structural test coverage metrics, DD-Path coverage and DU-Path coverage.

Table 8   DU-Path Coverage of Output Boundary Value Functional Test Cases

Case	locks	stocks	barrels	sales	commission	DU-Paths
1	1	1	1	100	10	1-23, 27, 33
2	1	1	2	125	12.5	1-23, 27, 33
3	1	2	1	130	13	1-23, 27, 33
4	2	1	1	145	14.5	1-23, 27, 33
5	10	10	9	975	97.5	1-23, 27, 33
6	10	9	10	970	97	1-23, 27, 33
7	9	10	10	955	95.5	1-23, 27, 33
8	5	5	5	500	50	1-23, 27, 33
9	10	10	10	1000	100	1-23, 27, 33
10	10	10	11	1025	103.75	1-23, 25, 26, 31, 32
11	10	11	10	1030	104.5	1-23, 25, 26, 31, 32
12	11	10	10	1045	106.75	1-23, 25, 26, 31, 32
13	14	14	14	1400	160	1-23, 25, 26, 31, 32
14	18	18	17	1775	216.25	1-23, 25, 26, 31, 32
15	18	17	18	1770	215.5	1-23, 25, 26, 31, 32
16	17	18	18	1755	213.25	1-23, 25, 26, 31, 32
17	18	18	18	1800	220	1-23, 25, 26, 31, 32
18	18	18	19	1825	225	1-23, 24, 28-30
19	18	19	18	1830	226	1-23, 24, 28-30
20	19	18	18	1845	229	1-23, 24, 28-30
21	48	48	48	4800	820	1-23, 24, 28-30
22	70	80	89	7775	1415	1-23, 24, 28-30
23	70	79	90	7770	1414	1-23, 24, 28-30
24	69	80	90	7755	1411	1-23, 24, 28-30
25	70	80	90	7800	1420	1-23, 24, 28-30

Since both functional testing methods attained complete DD-Path coverage, the net redundancy metric is omitted from Table 9.

Table 9   Comparison of Three Structural Testing Metrics

Metric	m	n	s	C(M, S)=n/s	R(M, S)=m/s
DD-Path	25	11	11	1	2.27
DU-Path	25	33	33	1	0.76
Slices	25	40	40	1	0.63

This also bears out what we would expect: redundancy is reduced when a more stringent test coverage metric is imposed. In general, the more sophisticated structural metrics result in more elements (the quantity s), hence a given functional methodology will tend to become less effective when evaluated in terms of more rigorous structural metrics. This is intuitively appealing, and it is supported by our examples. The data for slices is misleading; in fact, this is a good example of how metrics are misused if they are misunderstood. Since the slices are a lattice, test cases that cover the "bottom" slice will necessarily cover all subset slices. In that sense, there is massive redundancy. We will revisit this in Section 11.3.

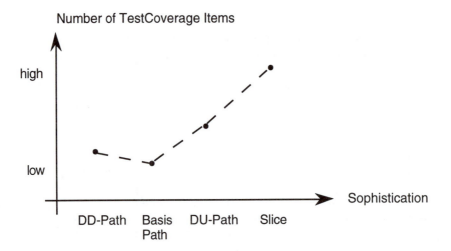

Figure 11.2 Trendline of Test Coverage Items

Figure 11.2 shows the growth of test coverage items in terms of increasingly sophisticated structural coverage metrics; this shape is echoed with our data for the Lock, Stock, and Barrel problem in Figure 11.3. In most programs, there are more DD-Paths than basis paths, hence the dip. There are also more DU-Paths than DD-Paths, but the relationship between DU-Paths and slices is less clear. Since we can always make a slice at a USE node, there should be at least as many slices as DU-Paths.

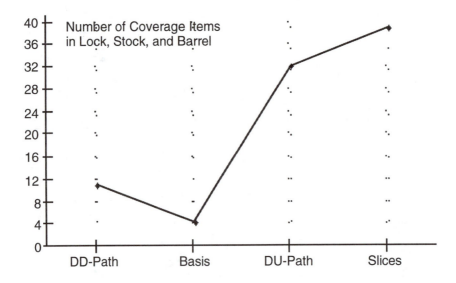

Figure 11.3 Test Coverage Items for Lock, Stock, and Barrel

The trendline of effort to identify structural coverage items is shown in Figure 11.4. Notice that the dip in the number of basis paths is accompanied by an increase in effort; this is due to the problem of finding feasible basis paths, rather than topologically possible ones.

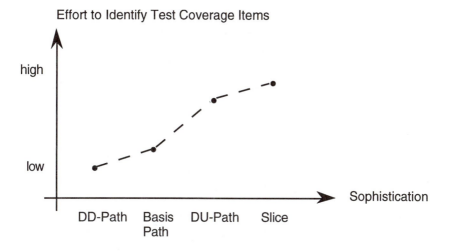

11.4 Trendline of Test Case Identification Effort

11.3 FUNCTIONAL-STRUCTURAL HYBRID TESTING

Our study of functional and structural testing is complete. Along the way, we have alluded to the possibility of combining the two approaches. We conclude this portion of the text with an example of "good practice" hybrid testing; the starting point is the test objectives for the slices of the Lock, Stock, and Barrel program, repeated below in Table 10.

Table 10   Slice Testing for Lock, Stock, and Barrel

Equivalent Slices	Sub-Function	Test Objective
1, 2, 3	1	salesman read and written correctly
4	2	locks read correctly
5, 6	3	locks sentinel correct
7	4	additional locks read correctly
8, 9 (10, 11)	5	iterative read of stocks correct
(8, 9) 10, 11	6	iterative read of barrels correct
12	7	num_locks initialized correctly
13, 14, 15	8	num_locks computed correctly
16	9	num_stocks initialized correctly
17, 18, 19	10	num_stocks computed correctly
20	11	num_barrels initialized correctly
21, 22, 23	12	num_barrels computed correctly
24	13	lock_price constant definition correct
25	14	stock_price constant definition correct
26	15	barrel_price constant definition correct

Table 10   Continued

27, 28, 29, 30, 31, 32, 33	16	sales computed correctly
34	17	commission on first 1000 correct for sales >1800
35	18	commission on next 800 correct for sales >1800
36	19	commission on excess over 1800 correct for sales >1800
37	20	commission on first 1000 correct for 1000 <sales <1800
38	21	commission on excess over 1000 correct for 1000 <sales <1800
39	22	commission on sales < 1000 correct
40	23	commission written correctly

We proceed by testing each sub-function as a separate slice (as recommended in Chapter 10). Imagine that we program each sub-function as a compilable slice, and that, after slices are individually tested, they are composed (spliced) together into the full program. The advantage of this procedure is that the sub-functions are easier to test because of their simplicity. The paragraph numbers that follow refer to the sub-function numbers in Table 8. The important source statements are given, but not the full compilable slice.

1.   Sub-function 1 is easy—it simply reads the salesperson's name and writes it out in the output report.

```
6     type
7          STRING_30 = string[30];    {Salesman's Name}
8     var
12         salesman : STRING_30;
17            READLN(salesman);
18            WRITELN ('Salesman is ', salesman);
32         WRITELN('Sales for ',salesman);
```

Since the salesman variable is defined to be of type string_30, we know it is a string of up to 30 characters. Special value testing is a good choice here; we might test with names such as 'Annie Oakley', ' ', and 'aThirtyTwoCharacterNameThatIsOdd'.

2-4.   We combine sub-functions 2 through 4 into a single function: the loop that is controlled by the sentinel variable locks and reads successive records.

```
22              READ(locks);
23              WHILE locks <> -1 DO
24                 BEGIN
( 25                 READLN(stocks, barrels);)
29                    READ(locks);
30                 END; {WHILE locks}
```

Huang's Theorem (see Chapter 8) requires two traversals of the loop, a drop through and a repetition. Even though the values of stocks and barrels are not read, the READLN statement consumes the end-of-line (EOL) character. Traditional equivalence class and two special value test cases are shown in Table 11.

Case 5 in Table 11 reveals a fault of omission: negative values shouldn't be tolerated; as it stands, they will arithmetically decrease the quantity num_locks. This might be used as a mechanism to process returned items, and thereby reduce a salesperson's commission, but it is not in the problem statement.

Table 11   Traditional Equivalence Class Test Cases for locks

Case	locks	stocks	barrels	Description
1	3			normal case
	14			
	-1			
2	0			nothing sold
	-1			
3	-1			drop-through case
4	5			
	-1			
5	-2			illegal value of locks
6	maxint+1			equals -1 in 2's complement

5, 6   Sub-functions 5 and 6 add the input of stocks and barrels to the loop controlled by locks. (Since both of these are in the same statement, we merge the slices.)

```
22              READ(locks);
23              WHILE locks <> -1 DO
24                  BEGIN
25                      READLN(stocks, barrels);
29                      READ(locks);
30                  END; {WHILE locks}
```

Since the values of stocks and barrels are never used in this slice, there isn't much to test except for a subtlety of Pascal: the difference between a READ and a READLN statement is that the latter also reads the End-Of-Line character. Thus there would be Pascal-specific tests (EOL before the barrels value), but not much else. Since this is also tested in sub-functions 9 and 10, we skip it here.

7, 8   Sub-functions 7 and 8 initialize and accumulate the value of num_locks as the sum of individual values for the locks variable as they are read in the slice for sub-functions 2-4.

```
19              num_locks := 0;
22              READ(locks);
23              WHILE locks <> -1 DO
24                  BEGIN
26                      num_locks := num_locks + locks;
29                      READ(locks);
30                  END; {WHILE locks}
```

To test this slice, we could re-use the test cases in Table 9. Pass/fail decisions would be based on expected values of num_locks.

9, 10   Sub-functions 9 and 10 initialize and accumulate the value of num_stocks as the sum of individual values for the stocks variable as they are read in the slice for sub-functions 2-4.

```
20              num_stocks := 0;
22              READ(locks);
23              WHILE locks <> -1 DO
24                  BEGIN
25                      READLN(stocks, barrels);
27                      num_stocks := num_stocks + stocks;
29                      READ(locks);
30                  END; {WHILE locks}
```

To test this slice, we could extend the test cases in Table 9 to include values for stocks (see Table 12). Pass/fail decisions would be based on expected values of num_stocks.

Table 12   Traditional Equivalence Class Test Cases for num_stocks

Case	locks	stocks	barrels	Description
1	3	22		normal case
	14	8		
	-1			
2	0	0		nothing sold
	-1			
3	-1			drop-through case
4	5	5		
	-1			
5	-2	-2		illegal value of stocks

11, 12 Sub-functions 11 and 12 initialize and accumulate the value of num_barrels as the sum of individual values for the barrels variable as they are read in the slice for sub-functions 2-4.

```
21              num_barrels := 0;
22              READ(locks);
23              WHILE locks <> -1 DO
24                BEGIN
25                  READLN(stocks, barrels);
28                  num_barrels := num_barrels + barrels;
29                  READ(locks);
30                END; {WHILE locks}
```

To test this slice, we could extend the test cases in Table 12 to include values for barrels (see Table 13). Pass/fail decisions would be based on expected values of num_barrels.

Table 13   Traditional Equivalence Class Test Cases for num_barrels

Case	locks	stocks	barrels	Description
1	3	22	6	normal case
	14	8	13	
	-1			
2	0	0	0	nothing sold
	-1			
3	-1			drop-through case
4	5	5	5	
	-1			
5	-2	-2	-2	illegal value of barrels

13-15 These sub-functions are just the constant definitions of values for lock_price, stock_price, and barrel_price. No testing is required.

```
3              lock_price   = 45.0;
4              stock_price  = 30.0;
5              barrel_price = 25.0;
```

16   These slices all refer to the sales variable; slice 27 (on sales at fragment 36) is where the value of sales is computed.

```
3              lock_price   = 45.0;
4              stock_price  = 30.0;
5              barrel_price = 25.0;
19                num_locks  := 0;
20                num_stocks := 0;
21                num_barrels := 0;
22                READ(locks);
23                WHILE locks <> -1 DO
24                  BEGIN
25                    READLN(stocks, barrels);
26                    num_locks := num_locks + locks;
27                    num_stocks := num_stocks + stocks;
28                    num_barrels := num_barrels + barrels;
29                    READ(locks);
30                  END; {WHILE locks}
36            sales := lock_price*num_locks + stock_price*num_stocks
                           + barrel_price*num_barrels;
```

By the time we reach this point in development and testing, we know that the prices and the quantities are correct (symmetric differences of slices), so our main concern is the computation at statement 36. Since the decision table test cases provide good coverage, this would be a good time to use them (see Table 14).

Table 14   Decision Table Test Cases for Sales Computation

Case	locks	stocks	barrels	Description
1	0	0	0	nothing sold
	-1			
2	5	5	5	sales = 500
	-1			
3	15	15	15	sales = 1500
	-1			
4	25	25	25	sales = 2500
	-1			

17-19   These sub-functions compute the commission when sales exceeds $1800. (See case 3 in Table 15.)

```
3              lock_price   = 45.0;
4              stock_price  = 30.0;
5              barrel_price = 25.0;
19                num_locks  := 0;
20                num_stocks := 0;
21                num_barrels := 0;
22                READ(locks);
23                WHILE locks <> -1 DO
24                  BEGIN
25                    READLN(stocks, barrels);
26                    num_locks := num_locks + locks;
27                    num_stocks := num_stocks + stocks;
28                    num_barrels := num_barrels + barrels;
```

```
29                      READ(locks);
30                  END;  {WHILE locks}
36          sales  :=  lock_price*num_locks  +  stock_price*num_stocks
                          +  barrel_price*num_barrels;
41              commission  :=  0.10  *  1000.0;
42              commission  :=  commission  +  0.15  *  800.0;
43              commission  :=  commission  +  0.20  *  (sales-1800.0);
```

The other slices would replace statements 41-43 with the following two sets of commission computations:

```
47              commission  :=  0.10  *  1000.0;
48              commission  :=  commission  +  0.15*(sales  -  1000.0);
```

and

```
50          ELSE  commission  :=  0.10  *  sales;
```

Table 15   Decision Table Test Cases for Commission Computations

Case	locks	stocks	barrels	Description
1	5	5	5	sales = 500
	-1			commission = 50
2	15	15	15	sales = 1500
	-1			commission = 175
3	25	25	25	sales = 2500
	-1			commission = 360

To see how these test cases reveal faults, suppose one of the constants in statement 41 was incorrect, as in the statement below:

```
41(bad)         commission  :=  0.10  *  100.0;
```

Test case 3 in Table 15 would fail, so we would know there was a problem somewhere in slices 34, 35, and 36, but not in slice 27. We would follow the lattice and first test slice 35; this test would also fail. If we determined that statement 42 was indeed correct, we would then test slice 34 (statement 41), and this test would also fail. Since all slices below (in the lattice) were already correct, we would know that the fault was in statement 41.

11.4 CLOSURE

We've come a long way since Chapter 1. We studied functional and structural testing techniques, both in terms of how they work and when they are appropriate. We have seen that neither approach, by itself, is adequate: functional testing is inevitably open to questions of gaps and redundancies, while the path-based forms of structural testing abstract so far away from the semantics of a program that they create new difficulties, namely infeasible paths. The dataflow forms of structural testing move back in the direction of functional testing by imposing semantically meaningful considerations onto the purely graph theoretic constructs of path-based testing. The bottom line is that well-chosen hybrids of functional and structural techniques are highly effective in revealing faults. We have moved software testing from an art to a craft.

In much of what we have done, there has been a latent assumption that the techniques are only for unit level testing. The illustrative examples reinforce this assumption, and it is partially true. The structural techniques do not scale up well, although there is commercial tool support for some of them. (Imagine identifying DU-Paths or slices in a program of 20,000 source statements.) While the specific structural techniques do not extend well to higher (integration and system) levels of testing, the basic interaction between functional and structural approaches is still important. Much of our task in Part IV is to develop structural constructs that are appropriate to integration and system level testing. Given such constructs, we will continue to enjoy (and exploit) the symbiosis between functional and structural testing.

EXERCISES

1. Repeat the gaps and redundancies analysis for the Triangle problem using the Pascal implementation in Chapter 2, and its DD-Path graph in Chapter 9.
2. Compute the coverage, redundancy, and net redundancy metrics for your study in question 1.
3. A major commercial software development corporation performs all its tests on an instrumented version of a product. When the instrumented version passes all tests, the original product version is released. Discuss this policy with respect to our four basic forms of structural testing: DD-Paths, basis paths, du-paths, and slices. Refine your discussion with respect to two forms of instrumentation: a passive form, with traces and value capturing output statements; and an active form, with assertions about program variables. The Department of Defense and other government software contracting agencies generally do not accept this form of testing. Are they justified?
4. Revise the Locks, Stocks, and Barrels program to correct the following faults:
   a. no check for maximum values of num_locks, num_stocks, and num_barrels.
   b. no check for negative values of locks, stocks, and barrels.
5. Choose one of the comparisons in this chapter and apply it to your improved program from question 4.

Part IV

Integration and System Testing

Chapter 12

Levels of Testing

In this chapter, we build a context for Part IV, with the immediate goal of identifying what we mean by levels of testing. We took a simplistic view in Chapter 1, where we identified three levels (unit, integration, and system) in terms of symmetries in the Waterfall Model of software development. This view has been relatively successful for decades, however, the advent of alternative life cycle models mandates changes to these views of testing. We begin with the traditional Waterfall model, mostly because it has enormous acceptance and similar expressive power. To ground our discussion in something concrete, we switch to the automated teller machine example.

12.1 TRADITIONAL VIEW OF TESTING LEVELS

The traditional model of software development is the Waterfall model, which is drawn as a V in Figure 12.1 to emphasize the basic levels of testing. In this view, information produced in one of the development phases constitutes the basis for test case identification at that level. Nothing controversial here: we certainly would hope that system test cases are somehow correlated with the requirements specification, and that unit test cases are derived from the detailed design of the unit. Two observations: there is a clear presumption of functional testing here, and there is an implied "bottom-up" testing order.

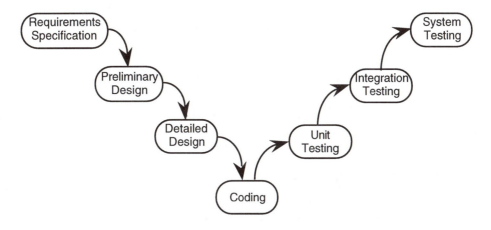

Figure 12.1 The Waterfall Life Cycle

Of the three traditional levels of testing (unit, integration, and system), unit testing is best understood. The testing theory and techniques we worked through in Parts I and II are directly applicable to unit testing. System testing is understood better than integration testing, but both need clarification. The bottom-up approach sheds some insight: test the individual components, and then integrate these into subsystems until the entire system is tested. System testing should be something that the customer (or user) understands, and it often borders on customer acceptance testing. Generally, system testing is functional rather than structural; this is mostly due to the absence of a structural basis for system test cases. In the traditional view, integration testing is what's left over: it's not unit testing, and it's not system testing. Most of the usual discussions on integration testing center on the order in which units are integrated: top-down, bottom-up, or the "big bang" (everything at once). Of the three levels, integration is the least well understood; we'll do something about that in this chapter and the next.

The waterfall model is closely associated with top-down development and design by functional decomposition. The end result of preliminary design is a functional decomposition of the entire system into a treelike structure of functional components. Figure 12.2 contains a partial functional decomposition of our ATM system. With this decomposition. top-down integration would begin with the main program, checking the calls to the three next level procedures (Terminal I/O, ManageSessions, and ConductTransactions). Following the tree, the ManageSessions procedure would be tested, and then the CardEntry, PIN Entry, and SelectTransaction procedures. In each case, the actual code for lower level units is replaced by a stub, which is a throw-away piece of code that takes the place of the actual code. Bottom-up integration would be the opposite sequence, starting with the CardEntry, PIN Entry, and SelectTransaction procedures, and working up toward the main program. In bottom-up integration, units at higher levels are replaced by drivers (another form of throw-away code) that emulate the procedure calls. The big bang approach simply puts all the units together at once, with no stubs or drivers. Whichever approach is taken, the goal of traditional integration testing is to integrate previously tested units with respect to the functional decomposition tree. While this describes integration testing as a process, discussions of this type offer little information about the goals or techniques. Before addressing these (real) issues, we need to understand the consequences of the alternative life cycle models.

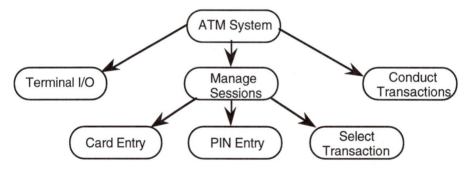

Figure 12.2   Partial Functional Decomposition of the ATM System

12.2 ALTERNATIVE LIFE CYCLE MODELS

Since the early 1980s, practitioners have devised alternatives in response to shortcomings of the traditional waterfall model of software development [Agresti 86]. Common to all of these alternatives is the shift away from the functional decomposition to an emphasis on composition. Decomposition is a perfect fit both to the top-down progression of the waterfall model and to the bottom-up testing order. One of the major weaknesses of waterfall development cited by [Agresti 86] is the over-reliance on this whole paradigm. Functional decomposition can only be well done when the system is completely understood, and it promotes analysis to the near exclusion of synthesis. The result is a very long separation between requirements specification and a completed system, and during this interval, there is no opportunity for feedback from the customer. Composition, on the other hand, is closer the way people work: start with something known and understood, then add to it gradually, and maybe remove undesired portions. There is a very nice analogy with positive and negative sculpture. In negative sculpture, work proceeds by removing unwanted material, as in the mathematician's view of sculpting Michelangelo's David: start with a piece of marble, and simply chip away all non-David. Positive sculpture is often done with a medium like wax. The central shape is approximated, and then wax is either added or removed until the desired shape is attained. Think about the consequences of a mistake: with negative sculpture, the whole work must be thrown away, and restarted. (There is a museum in Florence, Italy that contains half a dozen such false starts to The David.) With positive sculpture, the erroneous part is simply removed and replaced. The centrality of composition in the alternative models has a major implication for integration testing.

12.2.1 WATERFALL SPIN-OFFS

There are three mainline derivatives of the waterfall model: incremental development, evolutionary development, and the Spiral model [Boehm 88]. Each of these involves a series of increments or builds, as shown in Figure 12.3. Within a build, the normal waterfall phases from detailed design through testing occur, with one important difference: system testing is split into two steps, regression and progression testing.

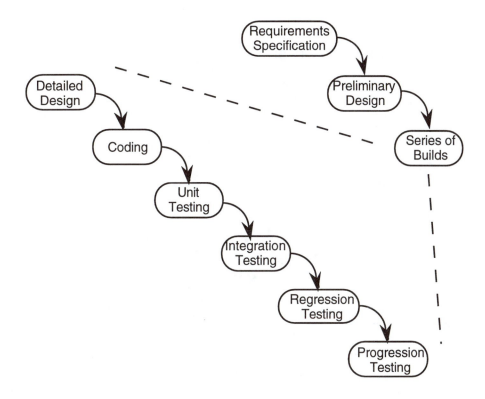

Figure 12.3 Life Cycle with a Build Sequence

It is important to keep preliminary design as an integral phase, rather than to try to amortize such high level design across a series of builds. (To do so usually results in unfortunate consequences of design choices made during the early builds that are regrettable in later builds.) Since preliminary design remains a separate step, we are tempted to conclude that integration testing is unaffected in the spin-off models. To some extent this is true: the main impact of the series of builds is that regression testing becomes necessary. The goal of regression testing is to assure that things that worked correctly in the previous build still work with the newly added code. Progression testing assumes that regression testing was successful, and that the new functionality can be tested. (We like to think that the addition of new code represents progress, not a regression.) Regression testing is an absolute necessity in a series of builds because of the well-known "ripple effect" of changes to an existing system. (The industrial average is that one change in five introduces a new fault.)

The differences among the three spin-off models are due to how the builds are identified. In incremental development, the motivation for separate builds is usually to level off the staff profile. With pure waterfall development, there can be a huge bulge of personnel for the phases from detailed design through unit testing. Most organizations cannot support such rapid staff fluctuations, so the system is divided into builds that can be supported by existing personnel. In evolutionary development, there is still the presumption of a build sequence, but only the first build is defined. Based on it, later builds are identified, usually in response to priorities set by the customer/user, so the system evolves to meet the changing needs of the user. The spiral model is a combination of rapid prototyping and evolutionary development, in which a build is defined first in terms of rapid prototyping, and then is subjected to a go/ no go decision based on technology-related risk factors. From this we see that keeping preliminary design as an integral step is difficult for the evolutionary and spiral models. To the extent that this cannot be maintained as an integral activity, integration testing is negatively affected.

Because a build is a set of deliverable end-user functionality, one advantage of these spin-off models is that all three yield earlier synthesis. This also results in earlier customer feedback, so two of the deficiencies of waterfall development are mitigated.

12.2.2 SPECIFICATION BASED MODELS

Two other variations are responses to the "complete understanding" problem. (Recall that functional decomposition is successful only when the system is completely understood.) When systems are not fully understood (by either the customer or the developer), functional decomposition is perilous at best. The rapid prototyping life cycle (Figure 12.4) deals with this by drastically reducing the specification-to-customer feedback loop to produce very early synthesis. Rather than build a final system, a "quick and dirty" prototype is built and then used to elicit customer feedback. Depending on the feedback, more prototyping cycles may occur. Once the developer and the customer agree that a prototype represents the desired system, the developer goes ahead and builds to a correct specification. At this point, any of the waterfall spin-offs might also be used.

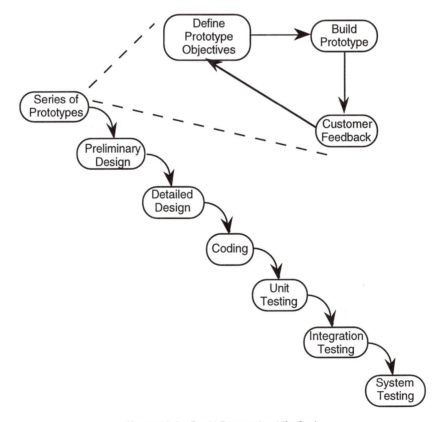

Figure 12.4 Rapid Prototyping Life Cycle

Rapid prototyping has interesting implications for system testing. Where are the requirements? Is the last prototype the specification? How are system test cases traced back to the prototype? One good answer to questions such as these is to use the prototyping cycle(s) as information gathering activities, and then produce a requirements specification in a more traditional manner. Another possibility is to capture what the customer does with the prototype(s), define these as scenarios that are important to the customer, and then use these as system test cases. The main contribution of rapid prototyping is that it brings the operational (or behavioral) viewpoint to the requirements specification phase. Usually, requirements specification techniques emphasize the structure of a system, not its behavior. This is unfortunate, because most customers don't care about the structure, and they do care about the behavior.

Executable specifications (Figure 12.5) are an extension of the rapid prototyping concept. With this approach, the requirements are specified in an executable format (such as finite state machines or Petri nets). The customer then executes the specification to observe the intended system behavior, and provides feedback as in the rapid prototyping model.

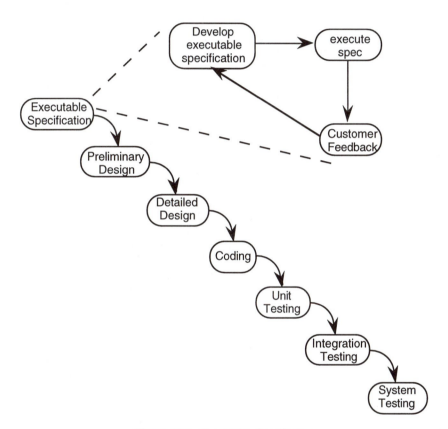

Figure 12.5   Executable Specification

One big difference is that the requirements specification document is explicit, as opposed to a prototype. More important, it is often a mechanical process to derive system test cases from an executable specification. We will see this in Chapter 16. Although more work is required to develop an executable specification, this is partially offset by the reduced effort to generate system test cases. Another important distinction: when system testing is based on an executable specification, we have a form of structural testing at the system level.

12.2.3 AN OBJECT-ORIENTED LIFE CYCLE MODEL

When software is developed with an object orientation, none of our life cycle models fit very well. The main reasons: the object orientation is highly compositional in nature, and there is dense interaction among the construction phases of object-oriented analysis, object-oriented design, and object-oriented programming. We could show this with pronounced feedback loops among waterfall phases, but the

164

fountain model [Henderson-Sellers 90] is a much more appropriate metaphor. In the fountain model, (see Figure 12.6) the foundation is the requirements analysis of real world systems.

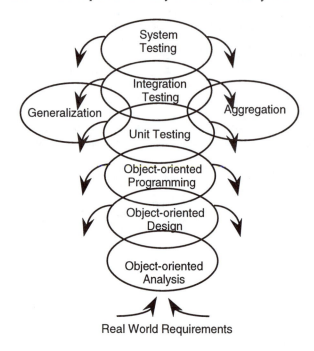

Figure 12.6   Fountain Model of Object-Oriented Software Development

As the object-oriented paradigm proceeds, details "bubble up" through specification, design, and coding phases, but at each stage, some of the "flow" drops back to the previous phase(s). This model captures the reality of the way people actually work (even with the traditional approaches).

12.3 FORMULATIONS OF THE SATM SYSTEM

In this and the next three chapters, we will relate our discussion to a higher level example, the Simple Automatic Teller Machine (SATM) system. The version developed here is a revision of that found in [Topper 93]; it is built around the fifteen screens shown in Figure 12.7. This is a greatly reduced system; commercial ATM systems have hundreds of screens and numerous time-outs.

The SATM terminal is sketched in Figure 12.8; in addition to the display screen, there are function buttons B1, B2, and B3, a digit keypad with a cancel key, slots for printer receipts and ATM cards, and doors for deposits and cash withdrawals. The SATM system is described here in two ways: with a structured analysis approach, and with an object-oriented approach. These descriptions are not complete, but they contain detail sufficient to illustrate the testing techniques under discussion.

12.3.1 SATM WITH STRUCTURED ANALYSIS

The structured analysis approach to requirements specification is the most widely used method in the world. It enjoys extensive CASE tool support as well as commercial training, and is described in numerous texts. The technique is based on three complementary models: function, data, and control. Here we use data flow diagrams for the functional models, entity/relationship models for data, and finite state machine models for the control aspect of the SATM system. The functional and data models were drawn with the Deft CASE tool from Sybase Inc. That tool identifies external devices (such as the terminal doors) with lower case letters, and elements of the functional decomposition with numbers (such as 1.5 for the Validate Card function). The open and filled arrowheads on flow arrows signify whether the flow item is simple or compound. The portions of the SATM system shown here pertain generally to the personal identification number (PIN) verification portion of the system.

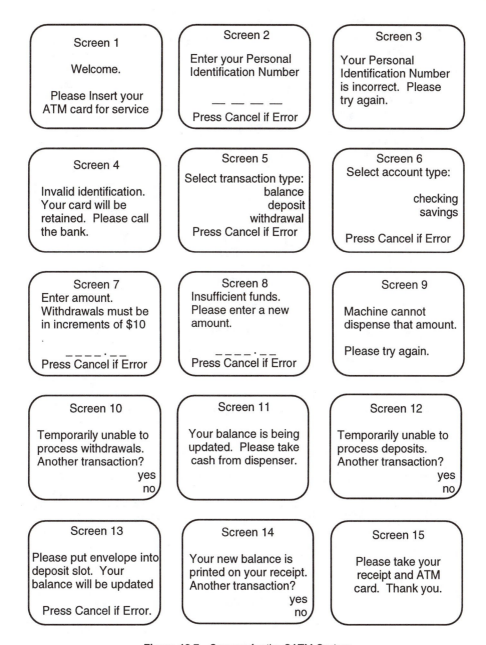

Figure 12.7   Screens for the SATM System

The Deft CASE tool distinguishes between simple and compound flows, where compound flows may be decomposed into other flows, which may themselves be compound. The graphic appearance of this choice is that simple flows have filled arrowheads, while compound flows have open arrowheads. As an example, the compound flow "screen" has the following decomposition:

screen is comprised of

screen1	welcome
screen2	enter PIN
screen3	wrong PIN
screen4	PIN failed, card retained
screen5	select trans type

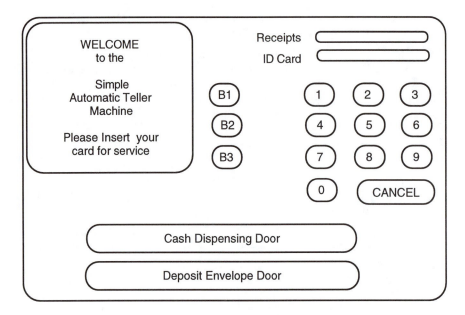

Figure 12.8 The SATM Terminal

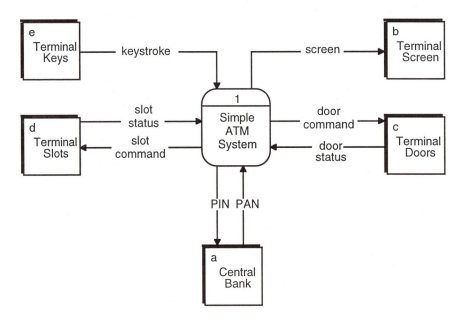

Figure 12.9 Context Diagram of the SATM System

screen6	select account type
screen7	enter amount
screen8	insufficient funds
screen9	cannot dispense that amount
screen10	cannot process withdrawals
screen11	take your cash
screen12	cannot process deposits
screen13	put dep envelop in slot
screen14	another transaction?
screen15	Thanks; take card and receipt

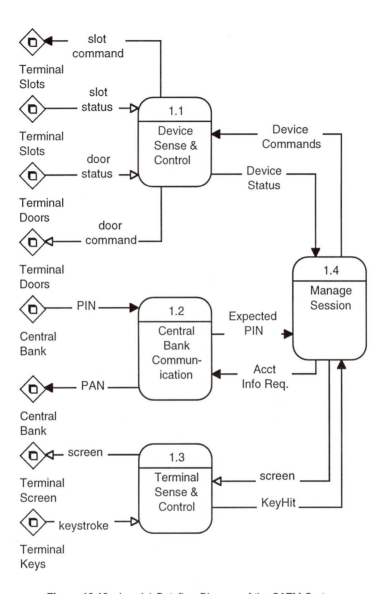

Figure 12.10 Level 1 Dataflow Diagram of the SATM System

Figure 12.11 is an (incomplete) Entity/Relationship diagram of the major data structures in the SATM system: Customers, Accounts, Terminals, and Transactions. Good data modeling practice dictates postulating an entity for each portion of the system that is described by data that is retained (and used by functional components). Among the data the system would need for each customer are the customer's identification and personal account number (PAN); these are encoded into the magnetic strip on the customer's ATM card. We would also want to know information about a customer's account(s), including the account numbers, the balances, the type of account (savings or checking), and the Personal Identification Number (PIN) of the account. At this point, we might ask why the PIN is not associated with the customer, and the PAN with an account. Some design has crept into the specification at this point: if the data were as questioned, a person's ATM card could be used by anyone; as it is, the present separation predisposes a security checking procedure. Part of the E/R model describes relationships among the entities: a customer HAS account(s), a customer conducts transaction(s) in a SESSION, and, independent of customer information, transaction(s) OCCUR at an ATM terminal. The single and double arrowheads signify the singularity or plurality of these relationships: one customer may have several accounts, and may conduct none or several transactions. Many transactions may occur at a terminal, but one transaction never occurs at a multiplicity of terminals.

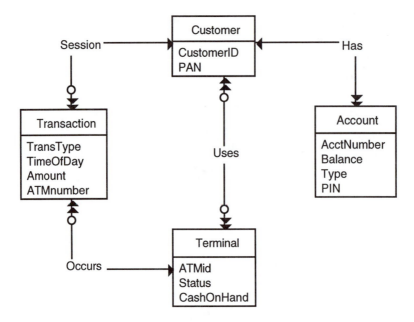

Figure 12.11 Entity/Relationship Model of the SATM System

The dataflow diagrams and the entity/relationship model contain information that is primarily structural. This is problematic for testers, because test cases are concerned with behavior, not with structure. As a supplement, the functional and data information are linked by a control model; here we use a finite state machine. Control models represent the point at which structure and behavior intersect; as such, they are of special utility to testers.

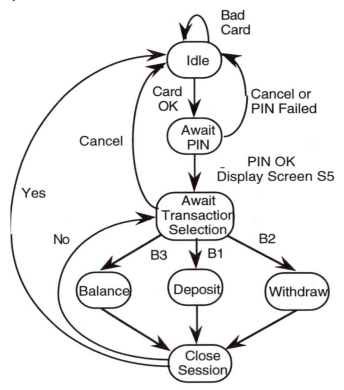

Figure 12.12 Upper Level SATM Finite State Machine

The upper level finite state machine in Figure 12.12 divides the system into states that correspond to stages of customer usage. Other choices are possible, for instance, we might choose states to be screens being displayed (this turns out to be a poor choice). Finite state machines can be hierarchically decomposed in much the same way as dataflow diagrams. The decomposition of the Await PIN state is shown in Figure 12.13. In both of these figures, state transitions are caused either by events at the ATM terminal (such as a keystroke) or by data conditions (such as the recognition that a PIN is correct). When a transition occurs, a corresponding action may also occur. We choose to use screen displays as such actions; this choice will prove to be very handy when we develop system level test cases.

The function, data, and control models are the basis for design activities in the waterfall model (and its spin-offs). During design, some of the original decisions may be revised based on additional insights and more detailed requirements (for example, performance or reliability goals). The end result is a functional decomposition such as the partial one shown in the structure chart in Figure 12.14. Notice that the original first level decomposition into four subsystems is continued: the functionality has beendecomposed to lower levels of detail. Choices such as these are the essence of design, and design is beyond the scope of this book. In practice, testers often have to live with the results of poor design choices.

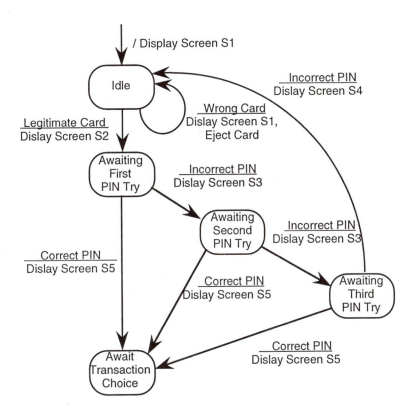

Figure 12.13 PIN Entry Finite State Machine

If we only use a structure chart to guide integration testing, we miss the fact that some (typically lower level) functions are used in more than one place. Here, for example, the ScreenDriver function is used by several other modules, but it only appears once in the functional decomposition. In the next chapter, we will see that a "call graph" is a much better basis for integration test case identification. We can develop the beginnings of such a call graph from a more detailed view of portions of the system. To support this, we need a numbered decomposition, and a more detailed view of two of the components.

Here is the functional decomposition carried further in outline form: the numbering scheme preserves the levels of the components in Figure 12.14.

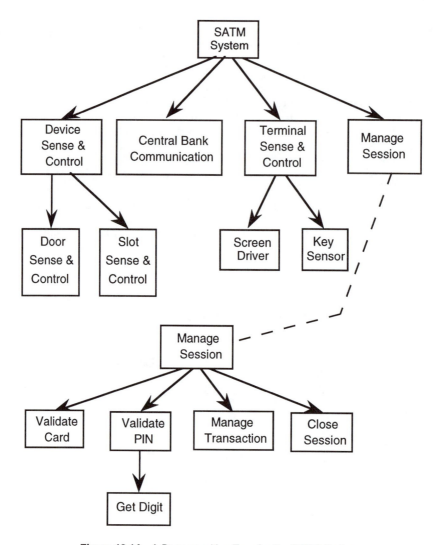

Figure 12.14 A Decomposition Tree for the SATM System

1 SATM System
  1.1 Device Sense & Control
      1.1.1 Door Sense & Control
          1.1.1.1 Get Door Status
          1.1.1.2 Control Door
          1.1.1.3 Dispense Cash
      1.1.2 Slot Sense & Control
          1.1.2.1 WatchCardSlot
          1.1.2.2 Get Deposit Slot Status
          1.1.2.3 Control Card Roller
          1.1.2.3 Control Envelope Roller
          1.1.2.5 Read Card Strip
  1.2 Central Bank Comm.
      1.2.1 Get PIN for PAN
      1.2.2 Get Account Status
      1.2.3 Post Daily Transactions
  1.3 Terminal Sense & Control
      1.3.1 Screen Driver
      1.3.2 Key Sensor

1.4 Manage Session
    1.4.1 Validate Card
    1.4.2 Validate PIN
        1.4.2.1 GetPIN
    1.4.3 Close Session
        1.4.3.1 New Transaction Request
        1.4.3.2 Print Receipt
        1.4.3.3 Post Transaction Local
    1.4.4 Manage Transaction
        1.4.4.1 Get Transaction Type
        1.4.4.2 Get Account Type
        1.4.4.3 Report Balance
        1.4.4.4 Process Deposit
        1.4.4.5 Process Withdrawal

As part of the specification and design process, each functional component is normally expanded to show its inputs, outputs, and mechanism. We do this here with pseudo-code (or PDL, for program design language) for three modules. This particular PDL is loosely based on Pascal; the point of any PDL is to communicate, not to develop something that can be compiled. The main program description follows the finite state machine description given in Figure 12.12. States in that diagram are "implemented" with a Case statement.

```
Main Program
State = AwaitCard
CASE State OF
AwaitCard:              ScreenDriver(1, null)
                        WatchCardSlot(CardSlotStatus)
                        WHILE CardSlotStatus is Idle DO
                                WatchCardSlot(CardSlotStatus)
                        ControlCardRoller(accept)
                        ValidateCard(CardOK, PAN)
                        IF CardOK    THEN  State = AwaitPIN
                                     ELSE  ControlCardRoller(eject)
                                           State = AwaitCard
AwaitPIN:               ValidatePIN(PINok, PAN)
                        IF PINok    THEN  ScreenDriver(2, null)
                                          State = AwaitTrans
                                    ELSE  ScreenDriver(4, null)
                                          State = AwaitCard
AwaitTrans:             ManageTransaction
                        State = CloseSession
CloseSession:           IF NewTransactionRequest
                                THEN  State = AwaitTrans
                                ELSE  PrintReceipt
                                      PostTransactionLocal
                                      CloseSession
                                      ControlCardRoller(eject)
                                      State = AwaitCard
End, (CASE State)
END. (Main program SATM)
```

The ValidatePIN procedure is based on another finite state machine shown in Figure 12.13, in which states refer to the number of PIN entry attempts.

```
Procedure ValidatePIN(PINok, PAN)
GetPINforPAN(PAN, ExpectedPIN)
Try = First
CASE Try OF
First:      ScreenDriver(2, null)
            GetPIN(EnteredPIN)
            IF EnteredPIN = ExpectedPIN
                  THEN   PINok = TRUE
                         RETURN
                  ELSE   ScreenDriver(3, null)
                         Try = Second
Second:     ScreenDriver(2, null)
            GetPIN(EnteredPIN)
            IF EnteredPIN = ExpectedPIN
                  THEN   PINok = TRUE
                         RETURN
                  ELSE   ScreenDriver(3, null)
                         Try = Third
Third:      ScreenDriver(2, null)
            GetPIN(EnteredPIN)
            IF EnteredPIN = ExpectedPIN
                  THEN   PINok = TRUE
                         RETURN
                  ELSE   ScreenDriver(4, null)
                         PINok = FALSE
END,  (CASE Try)
END.  (Procedure ValidatePIN)
```

The GetPIN procedure is based on another finite state machine in which states refer to the number of digits received, and in any state, either another digit key can be touched, or the cancel key can be touched. Rather than another CASE statement implementation, the "states" are collapsed into iterations of a WHILE loop.

```
Procedure GetPIN(EnteredPIN, CancelHit)
Local Data: DigitKeys = {0, 1, 2, 3, 4, 5, 6, 7, 8, 9}
BEGIN
CancelHit = FALSE
EnteredPIN = null string
DigitsRcvd=0
WHILE NOT(DigitsRcvd=4 OR CancelHit) DO
   BEGIN
       KeySensor(KeyHit)
       IF KeyHit IN DigitKeys
       THEN BEGIN
            EnteredPIN = EnteredPIN + KeyHit
            INCREMENT(DigitsRcvd)
            IF DigitsRcvd=1 THEN ScreenDriver(2,'X—')
            IF DigitsRcvd=2 THEN ScreenDriver(2,'XX—')
            IF DigitsRcvd=3 THEN ScreenDriver(2,'XXX-')
            IF DigitsRcvd=4 THEN ScreenDriver(2,'XXXX')
            END
   END   {WHILE}
END.  (Procedure GetPIN)
```

If we follow the pseudocode in these three modules, we can identify the "uses" relationship among the modules in the functional decomposition. In Chapter 13, we shall see how this provides useful insights into integration testing.

Module	Uses Modules
SATM Main	WatchCardSlot
	Control Card Roller
	Screen Driver
	Validate Card
	Validate PIN
	Manage Transaction
	New Transaction Request
ValidatePIN	GetPINforPAN
	GetPIN
	Screen Driver
GetPIN	KeySensor
	Screen Driver

Notice that the "uses" information is not readily apparent in the functional decomposition. This information is developed (and extensively revised) during the more detailed phases of the design process. We will revisit this in Chapter 13.

12.3.3 OBJECT-ORIENTED FORMULATION OF SATM

In two decades, the various flavors of structured analysis have coalesced into a fairly generic system. Naturally, there are differences, and those who postulate these differences defend them as essential. The various approaches to object-oriented software development are not yet at this stage of maturity. Some object-oriented flavors start with an entity/relationship model, postulate the entities as objects, build finite state machines for each object, and then develop methods (functions) for each object. Other flavors emphasize the inheritance and class aspects of object orientation. Here we use the latter approach; this version is from [Jorgensen 94].

As with the structured analysis formulation, the class hierarchy in Figure 12.15 focuses on the PIN Entry portion of the system. In this figure, the arrows indicate inheritance, and solid lines indicate object communication. Because objects encapsulate data and functionality, we can expect that the class hierarchy contains much of the information that is in the dataflow diagrams and the entity/relationship model of the SATM system. Most flavors of object-oriented analysis also include a behavioral model, which is usually a finite state machine such as the ones in Figures 12.12 and 12.13.

12.4 SEPARATING INTEGRATION AND SYSTEM TESTING

We are almost in a position to make a clear distinction between integration and system testing. We need this distinction to avoid gaps and redundancies across levels of testing, to clarify appropriate goals for these levels, and to understand how to identify test cases at different levels. This whole discussion is facilitated by a concept essential to all levels of testing: the notion of a "thread". A thread is a construct that refers to execution time behavior; when we test a system, we use test cases to select (and execute) threads. We can speak of levels of threads: system threads describe system level behavior, integration threads correspond to integration level behavior, and unit threads correspond to unit level behavior. Many authors use the term, but few define it, and of those that do, the offered definitions aren't very helpful. For now, we take "thread" to be a primitive term, much like function and data. In the next two chapters, we shall see that threads are most often recognized in terms of the way systems are described and developed. For example, we might think of a thread as a path through a finite state machine description of a system, or we might think of a thread as something that is determined by a data context and a sequence of port level input events, such as those in the context diagram of the SATM system. We could also think of a thread as a sequence of source statements, or as a sequence of machine instructions. The point is, threads are a generic concept, and they exist independently of how a system is described and developed.

We have already observed the structural versus behavioral dichotomy; here we shall find that both of these views help us separate integration and system testing. The structural view reflects both the process by which a system is built and the techniques used to build it. We certainly expect that test cases at various levels can be traced back to developmental information. While this is necessary, it fails to be sufficient: we will finally make our desired separation in terms of behavioral constructs.

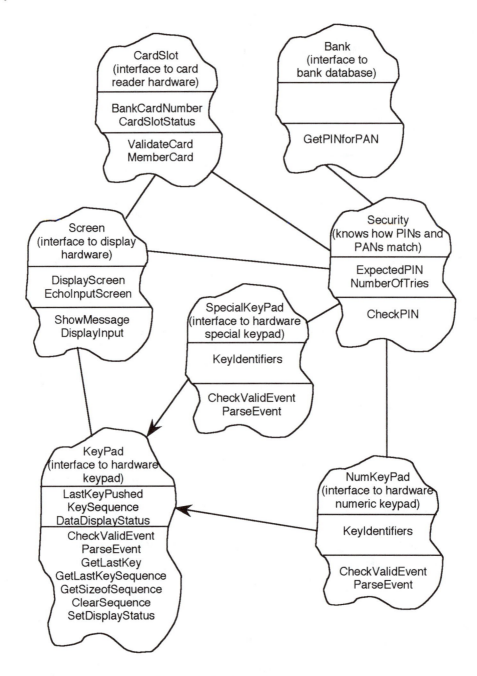

Figure 12.15 SATM Class Hierarchy

12.4.1 STRUCTURAL INSIGHTS

Everyone agrees that there must be some distinction, and that integration testing is at a more detailed level than system testing. There is also general agreement that integration testing can safely assume that the units have been separately tested, and that, taken by themselves, the units function correctly. One common view, therefore, is that integration testing is concerned with the interfaces among the units.

One possibility is to fall back on the symmetries in the waterfall life cycle model, and say that integration testing is concerned with preliminary design information, while system testing is at the level of the requirements specification. This is a popular academic view, but it begs an important question: how do we discriminate between specification and preliminary design? The pat academic answer to this is the what vs. how dichotomy: the requirements specification defines what, and the preliminary design describes how. While this sounds good at first, it doesn't stand up well in practice. Some scholars argue that just the choice of a requirements specification technique is a design choice

The life cycle approach is echoed by designers who often take a "Don't Tread On Me" view of a requirements specification: a requirements specification should neither predispose nor preclude a design option. With this view, when information in a specification is so detailed that it "steps on the designer's toes", the specification is too detailed. This sounds good, but it still doesn't yield an operational way to separate integration and system testing.

The models used in the development process provide some clues. If we follow the definition of the SATM system, we could first postulate that system testing should make sure that all fifteen display screens have been generated. (An output domain based, functional view of system testing.) The entity/relationship model also helps: the one-to-one and one-to-many relationships help us understand how much testing must be done. The control model (in this case, a hierarchy of finite state machines) is the most helpful. We can postulate system test cases in terms of paths through the finite state machine(s); doing this yields a system level analog of structural testing. The functional models (dataflow diagrams and structure charts) move in the direction of levels because both express a functional decomposition. Even with this, we cannot look at a structure chart and identify where system testing ends and integration testing starts. The best we can do with structural information is identify the extremes. For instance, the following threads are all clearly at the system level:

1. Insertion of an invalid card. (this is probably the "shortest" system thread)
2. Insertion of a valid card, followed by three failed PIN entry attempts.
3. Insertion of a valid card, a correct PIN entry attempt, followed by a balance inquiry.
4. Insertion of a valid card, a correct PIN entry attempt, followed by a deposit.
5. Insertion of a valid card, a correct PIN entry attempt, followed by a withdrawal.
6. Insertion of a valid card, a correct PIN entry attempt, followed by an attempt to withdraw more cash than the account balance.

We can also identify some integration level threads. Go back to the PDL descriptions of ValidatePIN and GetPIN. ValidatePIN calls GetPIN, and GetPIN waits for KeySensor to report when a key is touched. If a digit is touched, GetPIN echoes an "X" to the display screen, but if the cancel key is touched, GetPIN terminates, and ValidatePIN considers another PIN entry attempt. We could push still lower, and consider keystroke sequences such as two or three digits followed by cancel keystroke.

12.4.2 BEHAVIORAL INSIGHTS

Here is a pragmatic, explicit distinction that has worked well in industrial applications. Think about a system in terms of its port boundary, which is the location of system level inputs and outputs. Every system has a port boundary; the port boundary of the SATM system includes the digit keypad, the function buttons, the screen, the deposit and withdrawal doors, the card and receipt slots, and so on. Each of these devices can be thought of as a "port", and events occur at system ports. The port input and output events are visible to the customer, and the customer very often understands system behavior in terms of sequences of port events. Given this, we mandate that system port events are the "primitives" of a system test case, that is, a system test case (or equivalently, a system thread) is expressed as an interleaved sequence of port input and port output events. This fits our understanding of a test case, in which we specify pre-conditions, inputs, outputs, and post-conditions. With this mandate we can always recognize a level violation: if a test case (thread) ever requires an input (or an output) that is not visible at the port boundary, the test case cannot be a system level test case (thread). Notice that this is clear, recognizable, and enforceable. We will refine this in Chapter 14 when we discuss threads of system behavior.

Threads support a highly analytical view of testing. Unit level threads, for example, are sequences of source statements that execute (feasible paths). Integration level threads can be thought of as sequences of unit level threads, where we are concerned not with the "internals" of unit threads, but the interaction among them. Finally, system level threads can be interpreted as sequences of integration level threads. We will also be able to describe the interaction among system level threads. To end on a pun, the definitions of the next two chapters will tie these threads together.

13

Integration Testing

Craftspersons are recognized by two essential characteristics: they have a deep knowledge of the tools of their trade, and they have a similar knowledge of the medium in which they work, so that they understand their tools in terms of how they "work" with the medium. In Parts II and III, we focused on the tools (techniques) available to the testing craftsperson. Our goal there was to understand testing techniques in terms of their advantages and limitations with respect to particular types of faults. Here we shift our emphasis to the medium, with the goal that a better understanding of the medium will improve the testing craftsperson's judgment.

We make a deliberate separation here: this chapter and the next address testing for software that has been defined, designed, and developed with the traditional models for function, data, control, and structure. Testing for object-oriented software is deferred to Chapter 15. We continue our "development" of the SATM system in this chapter, and use it to illustrate three distinct approaches to integration testing. For each approach, we begin with its basis and then discuss various techniques that use the base information. To continue the craftsperson metaphor, we emphasize the advantages and limitations of each integration testing technique.

13.1 A CLOSER LOOK AT THE SATM SYSTEM

In Chapter 12, we described the SATM system in terms of its output screens (Figure 12.7), the terminal itself (Figure 12.8), its context and partial dataflow (Figures 12.9 and 12.10), an entity/relationship model of its data (Figure 12.11), finite state machines describing some of its behavior (Figures 12.12 and 12.13), and a partial functional decomposition (Figure 12.14). We also developed a PDL description of the main program and two units, ValidatePIN and GetPIN.

We begin here by expanding the functional decomposition that was started in Figure 12.12; the numbering scheme preserves the levels of the components in that figure. For easier reference, each component that appears in our analysis is given a new (shorter) number; these numbers are given in Table 1. (The only reason for this is to make the figures and spreadsheet more readable.) If you look closely at the units that are designated by letters, you see that they are packaging levels in the decomposition; they are never called as procedures.

The decomposition in Table 1 is pictured as a decomposition tree in Figure 13.1. This decomposition is the basis for the usual view of integration testing. It is important to remember that such a decomposition is primarily a packaging partition of the system. As software design moves into more detail, the added information lets us refine the functional decomposition tree into a unit calling graph. The unit calling graph is the directed graph in which nodes are program units and edges correspond to program calls; that is, if unit A calls unit B, there is a directed edge from node A to node B. We began the development of the call graph for the SATM system in Chapter 12 when we examined the calls made by the main program and the ValidatePIN and GetPIN modules. That information is captured in the adjacency matrix given below in Table 2. This matrix was created with a spreadsheet; this turns out to be a handy tool for testers.

Table 1: SATM Units and Abbreviated Names

Unit Number	Level Number	Unit Name
1	1	SATM System
A	1.1	Device Sense & Control
D	1.1.1	Door Sense & Control
2	1.1.1.1	Get Door Status
3	1.1.1.2	Control Door
4	1.1.1.3	Dispense Cash
E	1.1.2	Slot Sense & Control
5	1.1.2.1	WatchCardSlot
6	1.1.2.2	Get Deposit Slot Status
7	1.1.2.3	Control Card Roller
8	1.1.2.3	Control Envelope Roller
9	1.1.2.5	Read Card Strip
10	1.2	Central Bank Comm.
11	1.2.1	Get PIN for PAN
12	1.2.2	Get Account Status
13	1.2.3	Post Daily Transactions
B	1.3	Terminal Sense & Control
14	1.3.1	Screen Driver
15	1.3.2	Key Sensor
C	1.4	Manage Session
16	1.4.1	Validate Card
17	1.4.2	Validate PIN
18	1.4.2.1	GetPIN
F	1.4.3	Close Session
19	1.4.3.1	New Transaction Request
20	1.4.3.2	Print Receipt
21	1.4.3.3	Post Transaction Local
22	1.4.4	Manage Transaction
23	1.4.4.1	Get Transaction Type
24	1.4.4.2	Get Account Type
25	1.4.4.3	Report Balance
26	1.4.4.4	Process Deposit
27	1.4.4.5	Process Withdrawal

The SATM call graph is shown in Figure 13.2 Some of the hierarchy is obscured to reduce the confusion in the drawing. One thing should be quite obvious: drawings of call graphs do not scale up well. Both the drawings and the adjacency matrix provide insights to the tester. Nodes with high degree will be important to integration testing, and paths from the main program (node 1) to the sink nodes can be used to identify contents of builds for an incremental development.

13.2 DECOMPOSITION BASED INTEGRATION

Most textbook discussions of integration testing only consider integration testing based on the functional decomposition of the system being tested. These approaches are all based on the functional decomposition, expressed either as a tree (Figure 13.1) or in textual form. These discussions inevitably center on the order in which modules are to be integrated. There are four choices: from the top of the tree downward (top down), from the bottom of the tree upward (bottom up), some combination of these (sandwich), or most graphically, none of these (the big bang). All of these integration orders presume that the units have been separately tested, thus the goal of decomposition based integration is to test the interfaces among separately tested units.

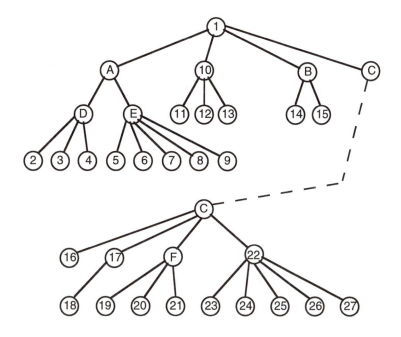

Figure 13.1 SATM Functional Decomposition Tree

Table 2: Adjacency Matrix for the SATM Call Graph

	2	3	4	5	6	7	8	9	10	11	12	13	14	15	16	17	18	19	20	21	22	23	24	25	26	27
1				X		X							X		X	X		X	X	X	X					
2																										
3																										
4																										
5																										
6																										
7																										
8																										
9																										
10																										
11																										
12																										
13																										
14																										
15																										
16						X	X		X																	
17							X						X				X									
18													X	X												
19													X	X												
20																										
21																										
22													X	X								X	X	X	X	X
23													X	X												
24													X	X												
25														X												
26	x	x			x		x					x	x	x												
27	x	x	x		x		x					x	x	x												

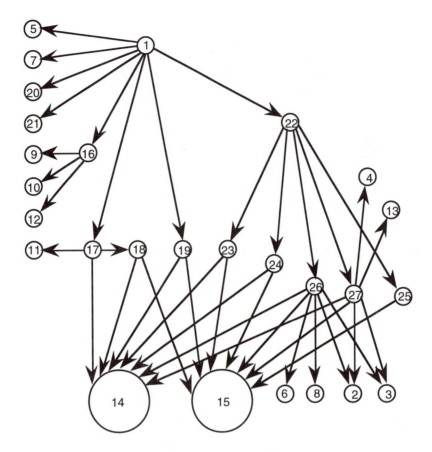

Figure 13.2 SATM Call Graph

We can dispense with the big bang approach most easily: in this view of integration, all the units are compiled together and tested at once. The drawback to this is that when (not if!) a failure is observed, there are few clues to help isolate the location(s) of the fault. (Recall the distinction we made in Chapter 1 between faults and failures.)

13.2.1 TOP-DOWN INTEGRATION

Top-down integration begins with the main program (the root of the tree). Any lower level unit that is called by the main program appears as a "stub", where stubs are pieces of throw-away code that emulate a called unit. If we performed top-down integration testing for the SATM system, the first step would be to develop stubs for all the units called by the main program: WatchCardSlot, Control Card Roller, Screen Driver, Validate Card, Validate PIN, Manage Transaction, and New Transaction Request. Generally, testers have to develop the stubs, and some imagination is required. Here are two examples of stubs.

```
Procedure GetPINforPAN(PAN, ExpectedPIN) STUB
IF PAN = '1123' THEN PIN := '8876';
IF PAN = '1234' THEN PIN := '8765';
IF PAN = '8746' THEN PIN := '1253';
End,

Procedure KeySensor(KeyHit) STUB
data: KeyStrokes STACK OF '8'. '8', '7', 'cancel'
KeyHit = POP (KeyStrokes)
End,
```

In the stub for GetPINforPAN, the tester replicates a table look-up with just a few values that will appear in test cases. In the stub for KeySensor, the tester must devise a sequence of port events that can occur once each time the KeySensor procedure is called. (Here, we provided the keystrokes to partially enter the PIN '8876', but the user hit the cancel button before the fourth digit.) In practice, the effort to develop stubs is usually quite significant. There is good reason to consider stub code as part of the software development, and maintain it under configuration management.

Once all the stubs for SATM main have been provided, we test the main program as if it were a stand-alone unit. We could apply any of the appropriate functional and structural techniques, and look for faults. When we are convinced that the main program logic is correct, we gradually replace stubs with the actual code. Even this can be problematic. Would we replace all the stubs at once? If we did, we would have a "small bang" for units with a high outdegree. If we replace one stub at a time, we retest the main program once for each replaced stub. This means that, for the SATM main program example here, we would repeat its integration test eight times (once for each replaced stub, and once with all the stubs).

13.2.2 BOTTOM-UP INTEGRATION
Bottom-up integration is a "mirror image" to the top-down order, with the difference that stubs are replaced by driver modules that emulate units at the next level up in the tree. In bottom-up integration, we start with the leaves of the decomposition tree (units like ControlDoor and DispenseCash), and test them with specially coded drivers. There is probably less throw-away code in drivers than there is in stubs. Recall we had one stub for each child node in the decomposition tree. Most systems have a fairly high fan-out near at the leaves, so in the bottom-up integration order, we won't have as many drivers. This is partially offset by the fact that the driver modules will be more complicated.

13.2.3 SANDWICH INTEGRATION
Sandwich integration is a combination of top-down and bottom-up integration. If we think about it in terms of the decomposition tree, we are really just doing big bang integration on a sub-tree. There will be less stub and driver development effort, but this will be offset to some extent by the added difficulty of fault isolation that is a consequence of big bang integration. (We could probably discuss the size of a sandwich, from dainty finger sandwiches to Dagwood-style sandwiches, but not now.)

13.2.4 PROS AND CONS
With the exception of big bang integration, the decomposition based approaches are all intuitively clear. Build with tested components. Whenever a failure is observed, the most recently added unit is suspected. Integration testing progress is easily tracked against the decomposition tree. (If the tree is small, it's a nice touch to shade in nodes as they are successfully integrated.) The top-down and bottom-up terms suggest breadth-first traversals of the decomposition tree, but this is not mandatory. (We could use full height sandwiches to test the tree in a depth-first manner.)

One of the most frequent objections to functional decomposition and waterfall development is that both are artificial, and both serve the needs of project management more than the needs of software developers. This holds true also for decomposition-based testing. The whole mechanism is that units are integrated with respect to structure; this presumes that correct behavior follows from individually correct units and correct interfaces. (Practitioners know better.) The development effort for stubs or drivers is another drawback to these approaches, and this is compounded by the retesting effort. Here is a formula that computes the number of integration test sessions for a given decomposition tree (a test session is one set of tests for a specific configuration actual code and stubs).

$$\text{Sessions} = \text{nodes} - \text{leaves} + \text{edges}.$$

For the SATM system, this is 42 integration testing sessions, which means 42 separate sets of integration test cases. For top-down integration, (nodes - 1) stubs are needed, and for bottom-up integration, (nodes - leaves) drivers are needed. For the SATM system, this is 32 stubs and 10 drivers.

13.3 CALL GRAPH BASED INTEGRATION
One of the drawbacks of decomposition based integration is that the basis is the functional decomposition tree. If we use the call graph instead, we mitigate this deficiency; we also move in the direction of behavioral testing. We are in a position to enjoy the investment we made in the discussion of graph theory.

Since the call graph is a directed graph, why not use it the way we used program graphs? This leads us to two new approaches to integration testing: we'll refer to them as pair-wise integration and neighborhood integration.

13.3.1 PAIR-WISE INTEGRATION

The idea behind pair-wise integration is to eliminate the stub/driver development effort. Rather than develop stubs and/or drivers, why not use the actual code? At first, this sounds like big bang integration, but we restrict a session to just a pair of units in the call graph. The end result is that we have one integration test session for each edge in the call graph (40 for the SATM call graph in Figure 13.2). This is not much of a reduction in sessions from either top-down or bottom-up (42 sessions), but it is a drastic reduction in stub/driver development.

13.3.2 NEIGHBORHOOD INTEGRATION

We can let the mathematics carry us still further by borrowing the notion of a "neighborhood" from topology. (This isn't too much of a stretch — graph theory is a branch of topology.) We (informally) define the neighborhood of a node in a graph to be the set of nodes that are one edge away from the given node. In a directed graph, this means all the immediate predecessor nodes and all the immediate successor nodes (notice that these correspond to the set of stubs and drivers of the node). The eleven neighborhoods for the SATM example (based on the call graph in Figure 13.2) are given in Table 3.

Table 3   SATM Neighborhoods

Node	Predecessors	Successors
16	1	9, 10, 12
17	1	11, 14, 18
18	17	14, 15
19	1	14, 15
23	22	14, 15
24	22	14, 15
26	22	14, 15, 6, 8, 2, 3
27	22	14, 15, 2, 3, 4, 13
25	22	15
22	1	23, 24, 26, 27, 25
1	n/a	5, 7, 2, 21, 16, 17, 19, 22

We can always compute the number of neighborhoods for a given call graph. There will be one neighborhood for each interior node, plus one extra in case there are leaf nodes connected directly to the root node. (An interior node has a non-zero indegree and a non-zero outdegree.) We have

$$\text{Interior nodes} = \text{nodes} - (\text{source nodes} + \text{sink nodes})$$
$$\text{Neighborhoods} = \text{interior nodes} + \text{source nodes}$$

which combine to

$$\text{Neighborhoods} = \text{nodes} - \text{sink nodes}$$

Neighborhood integration yields a drastic reduction in the number of integration test sessions (down to 11 from 40), and it avoids stub and driver development. The end result is that neighborhoods are essentially the sandwiches that we slipped past in the previous section. (There is a slight difference, because the base information for neighborhoods is the call graph, not the decomposition tree.) What they share with sandwich integration is more significant: neighborhood integration testing has the fault isolation difficulties of "medium bang" integration.

13.3.3 PROS AND CONS

The call graph based integration techniques move away from a purely structural basis toward a behavioral basis, thus the underlying assumption is an improvement. These techniques also eliminate the stub/driver development effort. In addition to these advantages, call graph based integration matches well with developments characterized by builds and composition. For example, sequences of neighborhoods can be used to define builds. Alternatively, we could allow adjacent neighborhoods to merge (into villages?) and provide an orderly, composition-based growth path. All of this supports the use of neighborhood based integration for systems developed by life cycles in which composition dominates.

The biggest drawback to call graph based integration testing is the fault isolation problem, especially for large neighborhoods. There is a more subtle, but closely related problem. What happens if (when) a fault is found in a node (unit) that appears in several neighborhoods? (For example, the screen driver unit appears is seven of the eleven neighborhoods.) Obviously, we resolve the fault, but this means changing the unit's code in some way, which in turn means that all the previously tested neighborhoods that contain the changed node need to be retested.

Finally, there is a fundamental uncertainty in any structural form of testing: the presumption that units integrated with respect to structural information will exhibit correct behavior. We know where we are going: we want system level threads of behavior to be correct. When integration testing is based on call graph information is complete, we still have quite a leap to get to system level threads. We resolve this by changing the basis from call graph information to special forms of paths.

13.4 PATH BASED INTEGRATION

Much of the progress in the development of mathematics comes from an elegant pattern: have a clear idea of where you want to go, and then define the concepts that take you there. We do this here for path based integration testing, but first we need to motivate the definitions.

We already know that the combination of structural and functional testing is highly desirable at the unit level; it would be nice to have a similar capability for integration (and system) testing. We also know that we want to express system testing in terms of behavioral threads. Lastly, we revise our goal for integration testing: rather than test interfaces among separately developed and tested units, we focus on interactions among these units. ("Co-functioning" might be a good term.) Interfaces are structural; interaction is behavioral.

When a unit executes, some path of source statements is traversed. Suppose that there is a call to another unit along such a path: at that point, control is passed from the calling unit to the called unit, where some other path of source statements is traversed. We cleverly ignored this situation in Part III, because this is a better place to address the question. There are two possibilities: abandon the single-entry, single exit precept and treat such calls as an exit followed by an entry, or "suppress" the call statement because control eventually returns to the calling unit anyway. The suppression choice works well for unit testing, but it is antithetical to integration testing.

13.4.1 NEW AND EXTENDED CONCEPTS

To get where we need to go, we need to refine some of the program graph concepts. As before, these refer to programs written in an imperative language, we allow statement fragments to be a complete statement, and statement fragments are nodes in the program graph.

Definition

A *source node* in a program is a statement fragment at which program execution begins or resumes.

The first "BEGIN" statement in a program is clearly a source node. Source nodes also occur immediately after nodes that transfer control to other units.

Definition

A *sink node* in a program is a statement fragment at which program execution terminates.

The final "END" statement in a program is clearly a sink node, so are statements that transfer control to other units.

Definition

A *module execution path* is a sequence of statements that begins with a source node and ends with a sink node, with no intervening sink nodes.

The effect of the definitions so far is that program graphs now have multiple source and sink nodes. This would greatly increase the complexity of unit testing, but integration testing presumes unit testing is complete.

Definition
A *message* is a programming language mechanism by which one unit transfers control to another unit.

Depending on the programming language, messages can be interpreted as subroutine invocations, procedure calls, and function references. We follow the convention that the unit that receives a message (the message destination) always eventually returns control to the message source. Messages can pass data to other units.

We can finally make the definitions for path based integration testing. Our goal is to have an integration testing analog of DD-Paths.

Definition
An *MM-Path* is an interleaved sequence of module execution paths and messages.

The basic idea of an MM-Path is that we can now describe sequences of module execution paths that include transfers of control among separate units. Since these transfers are by messages, MM-Paths always represent feasible execution paths, and these paths cross unit boundaries. We can find MM-Paths in an extended program graph in which nodes are module execution paths and edges are messages. The hypothetical example in Figure 13.3 shows an MM-Path (the dark line) in which module A calls module B, which in turn calls module C.

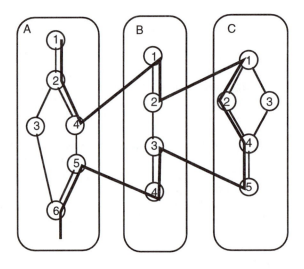

Figure 13.3 MM-Path Across Three Units

In module A, nodes 1 and 5 are source nodes, and nodes 4 and 6 are sink nodes. Similarly in module B, nodes 1 and 3 are source nodes, and nodes 2 and 4 are sink nodes. Module C has a single source node, 1, and a single sink node, 4. There are seven module execution paths in Figure 13.3:

$$MEP(A,1) = <1, 2, 3, 5>$$
$$MEP(A,2) = <1, 2, 4>$$
$$MEP(A,3) = <5, 6>$$
$$MEP(B,1) = <1, 2>$$
$$MEP(B,1) = <3, 4>$$
$$MEP(C,1) = <1, 2, 4, 5>$$
$$MEP(C,2) = <1, 3, 4, 5>$$

We can now define an integration testing analog of the DD-Path graph that serves unit testing so effectively.

Definition
Given a set of units, their ***MM-Path graph*** is the directed graph in which nodes are module execution paths and edges correspond to messages and returns from one unit to another.

Notice that MM-Path graphs are defined with respect to a set of units. This directly supports composition of units and composition based integration testing. We can even compose down to the level of individual module execution paths, but that is probably more detailed than necessary.

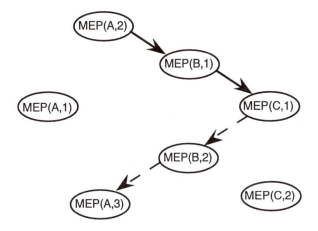

Figure 13.4   MM-Path Graph Derived from Figure 13.3

Figure 13.4 shows the MM-Path graph for the example in Figure 13.3. The solid arrows indicate messages; the corresponding returns are indicated by dotted arrows. We should consider the relationships among module execution paths, program path, DD-Paths, and MM-Paths. A program path is a sequence of DD-Paths, and an MM-Path is a sequence of module execution paths. Unfortunately, there is no simple relationship between DD-Paths and module execution paths. Either might be contained in the other, but more likely, they partially overlap. Since MM-Paths implement a function that transcends unit boundaries, we do have one relationship: consider the "intersection" of an MM-Path with a unit. The module execution paths in such an intersection are an analog of a slice with respect to the (MM-Path) function. Stated another way, the module execution paths in such an intersection are the restriction of the function to the unit in which they occur.

The MM-Path definition needs some practical guidelines. How long is an MM-Path? Nothing in the definition prohibits an MM-Path to cover an entire ATM session. (This extreme loses the forest because of the trees.) There are three observable behavioral criteria that put endpoints on MM-Paths. The first is "event quiescence", which occurs when a system is (nearly) idle, waiting for a port input event to trigger further processing. The SATM system exhibits event quiescence in several places: one is the tight loop at the beginning of SATM Main where the system has displayed the welcome screen and is waiting for a card to be entered into the card slot. Event quiescence is a system level property; there is an analog at the integration level: message quiescence. Message quiescence occurs when a unit that sends no messages is reached (like module C in Figure 13.3).

There is a still subtler form: data quiescence. This occurs when a sequence of processing culminates in the creation of stored data that is not immediately used. In the ValidateCard unit, the account balance is obtained, but it is not used until after a successful PIN entry. Figure 13.5 shows how data quiescence appears in a traditional dataflow diagram.

The first guideline for MM-Paths: points of quiescence are "natural" endpoints for an MM-Path. Our second guideline also serves to distinguish integration from system testing.

Definition
An ***atomic system function (ASF)*** is an action that is observable at the system level in terms of port input and output events.

An atomic system function begins with a port input event, traverses one or more MM-Paths, and terminates with a port output event. When viewed from the system level, there is no compelling reason

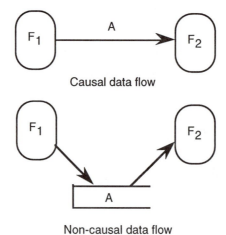

Causal data flow

Non-causal data flow

Figure 13.5 Data Quiescence

to decompose an ASF into lower levels of detail (hence the atomicity). In the SATM system, digit entry is a good example of an ASF, so are card entry, cash dispensing, and session closing. PIN entry is probably too big, it might be called a molecular system function.

Our second guideline: atomic system functions are an upper limit for MM-Paths: we don't want MM-Paths to cross ASF boundaries. This means that ASFs represent the seam between integration and system testing. They are the largest item to be tested by integration testing, and the smallest item for system testing. We can test an ASF at both levels. Again, the digit entry ASF is a good example. During system testing, the port input event is a physical key press that is detected by KeySensor and sent to GetPIN as a string variable. (Notice that KeySensor performs the physical to logical transition.) GetPIN determines whether a digit key or the cancel key was pressed, and responds accordingly. (Notice that button presses are ignored.) The ASF terminates with either screen 2 or 4 being displayed. Rather than require system keystrokes and visible screen displays, we could use a driver to provide these, and test the digit entry ASF via integration testing. We can see this using our continuing example.

13.4.2 MM-PATHS AND ASFS IN THE SATM SYSTEM

The PDL descriptions developed in Chapter 12 are repeated for convenient reference; statement fragments are numbered as we did to construct program graphs.

```
 1. Main Program
 2. State = AwaitCard
 3. CASE State OF
 4. AwaitCard:        ScreenDriver(1, null)
 5.                   WatchCardSlot(CardSlotStatus)
 6.                   WHILE CardSlotStatus is Idle DO
 7.                       WatchCardSlot(CardSlotStatus)
 8.                   ControlCardRoller(accept)
 9.                   ValidateCard(CardOK, PAN)
10.                   IF CardOK THEN State = AwaitPIN
11.                           ELSE ControlCardRoller(eject)
12.                                    State = AwaitCard
13. AwaitPIN:         ValidatePIN(PINok, PAN)
14.                   IF PINok THEN ScreenDriver(5, null)
15.                                    State = AwaitTrans
16.                           ELSE ScreenDriver(4, null)
17.                                    State = AwaitCard
```

```
18. AwaitTrans:        ManageTransaction
19.                     State = CloseSession
20. CloseSession:      IF NewTransactionRequest
21.                         THEN State = AwaitTrans
22.                         ELSE PrintReceipt
23.                              PostTransactionLocal
24.                              CloseSession
25.                              ControlCardRoller(eject)
26.                              State = AwaitCard
27. End, (CASE State)
28. END.   (Main program SATM)


29. Procedure ValidatePIN(PINok, PAN)
30. GetPINforPAN(PAN, ExpectedPIN)
31. Try = First
32. CASE Try OF
33. First:    ScreenDriver(2, null)
34.           GetPIN(EnteredPIN)
35.           IF EnteredPIN = ExpectedPIN
36.               THEN PINok = TRUE
37.                    RETURN
38.               ELSE ScreenDriver(3, null)
39.                    Try = Second
40. Second:   ScreenDriver(2, null)
41.           GetPIN(EnteredPIN)
42.           IF EnteredPIN = ExpectedPIN
43.               THEN PINok = TRUE
44.                    RETURN
45.               ELSE ScreenDriver(3, null)
46.                    Try = Third
47. Third:    ScreenDriver(2, null)
48.           GetPIN(EnteredPIN)
49.           IF EnteredPIN = ExpectedPIN
50.               THEN PINok = TRUE
51.                    RETURN
52.               ELSE ScreenDriver(4, null)
53.                    PINok = FALSE
54.  END, (CASE Try)
55.  END.   (Procedure ValidatePIN)
56.  Procedure GetPIN(EnteredPIN, CancelHit)
57.  Local Data: DigitKeys = {0, 1, 2, 3, 4, 5, 6, 7, 8, 9}
58.  BEGIN
59.  CancelHit = FALSE
60.  EnteredPIN = null string
61.  DigitsRcvd=0
62.  WHILE NOT(DigitsRcvd=4 OR CancelHit) DO
63.      BEGIN
64.          KeySensor(KeyHit)
65.          IF KeyHit IN DigitKeys
66.          THEN  BEGIN
67.                EnteredPIN = EnteredPIN + KeyHit
```

```
68.                    INCREMENT(DigitsRcvd)
69.                    IF DigitsRcvd=1 THEN ScreenDriver(2,'X—')
70.                    IF DigitsRcvd=2 THEN ScreenDriver(2,'XX—')
71.                    IF DigitsRcvd=3 THEN ScreenDriver(2,'XXX-')
72.                    IF DigitsRcvd=4 THEN ScreenDriver(2,'XXXX')
73.                    END
74.        END   {WHILE}
75.   END.    (Procedure GetPIN)
```

There are 20 source nodes in SATM Main: 1, 5, 6, 8, 9, 10, 12, 14, 15, 17, 18, 19, 20, 21, 22, 23, 24, 25, 26, 27. ValidatePIN has 11 source nodes: 29, 31, 34, 35, 39, 41, 46, 47, 48, 53; and in GetPIN there are 6 source nodes: 56, 65, 70, 71, 72, 73.

SATM Main contains 16 sink nodes: 4, 5, 7, 8, 9, 11, 13, 14, 16, 18, 20, 22, 23, 24, 25, 28. There are 14 sink nodes in ValidatePIN : 30, 33, 34, 37, 38, 40, 41, 44, 47, 48, 51, 52, 55; and 5 sink nodes in GetPIN: 64, 69, 70, 71, 72.

Most of the module execution paths in SATM Main are very short; this pattern is due to the high density of messages to other units. Here are the first two module execution paths in SATM Main: <1, 2, 3, 4>, <5> and <6, 7>, <8> . The module execution paths in ValidatePIN are slightly longer: <29, 30>, <31, 32, 33>, <34>, <35, 36, 37>, and so on. The beginning portion of GetPIN is a good example of a module execution path: the sequence < 58, 59, 60, 61, 62, 63, 64> begins with a source node (58) and ends with a sink node (64) which is a call to the KeyHit procedure. This is also a point of "event quiescence", where nothing will happen until the customer touches a key.

There are four MM-Paths in statements 64 through 72: each begins with KeySensor observing a port input event (a keystroke) and ends with a closely knit family of port output events (the calls to ScreenDriver with different PIN echoes). We could name these four MM-Paths GetDigit1, GetDigit2, GetDigit3, and GetDigit4. They are slightly different because the later ones include the earlier IF statements. (If the tester was the designer, this module might be reworked so that the WHILE loop repeated a single MM-Path.) Technically, each of these is also an atomic system function since they begin and end with port events.

There are interesting ASFs in ValidatePIN. This unit controls all screen displays relevant to the PIN entry process. It begins with the display of screen 2 (which asks the customer to enter his/her PIN). Next, GetPIN is called, and the system is event quiescent until a keystroke occurs. These keystrokes initiate the GetDigit ASFs we just discussed. Here we find a curious integration fault. Notice that screen 2 is displayed in two places: by the THEN clauses in the WHILE loop in GetPIN and by the first statements in each CASE clause in ValidatePIN. We could fix this by removing the screen displays from GetPIN and simply returning the string (e.g., 'X—') to be displayed.

This portion of the SATM system also illustrates the difference between unit and integration testing. When GetPIN is unit tested, its inputs come from KeySensor (which acts like an input statement similar to a READ). The input space of GetPIN contains the digits 0 through 9 and the cancel key. (These would likely be treated as string or character data.) We could add inputs for the function keys B1, B2, and B3; if we did, traditional equivalence class testing would be a good choice. The function we test is whether or not GetDigit reconstructs the keystrokes into a digit string, and whether or not the boolean indication for the cancel key is correct.

13.4.3 PROS AND CONS

The two new constructs, MM-Paths and Atomic System Functions, are a hybrid of functional and structural testing. They are functional, in the sense that each represents an action with inputs and outputs. As such, all the functional testing techniques are potentially applicable. The structural side comes from how they are identified, particularly the MM-Path graph. The net result is that the cross check of the functional and structural approaches is consolidated into the constructs for path based integration testing. We therefore avoid the pitfall of structural testing, and at the same time, integration testing gains a fairly seamless junction with system testing. Path based integration testing works equally well for software developed in the traditional waterfall process or with one of the composition based alternative life cycle models. We will revisit these concepts again in Chapter 15; there we will see that the concepts are equally applicable to object-oriented software testing. The most important advantage of path based integration testing is that the testing is closely coupled with actual system behavior, rather than the structural motivation of decomposition and call graph based integration.

The advantages of path based integration come at a price: there is more effort to identify the MM-Paths and ASFs. This effort is probably offset by the elimination of stub and driver development. Another disadvantage is that path based integration testing is a mild form of technical overkill for ordinary data processing applications (i.e., those that are not usually thought of as being event driven).

Chapter 14

System Testing

Of the three levels of testing, the system level is closest to everyday experience. We test many things: a used car before we buy it, an on-line network service before we subscribe, and so on. A common pattern in these familiar forms is that we evaluate a product in terms of our expectations; not with respect to a specification or a standard. Consequently, the goal is not to find faults, but to demonstrate performance. Because of this, we tend to approach system testing from a functional standpoint rather than from a structural one. Since it is so intuitively familiar, system testing in practice tends to be less formal than it might be, and this is compounded by the reduced testing interval that usually remains before a delivery deadline.

The craftsperson metaphor continues to serve us. We need a better understanding of the medium; as we said in Chapter 12, we will view system testing in terms of threads of system level behavior. We begin with further elaboration on the thread concept, highlighting some of the practical problems of thread-based system testing. Since system testing is closely coupled with requirements specification, we will discuss how to find threads in common notations. All of this leads to an orderly thread-based system testing strategy that exploits the symbiosis between functional and structural testing; we will apply the strategy to our SATM system.

14.1 THREADS

Threads are hard to define, in fact some published definitions are counter-productive, misleading, and/ or wrong. It's possible to simply treat threads as a primitive concept which needs no formal definition. For now we will use examples to develop a "shared vision". Here are several views of a thread:

- a scenario of normal usage
- a system level test case
- a stimulus/response pair
- behavior that results from a sequence of system level inputs
- an interleaved sequence of port input and output events
- a sequence of transitions in a state machine description of the system
- an interleaved sequence of object messages and method executions
- a sequence of machine instructions
- a sequence of source instructions
- a sequence of atomic system functions

Threads have distinct levels. A unit level thread is usefully understood as an execution-time path of source instructions, or alternatively as a path of DD-Paths. An integration level thread is a sequence of MM-Paths that implements an atomic system function. We might also speak of an integration level thread as an alternating sequence of module executions and messages. If we continue this pattern, a system level thread is a sequence of atomic system functions. Because atomic system functions have port events as their inputs and outputs, the sequence of atomic system functions implies an interleaved sequence of port input and output events. The end result is that threads provide a unifying view of our three levels of testing. Unit testing tests individual functions, integration testing examines interactions among units, and system testing examines interactions among atomic system functions. In this chapter, we focus on system level threads and we answer some fundamental questions: How big is a thread? Where do we find them? How do we test them?

14.1.1 THREAD POSSIBILITIES

Defining the endpoints of a system level thread is a little awkward. We motivate a tidy, graph theory based definition by working backwards from where we want to go with threads. Here are three candidate threads:

- Entry of a digit
- Entry of a Personal Identification Number (PIN)
- A simple transaction: ATM Card Entry, PIN entry, select transaction type (deposit, withdraw), present account details (checking or savings, amount), conduct the operation, and report the results.
- An ATM session, containing two or more simple transactions.

Digit entry is a good example of a minimal atomic system function that is implemented with a single MM-Path. It begins with a port input event (the digit keystroke) and ends with a port output event (the screen digit echo), so it qualifies as a stimulus/response pair. This level of granularity is too fine for the purposes of system testing. We saw this to be an appropriate level for integration testing.

The second candidate, PIN Entry, is a good example of an upper limit to integration testing, and at the same time, a starting point of system testing. PIN Entry is a good example of an atomic system function. It is also a good example of a family of stimulus/response pairs (system level behavior that is initiated by a port input event, traverses some programmed logic, and terminates in one of several possible responses [port output events]). As we saw in Chapter 13, PIN Entry entails a sequence of system level inputs and outputs:

1. A screen requesting PIN digits
2. An interleaved sequence of digit keystrokes and screen responses
3. The possibility of cancellation by the customer before the full PIN is entered
4. A system disposition: (A customer has three chances to enter the correct PIN. Once a correct PIN has been entered, the user sees a screen requesting the transaction type; otherwise a screen advises the customer that the ATM card will not be returned, and no access to ATM functions is provided.)

This is clearly in the domain of system level testing, and several stimulus/response pairs are evident. Other examples of ASFs include Card Entry, Transaction Selection, Provision of Transaction Details, Transaction Reporting, and Session Termination. Each of these is maximal in an integration testing sense, and minimal in a system testing sense. That is, we wouldn't want to integration test something larger than an ASF, and at the same time, we wouldn't want to system test anything smaller.

The third candidate, the simple transaction, has a sense of "end-to-end" completion. A customer could never execute PIN Entry all by itself (a Card Entry is needed), but the simple transaction is commonly executed. This is a good example of a system level thread; note that it involves the interaction of several ASFs.

The last possibility (the session) is really a sequence of threads. This is also properly a part of system testing; at this level, we are interested in the interactions among threads. Unfortunately, most system testing efforts never reach the level of thread interaction. (More on this in Chapter 16.)

14.1.2 THREAD DEFINITIONS

Definition
A **unit thread** is a path in the program graph of a unit.

There are two levels of threads used in integration testing: MM-Paths and atomic system functions. The definitions from Chapter 13 are repeated here so the coherence across the levels is more evident. Recall that MM-Paths are defined as paths in the directed graph in which module execution paths are nodes, and edges show execution time sequence.

Definition
An ***MM-Path*** is a path in the MM-Path graph of a set of units.

Definition
Given a system defined in terms of atomic system functions, the ***ASF Graph*** of the system is the directed graph in which nodes are atomic system functions and edges represent sequential flow.

Definition
A ***source ASF*** is an atomic system function that appears as a source node in the ASF graph of a system; similarly, a ***sink ASF*** is an atomic system function that appears as a sink node in the ASF graph.

In the SATM system, the Card Entry ASF is a source ASF, and the session termination ASF is a sink ASF. Notice that intermediary ASFs could never be tested at the system level by themselves — they need the predecessor ASFs to "get there".

Definition
A ***system thread*** is a path from a source ASF to a sink ASF in the ASF graph of a system.

Definition
Given a system defined in terms of system threads, the ***Thread Graph*** of the system is the directed graph in which nodes are system threads and edges represent sequential execution of individual threads.

This set of definitions provides a coherent set of increasingly broader views of threads, starting with threads within a unit and ending with interactions among system level threads. We can use these views as the ocular on a microscope, switching views to get to different levels of granularity. Having these concepts is only part of the problem, supporting them is another. We next take a tester's view of requirements specification to see how to identify threads.

14.2 BASIS CONCEPTS FOR REQUIREMENTS SPECIFICATION

Recall the notion of a basis of a vector space: a set of independent elements from which all the elements in the space can be generated. Rather than anticipate all the variations in scores of requirements specification methods, notations, and techniques, we will discuss system testing with respect to a basis set of requirements specification constructs: data, actions, ports, events, and threads. Every system can be expressed in terms of these five fundamental concepts (and every requirements specification technique is some combination of these). We examine these fundamental concepts here to see how they support the tester's process of thread identification.

14.2.1 DATA

When a system is described in terms of its data, the focus is on the information used and created by the system. We describe data in terms of variables, data structures, fields, records, data stores, and files. Entity/relationship models are the most common choice at the highest level, and some form of a regular expression (e.g., Jackson diagrams or data structure diagrams) is used at a more detailed level. The data-centered view is also the starting point for several flavors of object-oriented analysis. Data refers to information that is either initialized, stored, updated, or (possibly) destroyed. In the SATM system, initial data describe the various accounts (PANs) and their PINs, and each account has a data structure with information such as the account balance. As ATM transactions occur, the results are kept as created data and used in the daily posting of terminal data to the central bank. For many systems, the data centered view dominates. These systems are often developed in terms of CRUD actions (Create, Retrieve, Update, Delete). We could describe the transaction portion of the SATM system in this way, but it wouldn't work well for the user interface portion.

Sometimes threads can be identified directly from the data model. Relationships between data entities can be one-to-one, one-to-many, many-to-one, or many-to-many; these distinctions all have implications for threads that process the data. For example, if bank customers can have several accounts, each account will need a unique PIN. If several people can access the same account, they will need ATM cards with identical PANs. We can also find initial data (such as PAN, ExpectedPIN pairs) that are read but never written. Such read-only data must be part of the system initialization process. If not, there must be threads that create such data. Read-only data is therefore an indicator of source ASFs.

14.2.2 ACTIONS

Action-centered modeling is by far the most common requirements specification form. This is a historical outgrowth of the action-centered nature of imperative programming languages. Actions have inputs and outputs, and these can be either data or port events. Here are some methodology-specific synonyms for actions: transform, data transform, control transform, process, activity, task, method, and service. Actions can also be decomposed into lower level actions, as we saw with the dataflow diagrams in Chapter 12. The input/output view of actions is exactly the basis of functional testing, and the decomposition (and eventual implementation) of actions is the basis of structural testing.

14.2.3 PORTS

Every system has ports (and port devices); these are the sources and destinations of system level inputs and outputs (port events). The slight distinction between ports and port devices is sometimes helpful to testers. Technically, a port is the point at which an I/O device is attached to a system, as in serial and parallel ports, network ports, and telephone ports. Physical actions (keystrokes and light emissions from a screen) occur on port devices, and these are translated from physical to logical (or logical to physical). In the absence of actual port devices, much of system testing can be accomplished by "moving the port boundary inward" to the logical instances of port events. From now on, we will just use the term "port" to refer to port devices. The ports in the SATM system include the digit and cancel keys, the function keys, the display screen, the deposit and withdrawal doors, the card and receipt slots, and several less obvious devices, such as the rollers that move cards and deposit envelopes into the machine, the cash dispenser, the receipt printer, and so on.

Thinking about the ports helps the tester define both the input space that functional system testing needs; and similarly, the output devices provide output-based functional test information. (For example, we would like to have enough threads to generate all 15 SATM screens.)

14.2.4 EVENTS

Events are somewhat schizophrenic: they have some characteristics of data and some of actions. An event is a system level input (or output) that occurs at a port. Like data, events can be inputs to or outputs of actions. Events can be discrete (such as SATM keystrokes) or they can be continuous (such as temperature, altitude, or pressure). Discrete events necessarily have a time duration, and this can be a critical factor in real-time systems. We might picture input events as destructive read-out data, but it's a stretch to imagine output events as destructive write operations.

Events are like actions in the sense that they are the translation point between real-world physical events and internal logical manifestations of these. Port input events are physical-to-logical translations, and symmetrically, port output events are logical-to-physical translations. System testers should focus on the physical side of events, not the logical side (the focus of integration testers). There are situations where the context of present data values changes the logical meaning of physical events. In the SATM system, for example, the port input event of depressing button B1 means "Balance" when screen 5 is being displayed, "checking" when screen 6 is being displayed, and "yes" when screens 10, 11, and 14 are being displayed. We refer to such situations as "context sensitive port events", and we would expect to test such events in each context.

14.2.5 THREADS

Unfortunately for testers, threads are the least frequently used of the five fundamental constructs. Since we test threads, it usually falls to the tester to find them in the interactions among the data, events, and actions. About the only place that threads appear *per se* in a requirements specification is when rapid prototyping is used in conjunction with a scenario recorder. It's easy to find threads in control models, as we will soon see. The problem with this is that control models are just that — they are models, not the reality of a system.

14.2.6 RELATIONSHIPS AMONG BASIS CONCEPTS

Figure 14.1 is an entity/relationship model of our basis concepts. Notice that all relationships are many-to-many: Data and Events are generalized into an entity; the two relationships to the Action entity are for inputs and outputs. The same event can occur on several ports, and typically many events occur on a single port. Finally, an action can occur in several threads, and a thread is composed of several actions. This diagram demonstrates some of the difficulty of system testing. Testers must use events and threads to ensure that all the many-to-many relationships among the five basis concepts are correct.

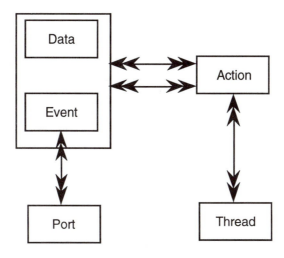

Figure 14.1 E/R Model of Basis Concepts

14.2.7 MODELING WITH THE BASIS CONCEPTS

All flavors of requirements specification develop models of a system in terms of the basis concepts. Figure 14.2 shows three fundamental forms of requirements specification models: structural, contextual, and behavioral. Structural models are used for development; these express the functional decomposition and data decomposition, and the interfaces among components. Contextual models are often the starting point of structural modeling. They emphasize system ports and, to a lesser extent, actions, and threads very indirectly. The models of behavior (also called control models) are where four of the five basis constructs come together. Selection of an appropriate control model is the essence of requirements specification: models that are too weak cannot express important system behaviors, while models that are too powerful typically obscure interesting behaviors. As a general rule, decision tables are a good choice only for computational systems, finite state machines are good for menu-driven systems, and Petri nets are the model of choice for concurrent systems. Here we use finite state machines for the SATM system, and in Chapter 16, we will use Petri nets to analyze thread interaction.

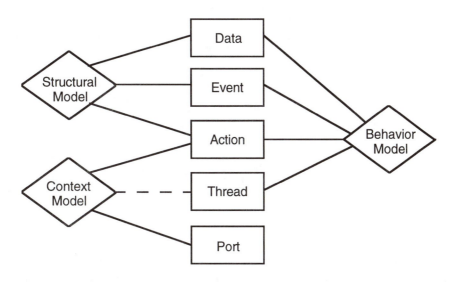

Figure 14.2 Modeling Relationships Among Basis Constructs

We must make an important distinction between a system itself (reality) and models of a system. Consider a system in which some function F cannot occur until two prerequisite events E1 and E2 have occurred, and that they can occur in either order. We could use the notion of event partitioning to model this situation. The result would be a diagram like that in Figure 14.3.

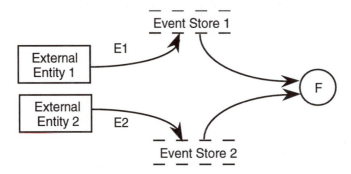

Figure 14.3   Event Partitioning View of Function F

In the event partitioning view, events E1 and E2 occur from their respective external entities. When they occur, they are held in their respective event stores. (An event store acts like a destructive read operation.) When both events have occurred, function F gets its prerequisite information from the event stores. Notice we cannot tell from the model which event occurs first; we only know that both must occur.

We could also model the system as a finite state machine (Figure 14.4), in which states record which event has occurred. The state machine view explicitly shows the two orders of the events.

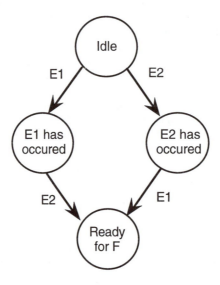

Figure 14.4   FSM for Function F

Both of these models express the same prerequisites for the function F, and neither is the reality of the system. Of these two models, the state machine is more useful to the tester, because paths are instantly convertible to threads.

14.3 FINDING THREADS

The finite state machine models of the SATM system are the best place to look for system testing threads. We'll start with a hierarchy of state machines; the upper level is shown in Figure 14.5. At this level, states correspond to stages of processing, and transitions are caused by logical (rather than port) events. The

Card Entry "state" for example, would be decomposed into lower levels that deal with details like jammed cards, cards that are upside-down, stuck card rollers, and checking the card against the list of cards for which service is offered. Once the details of a macro-state are tested, we use an easy thread to get to the next macro-state.

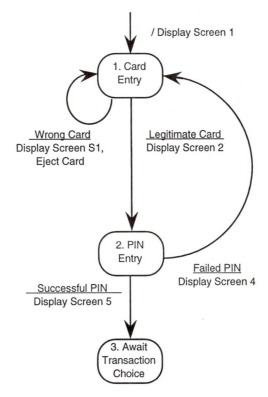

Figure 14.5 Top Level SATM State Machine

The PIN Entry state is decomposed into the more detailed view in Figure 14.6, which is a slight revision of the version in Chapter 12. The adjacent states are shown because they are sources and destinations of transitions from the PIN Entry portion. At this level, we focus on the PIN retry mechanism; all of the output events are true port events, but the input events are still logical events. The states and edges are numbered for reference later when we discuss test coverage.

To start the thread identification process, we first list the port events shown on the state transitions; they appear in Table 1. We skipped the eject card event because it isn't really part of the PIN Entry component.

Table 1   Events in the PIN Entry Finite State Machine

Port Input Events	Port Output Events
Legitimate Card	Display screen 1
Wrong Card	Display screen 2
Correct PIN	Display screen 3
Incorrect PIN	Display screen 4
Canceled	Display screen 5

Notice that Correct PIN and Incorrect PIN are really compound port input events. We can't actually enter an entire PIN, we enter digits, and at any point, we might hit the cancel key. These more detailed possibilities are shown in Figure 14.7. A truly paranoid tester might decompose the digit port input event into the actual choices (0-pressed, 1-pressed, ...,9-pressed), but this should have been tested at a lower level. The port events in the PIN Try finite state machine are in Table 2.

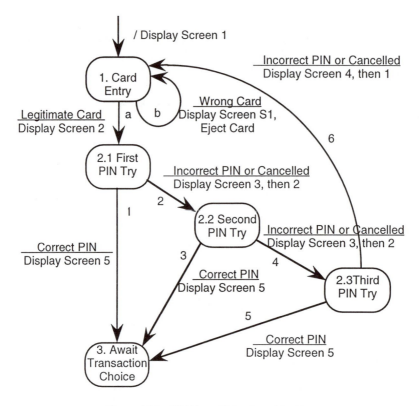

Figure 14.6 PIN Entry Finite State Machine

The "x" in the state names in the PIN Try machine refers to which try (first, second, or third) is passing through the machine.

Table 2   Port Events in the PIN Try Finite State Machine

Port Input Events	Port Output Events
digit	echo 'X---'
cancel	echo 'XX--'
	echo 'XXX-'
	echo 'XXXX'

In addition to the true port events in the PIN Try finite state machine, there are three logical output events (Correct PIN, Incorrect PIN, and Canceled); these correspond exactly to the higher level events in Figure 14.6.

The hierarchy of finite state machines multiplies the number of threads. There are 156 distinct paths form the First PIN Try state to the Await Transaction Choice or Card Entry states in Figure 14.6. Of these, 31 correspond to eventually correct PIN entries (1 on the first try, 5 on the second try, and 25 on the third try); the other 125 paths correspond to those with incorrect digits or with cancel keystrokes. This is a fairly typical ratio. The input portion of systems, especially interactive systems, usually has a large number of threads to deal with input errors and exceptions.

It is "good form" to reach a state machine in which transitions are caused by actual port input events, and the actions on transitions are port output events. If we have such a finite state machine, generating system test cases for these threads is a mechanical process — just follow a path of transitions, and note the port inputs and outputs as they occur along the path. This interleaved sequence is performed by the test executor (person or program). Tables 3 and 4 follow two paths through the hierarchic state machines.

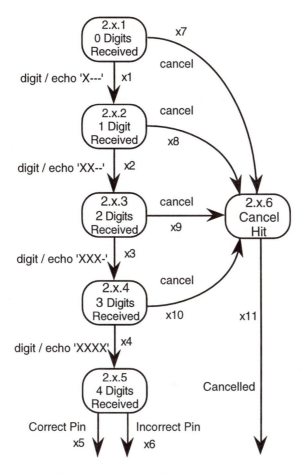

Figure 14.7 PIN Try Finite State Machine

Table 3 corresponds to a thread in which a PIN is correctly entered on the first try. Table 4 corresponds to a thread in which a PIN is incorrectly entered on the first try, cancels after the third digit on the second try, and gets it right on the third try. To make the test case explicit, we assume a pre-condition that the expected PIN is '1234'.

Table 3   Port Event Sequence for Correct PIN on First Try

Port Input Event	Port Output Event
	Screen 2 displayed with '----'
1 pressed	
	Screen 2 displayed with 'X---'
2 pressed	
	Screen 2 displayed with 'XX--'
3 pressed	
	Screen 2 displayed with 'XXX-'
4 pressed	
	Screen 2 displayed with 'XXXX'
(Correct PIN)	Screen 5 displayed

The event in parentheses in the last row of Table 3 is the logical event that "bumps up" to the parent state machine and causes a transition there to the Await Transaction Choice state.

Table 4   Port Event Sequence for Correct PIN on Third Try

Port Input Event	Port Output Event
	Screen 2 displayed with '----'
1 pressed	
	Screen 2 displayed with 'X---'
2 pressed	
	Screen 2 displayed with 'XX--'
3 pressed	
	Screen 2 displayed with 'XXX-'
5 pressed	
	Screen 2 displayed with 'XXXX'
(Incorrect PIN)	Screen 3 displayed
(second try)	Screen 2 displayed with '----'
1 pressed	
	Screen 2 displayed with 'X---'
2 pressed	
	Screen 2 displayed with 'XX--'
3 pressed	
	Screen 2 displayed with 'XXX-'
cancel key pressed	
(end of second try)	Screen 3 displayed
	Screen 2 displayed with '----'
1 pressed	
	Screen 2 displayed with 'X---'
2 pressed	
	Screen 2 displayed with 'XX--'
3 pressed	
	Screen 2 displayed with 'XXX-'
4 pressed	
	Screen 2 displayed with 'XXXX'
(Correct PIN)	Screen 5 displayed

If you look closely at Tables 3 and 4, you will see that the bottom third of Table 4 is exactly Table 3; thus a thread can be a subset of another thread.

14.4 STRUCTURAL STRATEGIES FOR THREAD TESTING

While generating thread test cases is easy, deciding which ones to actually use is more complex. (If you have an automatic test executor, this is not a problem.) We have the same path explosion problem at the system level that we had at the unit level. Just as we did there, we can use the directed graph insights to make an intelligent choice of threads to test.

14.4.1 BOTTOM-UP THREADS

When we organize state machines in a hierarchy, we can work from the bottom up. There are six paths in the PIN Try state machine. If we traverse these six, we test for three things: correct recognition and echo of entered digits, response to the cancel keystroke, and matching expected and entered PINs. These paths are described in Table 5 as sequences of the transitions in Figure 14.7. A thread that traverses the path is described in terms of its input keystrokes, thus the input sequence 1234 corresponds to the thread described in more detail in Table 3 (the cancel keystroke is indicated with a 'C').

Once this portion is tested, we can go up a level to the PIN Entry machine, where there are four paths. These four are concerned with the three try mechanism and the sequence of screens presented to the user. In Table 6, the paths in the PIN Entry state machine (Figure 14.6) are named as transition sequences.

Table 5   Thread Paths in the PIN Try FSM

Input Event Sequence	Path of Transitions
1234	x1, x2, x3, x4, x5
1235	x1, x2, x3, x4, x6
C	x7, x11
1C	x1, x8, x11
12C	x1, x2, x9, x11
123C	x1, x2, x3, x10, x11

Table 6   Thread Paths in the PIN Entry FSM

Input Event Sequence	Path of Transitions
1234	1
12351234	2, 3
1235C1234	2,4,5
CCC	2, 4, 6

These threads were identified with the goal of path traversal in mind. Recall from our discussion of structural testing that these goals can be misleading. The assumption is that path traversal uncovers faults, and traversing a variety of paths reduces redundancy. The last path in Table 6 illustrates how structural goals can be counter-productive. Hitting the cancel key three times does indeed cause the three try mechanism to fail, and returns the system to the Card Entry state, but it seems like a degenerate thread. There is a more serious flaw with these threads: we could not really execute them "by themselves", because of the hierarchic state machines. What really happens with the '1235' input sequence in Table 5? It traverses an interesting path in the PIN Try machine, and then it "returns" to the PIN Entry machine where it is seen as a logical event (incorrect PIN), which causes a transition to state 2.2 (Second PIN Try). If no additional keystrokes occur, this machine would remain in state 2.2. We show how to overcome such situations next.

14.4.2 NODE AND EDGE COVERAGE METRICS

Because the finite state machines are directed graphs, we can use the same test coverage metrics that we applied at the unit level. The hierarchic relationship means that the upper level machine must treat the lower machine as a procedure that is entered and returned. (Actually, we need to do this for one more level to get to true threads that begin with the Card Entry state.) The two obvious choices are node coverage and edge coverage. Table 7 is extended from Table 4 to show the node and edge coverage of the three-try thread.

Node (state) coverage is analogous to statement coverage at the unit level — it is the bare minimum. In the PIN Entry example, we can attain node coverage without ever executing a thread with a correct PIN. If you examine Table 8, you will see that two threads (initiated by C1234 and 123C1C1C) traverse all the states in both machines.

Edge (state transition) coverage is a more acceptable standard. If the state machines are "well formed" (transitions in terms of port events), edge coverage also guarantees port event coverage. The threads in Table 9 were picked in a structural way, to guarantee that the less traveled edges (those caused by cancel keystrokes) are traversed.

14.5 FUNCTIONAL STRATEGIES FOR THREAD TESTING

The finite state machine based approaches to thread identification are clearly useful, but what if no behavioral model exists for a system to be tested? The testing craftsperson has two choices: develop a behavioral model, or resort to the system level analogs of functional testing. Recall that when functional test cases are identified, we use information from the input and output spaces as well as the function itself. We describe functional threads here in terms of coverage metrics that are derived from three of the basis concepts (events, ports, and data).

Table 7 Node and Edge Traversal of a Thread

Port Input Event	Port Output Event	Nodes	Edges
	Screen 2 displayed with '----'	2.1	a
1 pressed		2.1.1	
	Screen 2 displayed with 'X---'		x1
2 pressed		2.1.2	
	Screen 2 displayed with 'XX--'		x2
3 pressed		2.1.3	
	Screen 2 displayed with 'XXX-'		x3
5 pressed		2.1.4	
	Screen 2 displayed with 'XXXX'		x4
(Incorrect PIN)	Screen 3 displayed	2.1.5, 3	x6, 2
(second try)	Screen 2 displayed with '----'	2.2	
1 pressed		2.2.1	
	Screen 2 displayed with 'X---'		x1
2 pressed		2.2.2	
	Screen 2 displayed with 'XX--'		x2
3 pressed		2.2.3	
	Screen 2 displayed with 'XXX-'		x3
cancel pressed		2.2.4	x10
(end of 2nd try)	Screen 3 displayed	2.2.6	x11
	Screen 2 displayed with '----'	2.3	4
1 pressed		2.3.1	
	Screen 2 displayed with 'X---'		x1
2 pressed		2.3.2	
	Screen 2 displayed with 'XX--'		x2
3 pressed		2.3.3	
	Screen 2 displayed with 'XXX-'		x3
4 pressed		2.3.4	
	Screen 2 displayed with 'XXXX'		x4
(Correct PIN)	Screen 5 displayed	2.3.5, 3	x5, 5

Table 8   Thread/State Incidence

Input Events	2.1	2.x1	2.x2	2.x3	2.x4	2.x5	2.2.6	2.2	2.3	3	1
1234	x	x	x	x	x	x				x	
12351234	x	x	x	x	x	x		x		x	
C1234	x	x	x	x	x	x	x	x		x	
1C12C1234	x	x	x	x			x	x	x	x	
123C1C1C	x	x	x	x	x		x	x	x		x

Table 9   Thread/Transition Incidence

Input Events	x1	x2	x3	x4	x5	x6	x7	x8	x9	x10	x11	1	2	3	4	5	6
1234	x	x	x	x	x							x					
12351234	x	x	x	x	x	x							x	x			
C1234	x	x	x	x	x		x				x		x	x			
1C12C1234	x	x	x	x	x			x	x		x		x		x	x	
123C1C1C	x	x	x					x		x	x		x		x		x

14.5.1 EVENT-BASED THREAD TESTING

Consider the space of port input events. There are five port input thread coverage metrics of interest. Attaining these levels of system test coverage requires a set of threads such that:

- PI1: each port input event occurs
- PI2: common sequences of port input events occur
- PI3: each port input event occurs in every "relevant" data context
- PI4: for a given context, all "inappropriate" input events occur
- PI5: for a given context, all possible input events occur

The PI1 metric is a bare minimum, and is inadequate for most systems. PI2 coverage is the most common, and it corresponds to the intuitive view of system testing because it deals with "normal use". It is difficult to quantify, however. What is a "common" sequence of input events? What is an uncommon one?

The last three metrics are defined in terms of a "context". The best view of a context is that it is a point of event quiescence. In the SATM system, screen displays occur at the points of event quiescence. The PI3 metric deals with context sensitive port input events. These are physical input events that have logical meanings determined by the context within which they occur. In the SATM system, for example, a keystroke on the B1 function button occurs in five separate contexts (screens being displayed) and has three different meanings. The key to this metric is that it is driven by an event in all of its contexts. The PI4 and PI5 metrics are converses: they start with a context and seek a variety of events. The PI4 metric is often used on an informal basis by testers who try to break a system. At a given context, they want to supply unanticipated input events just to see what happens. In the SATM system for example, what happens if a function button is depressed during the PIN Entry stage? The appropriate events are the digit and cancel keystrokes. The inappropriate input events are the keystrokes on the B1, B2, and B3 buttons.

This is partially a specification problem: we are discussing the difference between prescribed behavior (things that should happen) and proscribed behavior (things that should not happen). Most requirements specifications have a hard time just describing prescribed behavior; it is usually testers that find proscribed behavior. The designer who maintains my local ATM system told me that once someone inserted a fish sandwich in the deposit envelope slot. (Apparently they thought it was a waste receptacle.) At any rate, no one at the bank ever anticipated insertion of a fish sandwich as a port input event. The PI4 and PI5 metrics are usually very effective, but they raise one curious difficulty. How does the tester know what the expected response should be to a proscribed input? Are they simply ignored? Should there be an output warning message? Usually, this is left to the tester's intuition. If time permits, this is a powerful point of feedback to requirements specification. It is also a highly desirable focus for either rapid prototyping or executable specifications.

We can also define two coverage metrics based on port output events:

- PO1: each port output event occurs
- PO2: each port output event occurs for each cause

PO1 coverage is an acceptable minimum. It is particularly effective when a system has a rich variety of output messages for error conditions. (The SATM system does not.) PO2 coverage is a good goal, but it is hard to quantify; we will revisit this in Chapter 16 when we examine thread interaction. For now, note that PO2 coverage refers to threads that interact with respect to a port output event.. Usually a given output event only has a small number of causes. In the SATM system, screen 10 might be displayed for three reasons: the terminal might be out of cash, it may be impossible to make a connection with the central bank to get the account balance, or the withdrawal door might be jammed. In practice, some of the most difficult faults found in field trouble reports are those in which an output occurs for an unsuspected cause. One example: my local ATM system (not the SATM) has a screen that informs me that "Your daily withdrawal limit has been reached". This screen should occur when I attempt to withdraw more than $300 in one day. When I see this screen, I used to assume that my wife has made a major withdrawal (thread interaction), so I request a lesser amount. I found out that the ATM also produces this screen when the amount of cash in the dispenser is low. Rather than provide a lot of cash to the first users, the central bank prefers to provide less cash to more users.

14.5.2 PORT-BASED THREAD TESTING

Port-based testing is a useful complement to event-based testing. With port-based testing, we ask, for each port, what events can occur at that port. We then seek threads that exercise input ports and output ports with respect to the event lists for each port. (This presumes such event lists have been specified; some requirements specification techniques mandate such lists.) Port-based testing is particularly useful for systems in which the port devices come from external suppliers. The main reason for port-based testing can be seen in the entity/relationship model of the basis constructs (Figure 14.1). The many-to-many relationship between ports and events should be exercised in both directions. Event based testing covers the one-to-many relationship from events to ports, and conversely, port-based testing covers the one-to many relationship from ports to events. The SATM system fails us at this point — there is no SATM event that occurs at more than one port.

14.5.3 DATA-BASED THREAD TESTING

Port and event based testing work well for systems that are primarily event driven. Such systems are sometimes called "reactive" systems because they react to stimuli (port input events), and often the reaction is in the from of port output events. Reactive systems have two important characteristics: they are "long-running" (as opposed to the short burst of computation we see in a payroll program) and they maintain a relationship with their environment. Typically, event driven, reactive systems do not have a very interesting data model (as we see with the SATM system), so data model based threads aren't particularly useful. But what about conventional systems which are data driven? These systems, described as "static" in [Topper 93], are transformational (rather than reactive); they support transactions on a database. When these systems are specified, the entity/relationship model is dominant, and is therefore a fertile source of system testing threads. To attach our discussion to something familiar, we use the entity/relationship model of a simple library system (see Figure 14.8) from [Topper 93] .

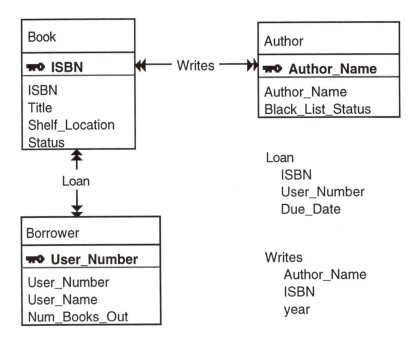

Figure 14.8   E/R Model of a Library

Here are some typical transactions in the library system:

1. Add a book to the library.
2. Delete a book from the library.
3. Add a borrower to the library.
4. Delete a borrower from the library.
5. Loan a book to a borrower.
6. Process the return of a book from a borrower.

These transactions are all mainline threads; in fact, they represent families of threads. For example, suppose the book loan transaction is attempted for a borrower whose current number of checked out books is at the lending limit (a nice boundary value example). We might also try to return a book that was never owned by the library. One more: suppose we delete a borrower that has some unreturned books. All of these are interesting threads to test, and all are at the system level.

We can identify each of these examples, and many more, by close attention to the information in the entity/relationship model. As we did with event-based testing, we describe sets of threads in terms of data-based coverage metrics. These refer to relationships for an important reason. Information in relationships is generally populated by system level threads, whereas that in the entities is usually handled at the unit level. (When entity/relationship modeling is the starting point of object-oriented analysis, this is enforced by encapsulation.)

- DM1: Exercise the cardinality of every relationship.
- DM2: Exercise the participation of every relationship.
- DM3: Exercise the functional dependencies among relationships.

Cardinality refers of the four possibilities of relationship that we discussed in Chapter 3: one-to-one, one-to-many, many-to-one, and many-to-many. In the library example, both the loan and the writes relationships are many-to-many, meaning that one author can write many books, and one book can have many authors; and that one book can be loaned to many borrowers (in sequence) and one borrower can borrow many books. Each of these possibilities results in a useful system testing thread.

Participation refers to whether or not every instance of an entity participates in a relationship. In the writes relationship, both the Book and the Author entities have mandatory participation (we cannot have a book with no authors, or an author of no books). In some modeling techniques, participation is expressed in terms of numerical limits; the Author entity, for example, might be expressed as "at least 1 and at most 12". When such information is available, it leads directly to obvious boundary value system test threads.

Sometimes transactions determine explicit logical connections among relationships; these are known as functional dependencies. For example, we cannot loan a book that is not possessed by the library, and we would not delete a book that is out on loan. Also, we would not delete a borrower who still has some books checked out. These kinds of dependencies are reduced when the database is normalized, but they still exist, and they lead to interesting system test threads.

14.6 SATM TEST THREADS

If we apply the discussion of this chapter to the SATM system, we get a set of threads that constitutes a thorough system level test. We develop such a set of threads here in terms of an overall state model in which states correspond to key atomic system functions. The macro-level states are: Card Entry, PIN Entry, Transaction Request, (and processing), and Session Management. The stated order is the testing order, because these stages are in prerequisite order. (We cannot enter a PIN until successful card entry, we cannot request a transaction until successful PIN entry, and so on.) We also need some pre-condition data that define some actual accounts with PANs, Expected PINs, and account balances. These are given in Table 10. Two less obvious pre-conditions are that the ATM terminal is initially displaying screen 1 and the total cash available to the withdrawal dispenser is $500 (in $10 notes).

Table 10   SATM Test Data

PAN	Expected PIN	Checking Balance	Savings Balance
100	1234	$1000.00	$800.00
200	4567	$100.00	$90.00
300	6789	$25.00	$20.00

We will express threads in tables in which pairs of rows correspond to port inputs and expected port outputs at each of the four major stages. We start with three basic threads, one for each transaction type (balance inquiry, deposit, and withdrawal).

Thread 1 (balance)	Card Entry (PAN)	PIN Entry	Transaction Request	Session Management
Port Inputs	100	1234	B1, B1	B2
Port Outputs	screen 2	screen 5	screen 6, screen 14 $1000.00	screen 15, eject card, screen 1

In thread 1, a valid card with PAN = 100 is entered, which causes screen 2 to be displayed. The PIN digits '1234' are entered, and since they match the expected PIN for the PAN, screen 5 inviting a transaction selection is displayed. When button B1 is touched the first time (requesting a balance inquiry), screen 6 asking which account is displayed. When B1 is pressed the second time (checking), screen 14 is displayed and the checking account balance ($1000.00) is printed on the receipt. When B2 is pushed, screen 15 is displayed, the receipt is printed, the ATM card is ejected, and then screen 1 is displayed.

Thread 2 is a deposit to checking: Same PAN and PIN, but B2 is touched when screen 5 is displayed, and B1 is touched when screen 6 is displayed. The amount 25.00 is entered when screen 7 is displayed and then screen 13 is displayed. The deposit door opens and the deposit envelope is placed in the deposit slot. Screen 14 is displayed, and when B2 is pushed, screen 15 is displayed, the receipt showing the new checking account balance of $1025.00 is printed, the ATM card is ejected, and then screen 1 is displayed.

Thread 2 (deposit)	Card Entry (PAN)	PIN Entry	Transaction Request	Session Management
Port Inputs	100	1234	B2, B1, 25.00 insert env.	B2
Port Outputs	screen 2	screen 5	screen 6, screen 7, screen 13, dep. door opens, screen 14, $1025.00	screen 15, eject card, screen 1

Thread 3 is a withdrawal from savings: Again the same PAN and PIN, but B3 is touched when screen 5 is displayed, and B2 is touched when screen 6 is displayed. The amount 30.00 is entered when screen 7 is displayed and then screen 11 is displayed. The withdrawal door opens and three $10 notes are dispensed. Screen 14 is displayed, and when B2 is pushed, screen 15 is displayed, the receipt showing the new savings account balance of $770.00 is printed, the ATM card is ejected, and then screen 1 is displayed.

Thread 3 (withdrawal)	Card Entry (PAN)	PIN Entry	Transaction Request	Session Management
Port Inputs	100	1234	B3, B2, 30.00	B2
Port Outputs	screen 2	screen 5	screen 6, screen 7, screen 11, withdrawal door opens, 3 $10 notes, screen 14, $770.00	screen 15, eject card, screen 1

A few of these detailed descriptions are needed to show the pattern; the remaining threads are described in terms of input and output events that are the objective of the test thread.

Thread 4 is the shortest thread in the SATM system, it consists of an invalid card, which is immediately rejected.

Thread 4	Card Entry (PAN)	PIN Entry	Transaction Request	Session Management
Port Inputs	400			
Port Outputs	eject card screen 1			

Following the macro-states along thread 1, we next perform variations on PIN Entry. We get four new threads from Table 9, which yield edge coverage in the PIN Entry finite state machines.

Thread 5 (balance)	Card Entry (PAN)	PIN Entry	Transaction Request	Session Management
Port Inputs	100	12351234	as in thread 1	
Port Outputs	screen 2	screens 3,2,5		

Thread 6 (balance)	Card Entry (PAN)	PIN Entry	Transaction Request	Session Management
Port Inputs	100	C1234	as in thread 1	
Port Outputs	screen 2	screens 3,2,5		

Thread 7 (balance)	Card Entry (PAN)	PIN Entry	Transaction Request	Session Management
Port Inputs	100	1C12C1234	as in thread 1	
Port Outputs	screen 2	screens 3,2, 3,2,5		

Thread 8 (balance)	Card Entry (PAN)	PIN Entry	Transaction Request	Session Management
Port Inputs	100	123C1C1C		
Port Outputs	screen 2	screens 3,2, 3,2,4,1		

Moving to the Transaction Request stage, there are variations with respect to the type of transaction (balance, deposit, or withdraw), the account (checking or savings) and several that deal with the amount requested. Threads 1, 2, and 3 cover the type and account variations, so we focus on the amount-driven threads. Thread 9 rejects the attempt to withdraw an amount not in $10 increments, Thread 10 rejects the attempt to withdraw more than the account balance, and Thread 11 rejects the attempt to withdraw more cash than the dispenser contains.

Thread 9 (withdrawal)	Card Entry (PAN)	PIN Entry	Transaction Request	Session Management
Port Inputs	100	1234	B3, B2, 15.00 Cancel	B2
Port Outputs	screen 2	screen 5	screens 6,7, 9, 7	screen 15, eject card, screen 1

Thread 10 (withdrawal)	Card Entry (PAN)	PIN Entry	Transaction Request	Session Management
Port Inputs	300	6789	B3, B2, 50.00 Cancel	B2
Port Outputs	screen 2	screen 5	screens 6,7,8	screen 15, eject card, screen 1

Thread 11 (withdrawal)	Card Entry (PAN)	PIN Entry	Transaction Request	Session Management
Port Inputs	100	1234	B3, B2, 510.00 Cancel	B2
Port Outputs	screen 2	screen 5	screens 6,7, 10	screen 15, eject card, screen 1

Having exercised the transaction processing portion, we proceed to the session management stage, where we test the multiple transaction option.

Thread 12 (balance)	Card Entry (PAN)	PIN Entry	Transaction Request	Session Management
Port Inputs	100	1234	B1, B1	B1, Cancel
Port Outputs	screen 2	screen 5	screen 6, screen 14 $1000.00	screen 15, screen 5, screen 15, eject card, screen 1

At this point, the threads provide coverage of all output screens except for screen 12, which informs the user that deposits cannot be processed. Causing this condition is problematic (maybe we should place a fish sandwich in the deposit envelope slot). This is an example of a thread selected by a pre-condition that is a hardware failure. We just give it a thread name here, it's thread 13. Next, we develop threads 14 through 22 to exercise context sensitive input events. They are shown in Table 11; notice that some of the first 13 threads exercise context sensitivity.

Table 11 Threads for Context Sensitive Input Events

Thread	Keystroke	Screen	Logical Meaning
6	cancel	2	PIN Entry error
14	cancel	5	transaction selection error
15	cancel	6	account selection error
16	cancel	7	amount selection error
17	cancel	8	amount selection error
18	cancel	13	deposit envelope not ready
1	B1	5	balance
1	B1	6	checking
19	B1	10	yes (a non-withdrawal transaction)
20	B1	12	yes (a non-deposit transaction)
12	B1	14	yes (another transaction)
2	B2	5	deposit
3	B2	6	savings
21	B2	10	no (no additional transaction)
22	B2	12	no (no additional transaction)
1	B2	14	no (no additional transaction)

These 22 threads comprise a reasonable test of the portion of the SATM system that we have specified. Of course there are untested aspects; one good example involves the balance of an account. Consider two threads, one that deposits $40 to an account, and a second that withdraws $80, and suppose that the balance obtained form the central bank at the Card Entry stage is $50. There are two possibilities: one is to use the central bank balance, record all transactions, and then resolve these when the daily posting occurs. The other is to maintain a running local balance, which is what would be shown on a balance inquiry transaction. If the central bank balance is used, the withdrawal transaction is rejected, but if the local balance is used, it is processed. This detail was not addressed in our specification; we will revisit when we discuss thread interaction in Chapter 16.

Another prominent untested portion of the SATM system is the Amount Entry process that occurs in screens 7 and 8. The possibility of a cancel keystroke at any point during amount entry produces a multiplicity greater than that of PIN Entry. There is a more subtle (and therefore more interesting) test for Amount Entry. What actually happens when we enter an amount? To be specific, suppose we wish to enter $40.00. We expect an echo after each digit keystroke, but in which position does the echo occur? Two obvious solutions: always require six digits to be entered (so we would enter '004000') or use the high order digits first and shift left as successive digits are entered, as shown in Figure 14.10. Most ATM systems use the shift approach, and this raises the subtle point: how does the ATM system know when all amount digits have been entered? The ATM system clearly cannot predict that the deposit amount is $40.00 instead of $400.00 or $4000.000 because there is no "enter" key to signify when the last digit has been entered. The reason for this digression is that this is a good example of the kind of detail discovered by testers that is often missing from a requirements specification. (Such details would likely be found with either Rapid Prototyping or using an executable specification.)

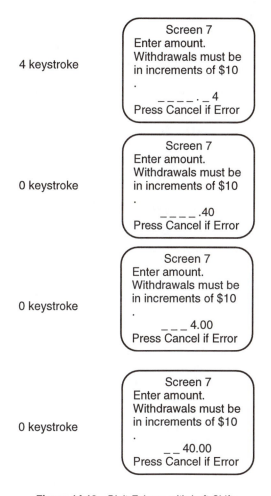

Figure 14.10 Digit Echoes with Left Shifts

14.7 SYSTEM TESTING GUIDELINES

If we disallow compound sessions (more than one transaction) and if we disregard the multiplicity due to Amount Entry possibilities, there are 435 distinct threads per valid account in the SATM system. Factor in the effects of compound sessions and the Amount Entry possibilities and there are tens of thousands of possible threads for the SATM system. We end this chapter with three strategies to deal with the thread explosion problem.

14.7.1 PSEUDO-STRUCTURAL SYSTEM TESTING

When we studied unit testing, we saw that the combination of functional and structural testing yields a desirable cross-check. We have something similar with system level threads: we defined ten system level, functional coverage metrics in Section 14.5, and two graph based metrics (node and edge coverage) in Section 14.4. We can use the graph based metrics as a cross-check on the functional threads in much the same way that we used DD-Paths at the unit level to identify gaps and redundancies in functional test cases. We can only claim pseudo-structural testing [Jorgensen 94], because the node and edge coverage metrics are defined in terms of a control model of a system, and are not derived directly from the system implementation. (Recall we started out with a concern over the distinction between reality and models of reality.) In general, behavioral models are only approximations of a system's reality, which is why we could decompose our models down to several levels of detail. If we made a true structural model, its size and complexity would make it too cumbersome to use. The big weakness of pseudo-structural metrics is that the underlying model may be a poor choice. The three most common behavioral models (decision tables, finite state machines, and Petri nets) are appropriate, respectively, to transformational, interactive, and concurrent systems.

Decision tables and finite state machines are good choices for ASF testing. If an ASF is described using a decision table, conditions typically include port input events, and actions are port output events. We can then devise test cases that cover every condition, every action, or most completely, every rule. As we saw for finite state machine models, test cases can cover every state, every transition, or every path.

Thread testing based on decision tables is cumbersome. We might describe threads as sequences of rules from different decision tables, but this becomes very messy to track in terms of coverage. We need finite state machines as a minimum, and if there is any form of interaction, Petri nets are a better choice. There we can devise thread tests that cover every place, every transition, and every sequence of transitions.

14.7.2 OPERATIONAL PROFILES

In its most general form, Zipf's Law holds that 80% of the activities occur in 20% of the space. Activities and space can be interpreted in numerous ways: people with messy desks hardly ever use most of their desktop clutter, programmers seldom use more than 20% of the features of their favorite programming language, and Shakespeare (whose writings contain an enormous vocabulary) uses a small fraction of his vocabulary most of the time. Zipf's Law applies to software (and testing) in several ways. The most useful interpretation for testers is that the space consists of all possible threads and activities are thread executions (or traversals). Thus for a system with many threads, 80% of the execution traverses only 20% of the threads.

Recall that a failure occurs when a fault is executed. The whole idea of testing is to execute test cases such that, when a failure occurs, the presence of a fault is revealed. We can make an important distinction: the distribution of faults in a system is only indirectly related to the reliability of the system. The simplest view of system reliability is the probability that no failure occurs during a specific time interval. (Notice no mention is even made of faults, the number of faults, or fault density.) If the only faults are "in the corners" on threads that are seldom traversed, the overall reliability is higher than if the same number of faults were on "high traffic" threads. The idea of operational profiles is to determine the execution frequencies of various threads, and to use this information to select threads for system testing. Particularly when test time is limited (usually!), operational profiles maximize the probability of finding faults by inducing failures in the most frequently traversed threads.

One way to determine the operational profile of a system is to use a decision tree. This works particularly well when system behavior is modeled in hierarchic state machines, as we did with the SATM system. For any state, we find (or estimate) the probability of each outgoing transition (the sum of these must be 1). When a state is decomposed into a lower level, the probabilities at the lower level become "split edges" at the upper level. Figure 14.11 shows the result of this with hypothetical transition probabilities. Given the transition probabilities, the overall probability of a thread is simply the product of the transition probabilities along the thread. Table 12 shows this calculation for the most and least frequent threads.

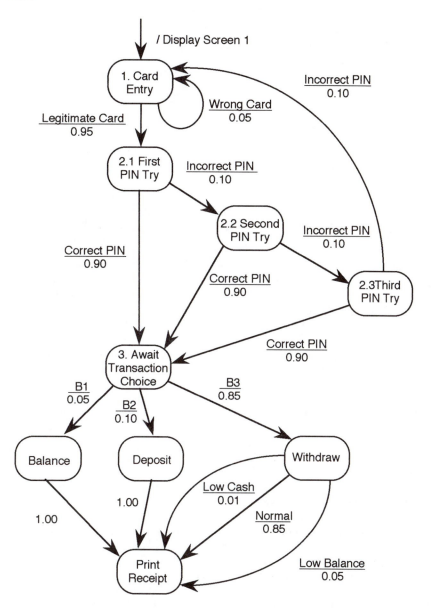

Figure 14.11   Transition Probabilities for SATM System

Operational profiles provide a feeling for the "traffic mix" of a delivered system. This is helpful for reasons other than just optimizing system testing. These profiles can also be used in conjunction with simulators to get an early indication of execution time performance and system transaction capacity. Many times, customers are a good source of traffic mix information, so this approach to system testing is often well received just because it makes an attempt to replicate the reality of a delivered system.

14.7.3 PROGRESSION VS. REGRESSION TESTING
When we discussed software development life cycles in Chapter 12, we mentioned that the use of builds induces the need for regression testing. When build 2 is added to build 1, we test the new material in build 2, and we also retest build 1 to see that the new material has no deleterious effect on build 1 contents.

Table 12   Thread Probabilities

Common Thread	Probabilities	Rare Thread	Probabilities
Legitimate Card	0.95	Legitimate Card	0.95
PIN ok 1st try	0.90	Bad PIN 1st try	0.10
Withdraw	0.85	Bad PIN 2nd try	0.10
Normal	0.85	PIN ok 3rd try	0.90
		Withdraw	0.85
		Low Cash	0.01
	0.6177375		0.00072675

(The industrial average for such "ripple effect" is that 20% of changes to an existing system induce new faults in the system.) If a project has several builds, regression testing implies a significant repetition of testing, especially for the early builds. We can reduce this by concentrating on the difference between progression and regression testing.

The most common approach to regression testing is to simply repeat the system tests. We can refine this (and drastically reduce the effort) by choosing test threads with respect to the goals of regression and progression testing. With progression testing, we are testing "new territory", so we expect a higher failure rate than with regression testing. Another difference: because we expect to find more faults with progression testing, we need to be able to locate the faults. This requires test cases with a "diagnostic" capability, that is, tests that can fail only a few ways. For thread based testing, progression testing should use shorter threads that can fail only in a few ways. These threads might be ordered as we did with the SATM thread test set, such that longer threads are built up from shorter (and previously tested) threads.

We have lower expectations of failure with regression testing, and we are less concerned with fault isolation. Taken together, this means regression testing should use longer threads that can fail in several ways. If we think in terms of coverage, both progression and regression testing will have thorough coverage, but the density is different. State and transition coverage matrices (like Tables 8 and 9) will be sparse for progression testing threads and dense for regression testing threads. This is somewhat antithetical to the use of operational profiles. As a rule, "good" regression testing threads will have low operational frequencies, and progression testing threads will have high operational frequencies.

EXERCISES

1. One of the problems of system testing, particularly with interactive systems, is to anticipate all the strange things the user might do. What happens in the SATM system if a customer enters three digits of a PIN and then walks away?
2. To remain "in control" of abnormal user behavior (the behavior is abnormal, not the user), the SATM system might introduce a timer with a 30 second time-out. When no port input event occurs for 30 seconds, the SATM system asks if the user needs more time. The user can answer yes or no. Devise a new screen and identify port events that would implement such a time-out event.
3. Suppose you add this time-out feature to the SATM system. What regression testing would you perform?
4. Make an additional refinement to the PIN Try finite state machine (Figure 14.6) to implement your time-out mechanism, then revise the thread test case in Table 3.
5. The text asserts that "the B1 function button occurs in five separate contexts (screens being displayed) and has three different meanings". Examine the fifteen screens (points of event quiescence) and decide whether there are three or five different logical meanings to a B1 keystroke.
6. Does it make sense to use test coverage metrics in conjunction with operational profiles? Discuss this.
7. Develop an operational profile for the NextDate problem. Use the decision table formulation, and provide individual condition probabilities. Since a rule is the conjunction of its conditions, the product of the condition entry probabilities is the rule probability.

Chapter 15

Object-Oriented Testing

One of the original hopes for object-oriented software was that objects could be re-used without modification or additional testing. This was based on well-conceived objects that encapsulate functions and data "that belong together", and once such objects are developed and tested, they become reusable components. The hoped-for economies, especially in testing, have not been realized. In fact, the contrary is emerging as a specter for object-oriented development: "It seems likely that more, not less, testing will be needed to obtain high reliability in object-oriented systems." [Binder 94a].

We begin our examination of object-oriented testing by taking an object-oriented view of the five basis constructs we discussed in Chapter 14, and then list testing issues raised by object-oriented software development. Next we extend our existing testing framework to address these issues, and after relating these ideas to our SATM example, we conclude with some recommendations for object-oriented testing. (We will be able to re-use much of the theory and techniques from traditional software testing.)

15.1 OBJECT ORIENTATION

Even after a decade of industrial use, object-oriented software development lacks a widely accepted general definition. In the late 1980s, a leading CASE tool vendor organized a symposium to identify the directions of object-oriented technology. After two days, the nearly fifty invited object-oriented experts failed to agree on a definition of an object. Not surprisingly, the development of object-oriented thinking has been a bottom-up process frequently driven by specific types of applications. Three distinct phases are generally recognized: object-oriented analysis (OOA), object-oriented design (OOD), and object-oriented programming (OOP); but these do not correspond well to system, integration, and unit testing. OOA is at the system level, and OOD and OOP are at the unit level; there is no direct counterpart for integration testing.

We can impose some order on the cacophony of object-oriented voices by revisiting the five basis system constructs (see Figure 14.1). The functional view of these constructs emphasizes actions that have events and data as inputs and outputs. If we reorganize the same base information, this is replaced by the encapsulation of actions (methods) with either data or ports (see Figure 15.1). The many-to-many relationship between ports and events remains, but objects are event driven.

As with traditional development, object-oriented software development proceeds via structural, contextual, and behavioral models. Structural models focus on the encapsulation between actions and data or ports, and at this point, inheritance is the central driver to design. Once objects are identified, they are components in contextual models in which port objects constitute the port boundary of a system. Behavioral models are usually finite state machines that describe the life history of an object. These life histories must be merged when objects are composed, and this is a vulnerable point of object-oriented software development.

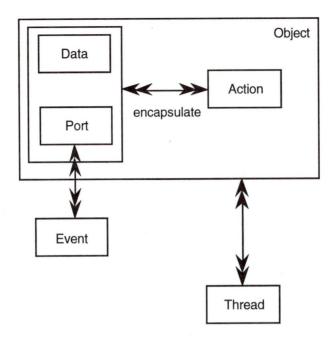

Figure 15.1 Five Basic Constructs Viewed as Objects

The greatest disparity among various object-oriented flavors is how object-oriented analysis is performed. One methodologist recommends that the analyst immerse him/herself in descriptions of the system, possibly for weeks or even months, until the system is "intuitively familiar" (my quotes). At that point, the analyst will be able to identify the objects in a natural, intuitive way. Other object-oriented thinkers begin with a narrative description of a system in which the nouns and verbs are highlighted. After a brief filtering process that collapses sets of synonyms onto one representative, the nouns are deemed to be objects and the verbs become methods. An incidence matrix is used to associate nouns and verbs, resulting in the encapsulation. Still other object-oriented flavors start with an entity/relationship model (that emphasizes inheritance features of a system) and declare that the entities are objects. Testers need to overcome all this disparity at the OOA level with formulations of system testing that transcend the differences.

15.2 ISSUES RAISED BY OBJECT ORIENTATION

The distinctive features of object-oriented software require special attention from testers. Here we highlight the most important of these, with the presumption that the reader is generally familiar with object-oriented terminology.

15.2.1 LEVELS OF TESTING

Because object-oriented software development typically does not follow a waterfall-like development life cycle, there is some confusion about levels of object-oriented testing. Some researchers hold that the class is the natural subject for unit level object-oriented testing. Other methodologists simply equate classes and objects, and don't even worry about instantiation. One problem with treating classes as units is that some methods can be very large. Also, what happens if a method appears in different objects?

At the other extreme, system level testing is generally unaffected by the object-orientation. Threads are still threads; in fact, we would like to think that threads are independent of the way in which a system is developed. System level coverage metrics clearly must relate to the object orientation. This leaves integration testing as an open question. Typically there is no decomposition tree to use as a basis of integration testing, so we need something else. Objects communicate by messages, so that seems like a good place to start. The replacement of decomposition with composition has a major effect; we discuss this next.

15.2.2 OBJECT COMPOSITION

One of the major differences between traditional and object-oriented software development is that the former is largely characterized by decomposition (of actions, data, and events), while the latter presumes composition instead. As a design strategy, composition avoids most of the pitfalls of decomposition, but it has its own unique problems. The most important is the impossibility of ever knowing the other objects with which a given object may be composed. Just think about the implications this has for integration testing. This point is as important as it is obscure. We'll make a digression here to illustrate it with an example, the Saturn Windshield Wiper system (see Chapter 2).

If we make an object formulation of the Saturn Windshield Wiper system, we find three natural port objects: the lever, the dial, and the wiper motor. These are shown in Figure 15.2, along with their methods (actions) and their attributes (data). The arrows indicate messages that are caused by port input events on either the lever or the dial.

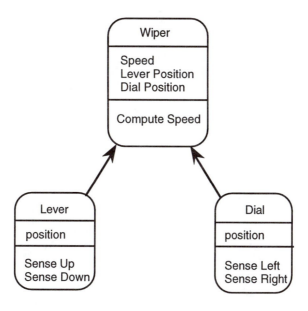

Figure 15.2   Saturn Windshield Wiper Objects

There are two events that occur on the lever: it can be moved up one position, or it can be moved down one position. Similarly, there are two events that occur on the dial: it can be moved clockwise or counter-clockwise. We can decompose these into the finer granularity shown in Table 1:

Table 1   Port Input Events in the Saturn Windshield Wiper

Port Input Event	Description
ie1	lever from OFF to INT
ie2	lever from INT to LOW
ie3	lever from LOW to HIGH
ie4	lever from HIGH to LOW
ie5	lever from LOW to INT
ie6	lever from INT to OFF
ie7	dial from 1 to 2
ie8	dial from 2 to 3
ie9	dial from 3 to 2
ie10	dial from 2 to 1

The Wiper object produces six port output events: the six different wiper speeds (expressed in wipes per minute); these are shown in Table 2.

Table 2   Port Output Events in the Saturn Windshield Wiper

Port Output Event	Description
oe1	0 w.p.m.
oe2	4 w.p.m.
oe3	6 w.p.m.
oe4	12 w.p.m.
oe5	30 w.p.m.
oe6	60 w.p.m.

The finite state machines for the Lever and Dial objects are given in Figure 15.3. Notice we can easily show the events that cause the state transitions, but some of the associated outputs (indicated by question marks) are indeterminate. For example, when we move the lever from OFF to INT, we cannot assert a specific port output event because we do not know the state of the Dial machine. We can assert no output events in the Dial machine, because we do not know if the Lever is in the INT position.

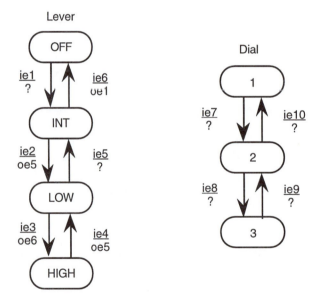

Figure 15.3 Lever and Dial Finite State Machines

Right here is where the problem with composition occurs. The attempt to show port output events on the state transitions in the Lever and Dial machines presumes that they will be composed. Instead, it is better to express the object state machines in terms of the messages they send, as in Figure 15.4. The messages m1 - m10 simply inform the wiper object of the new states of the Lever and Dial objects.

The encapsulation of the Lever and Dial objects implies that neither knows the internal state of the other. (If they did, they would be closely coupled, and this would reduce their potential for re-use.) The interaction between the Lever and the Dial machines determines the wiper speed, and the interaction is accomplished by composition. We get some help from the Wiper finite state machine (see Figure 15.5), where the states correspond to the number of wiper strokes per minute.

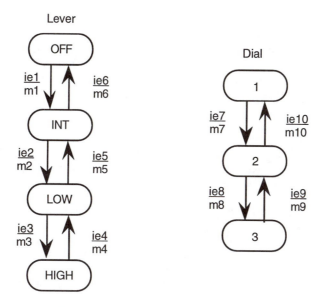

Figure 15.4 Message Responses to Events

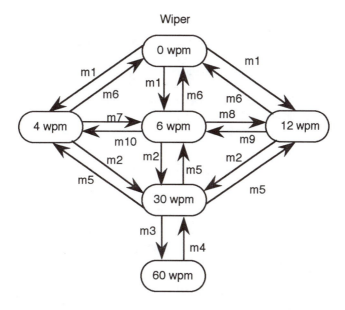

Figure 15.5 Wiper Object Finite State Machine

Now if we ask what causes the state transitions in the Wiper machine, we see that it is actually messages received from the Lever and Dial machines in conjunction with the states of the other two objects. We can relate the three finite state machines with a single decision table:

Lever	OFF	INT	INT	INT	LOW	HIGH
Dial	n/a	1	2	3	n/a	n/a
Wiper	0	4	6	12	30	60

To complete the discussion of composition, suppose the windshield wiper manufacturer had several systems: a four speed system controlled with the lever alone, the six speed one we described here, and a quasi-continuous one controlled by a dial with dozens of closely spaced, discrete positions. If we built objects intended for re-use, the lever and dial objects could have no information about each other. When two object instances are composed, the composition requires additional modification to the Wiper object. Notice that the composition has nothing to do with either unit or system testing, but it has everything to do with integration testing.

15.2.3 ESOTERIC OBJECT FEATURES

Three other features of object-oriented software have special implications for testing; in fact, they are topics of current research. The features are inheritance, dynamic binding, and polymorphism. When a class has subclasses, lower level classes can inherit both attributes and methods from higher classes. Where are these relationships tested: at the unit level? At the integration level? As part of the super class or part of the subclass? These demands are complicated by other considerations, for example, selective and multiple inheritance. Selective inheritance occurs when a class inherits some, but not all, of the attributes and methods from a super class, and multiple inheritance occurs when a class inherits these from more than one super class. (Multiple inheritance is usually thought of as being selective.) Dynamic binding occurs when a method is first associated with an object at execution time. We might refer to this as execution-time composition; the implications for integration testing are enormous. Finally, polymorphism refers to messages that elicit (or cause) different behavior with different recipients. We might refer to these as context-sensitive messages, and treat them like context sensitive port input events.

15.3 FRAMEWORK FOR OBJECT-ORIENTED TESTING

To deal with the diversity and lack of consensus among object-oriented thinkers, we develop a framework for object-oriented testing that makes sense. In this section, we extend and only slightly modify the definitions we made for integration and system testing. Information in this section also appears in [Jorgensen 94].

Behavior is dynamic, hence testing must operate with dynamic constructs. There are five levels at which we can test object-oriented software:

- a method
- message quiescence
- event quiescence
- thread testing
- inter-thread testing (thread interaction)

An individual method is programmed in an imperative language and performs a single, cohesive function. This directly corresponds to the unit level of traditional software testing, and both the traditional functional and structural techniques are applicable to testing object methods. By defining unit testing at the method level, the complexity introduced by inheritance is reduced. (This will be at the expense of integration testing, however.)

Message and event quiescence provide natural boundaries for integration level threads of object-oriented behavior. First, we refine two definitions from Chapter 13 to accommodate object-oriented concepts.

Definition
An **MM-Path** is a sequence of method executions linked by messages.

When we spoke of MM-Paths in traditional software, we used message to refer to the invocation among separate units (modules), and we spoke of module execution paths (module level threads) rather than full modules. Here we use the same acronym to refer to an alternating sequence of method executions separated by messages, hence Method/Message Path. Just as in traditional software, methods may have several internal execution paths; we choose not to operate at that level of detail for object-oriented integration testing.

An MM-Path starts with a method and ends when it reaches a method which does not issue any messages of its own; this is the point message quiescence. Since MM-Paths are composed of linked method-message pairs in an object network, they interleave and branch off from other MM-Paths.

The second object-oriented integration testing construct addresses the event driven nature of object-oriented software. Execution of object-oriented software begins with a port input event. This system level input triggers the method-message sequence of an MM-Path which may trigger other MM-Paths until finally, the sequence of MM-Paths ends with a port output event. When such a sequence ends, the system is quiescent, that is, the system is waiting for another port input event that initiates further processing.

Definition
An *Atomic System Function (ASF)* is an input port event, followed by a set of MM-Paths, and terminated by an output port event.

Notice that the only real change to ASFs is that the MM-Paths themselves are slightly different. An atomic system function (ASF) is still an elemental function visible at the system level. As in traditional software, ASFs still constitute the point at which integration and system testing meet. Again we have a more seamless junction between these two forms of testing.

MM-Paths and Atomic System Functions deal with message and event quiescence; taken together, they are the framework for object-oriented integration testing. Of the five testable items, the two that remain, threads and thread interaction, are at the system level. As with traditional software, these cannot be tested at a lower level, and we have the same problem/question of finding threads and thread interactions. Our framework begins at the unit level where individual object methods are tested. We might call this intra-object testing. Once the methods are individually tested, we move to integration testing, where we test the interaction among objects in terms of the MM-Path and ASF constructs. MM-Paths reflect the interaction among objects, and ASFs require the interaction among MM-Paths. If we simulate port events, ASF testing is clearly at the integration level; if we use actual port events, we are at the lowest level of system testing. These levels are illustrated with the SATM example next.

15.4 OBJECT-ORIENTED TESTING OF THE SATM SYSTEM

Figures in this section are loosely taken from the Booch, OMT, and Schlaer/Mellor object-oriented techniques. The presentation of the object-oriented formulation of the SATM system is generally top-down, but that is not the order in which the objects and classes were generated.

The uppermost levels of many object-oriented techniques are much like entity/relationship diagrams. We begin with a very high level view in Figure 15.6, which shows the major classes: The ATM Terminal, the Customer, the Central Bank, and the Account classes. At this level, most object-oriented techniques employ one of two forms of decomposition: generalization and aggregation.

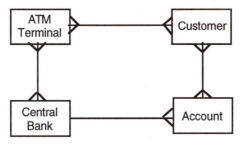

Figure 15.6 Uppermost SATM Classes

The ATM Terminal class is an aggregation of four classes. (Sometimes aggregation is described as the "A-Part-Of" relationship.) The ATM Terminal class, for example, is comprised of device-oriented classes for Screen, Door, Slot, and KeyPad, as shown in Figure 15.7 (the diamond is the OMT symbol for aggregation).

The Door, Slot, and KeyPad classes are reduced still further; we'll just look at the Door class in Figure 15.8, which is decomposed by generalization.

Both the Deposit Door and the Withdrawal Door classes inherit the status attribute and the open and close methods from the Door class. In addition, each subclass has its local methods, as shown.

The object modeling thus far has all been in the structural domain; we have very little information about behavior. Several object-oriented methodologies have a form of object communication diagram, similar to the one in Figure 15.9. Here we shift our focus from the general SATM system to the card and PIN entry portions, as we did in Chapter 14. (The event and variable names are re-used.)

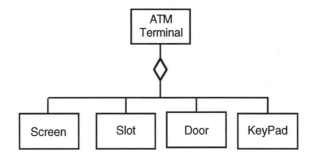

Figure 15.7 Members of the ATM Terminal Aggregation

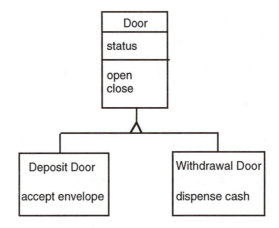

Figure 15.8 Subclasses of the Door Class

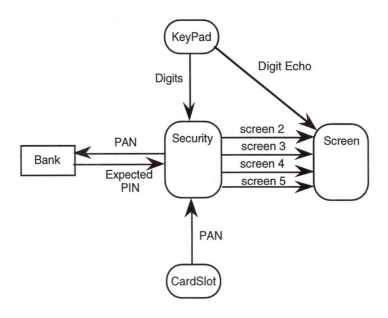

Figure 15.9 Object Communication Diagram

The object communication diagram starts to portray the operational behavior of the system. The flows here are about as helpful to testers as those in a dataflow diagram (not very). Object communication diagrams are usually supplemented with an event trace, such as the one in Figure 15.10. In these diagrams, objects are vertical lines, and the arrows between them show event flows. Also, by convention, time "starts" at the top and flows downward. Event traces represent families of closely related threads. These are sometimes difficult to draw, particularly when objects have a high outdegree. Notice we still cannot distinguish the keystroke level variations in the PIN Entry process.

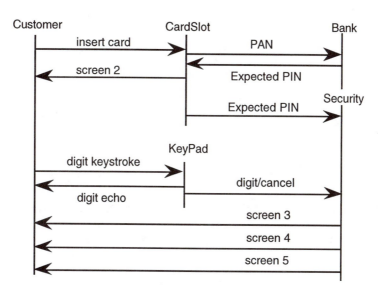

Figure 15.10 Event Trace for PIN Entry

We can see the general sequence of port events and the objects that receive/cause them. We also begin to see some of the interactions among the objects. Event traces are also the basis of an extremely useful "people-ware" technique, in which the trace serves as a skeleton of a play in which the designers of the objects personify and perform the roles of their respective objects:

Customer: I'm inserting a valid ATM card.
CardSlot: When I receive a card, I read the magnetic strip to get the card member bank code and the PAN. Once I determine that the card can be served by this terminal, I send a message to the central bank asking for the Expected PIN that goes with the PAN.
Bank: When I receive a request for an Expected PIN, I use the PAN in a table look-up and return the proper PIN.
CardSlot: When I receive the Expected PIN, I send screen 2 and then I pass the Expected PIN to the Security object.

This role playing is an effective way to create a shared vision of the execution-time behavior of a system at the inter-object level. We might refer to such episodes as rapid prototypes for designers (and testers). With the above scenario, the players (or the reader) might notice that the CardSlot should really send a message to the Screen object requesting the display of screen 2. What usually happens is the Screen object designer would speak up to say that (s)he displays screen 2.

Many object-oriented methods recommend using a finite state machine to describe an object's behavior. Figures 15.11, 15.12, and 15.13 contain state machines for (the easy) three objects: the KeyPad, the CardSlot, and the Bank. Since all of these are devices (the bank acts like an off-line storage unit), the state machines are fairly simple. Each begins with an Idle state (the point of event quiescence) and shows the device's response to port input events and messages.

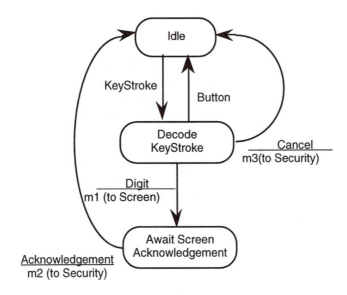

Figure 15.11 Finite State Machine for the KeyPad Object

The KeyPad object responds to a keystroke port input event. The function buttons are ignored, the cancel key generates the appropriate message (m3) to the Security object, and a digit keystroke results in two messages, one to the Screen object, and the other to the Security object.

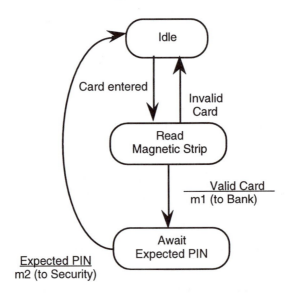

Figure 15.12 Finite State Machine for the CardSlot Object

There are a couple of stylistic details that are helpful to testers. Notice that the messages are given local names (m1, m2); this is necessary because the objects should have no knowledge of each other. Also, logical names are given to messages received from other objects (e.g., when the Bank object sends its message m1, the CardSlot object calls it Expected PIN).

Once the individual finite state machines are developed, they must be composed with each other. This is a point of extreme vulnerability for object-oriented development. It is also provides the basis for identification of MM-Paths and Atomic System Functions. Rather than attempt to compose objects into

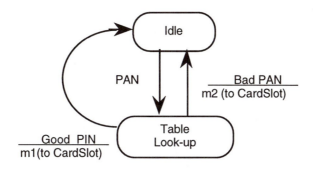

Figure 15.13   Finite State Machine for the Bank Object

one comprehensive state machine, it is more effective to create state machines at the ASF level. If an object occurs several ASFs, it will appear in as many different composed state machines. In this way, ASFs reflect the composition, and integration testing is forced to examine exactly the interactions among objects that actually occur. There is a contrived fault in the KeyPad object that would be revealed by this composition process. When the KeyPad object is used to accept digits that describe an amount to be deposited or withdrawn, the digit echo is the actual digit character, but when KeyPad is composed with the Security object, the confirming echo is an 'X'.

Figures 15.14 and 15.15 (from [Jorgensen 94]) illustrate this composition. Figure 15.14 shows a partial class hierarchy (in a Booch style cloud diagram) with those classes involved in the card and PIN entry ASFs. Only the relevant objects and methods are shown in Figure 15.15.

In Figure 15.15, messages are indicated by dotted lines, and MM-Paths are the heavy lines. An MM-Path begins with an open circle and ends (at the point of message quiescence) with a closed one. Most of the MM-Paths are short. Three ASFs in Figure 15.15 are described in Table 1.

Table 3   Card and PIN Entry ASFs

ASF	Description	MM-Path Sequence
1	Invalid card entered	1, 2
2	Valid card entered	1, 3, 2
3	Good PIN on first try	5, 6, 5, 6, 5, 6, 5, 4

15.5 GUIDELINES FOR OBJECT-ORIENTED TESTING

We can draw several conclusions about object-oriented testing from the SATM example. The most important is that integration testing is complicated by composition, and the MM-Path and ASF constructs correctly deal with the problems of composition. The second is that object-oriented testing is fairly dependent on the modeling notation used during development. Finally, object-oriented testing profits from attention to structural information. Several structural metrics for object-oriented software are proposed in [Binder 94b]. These can do double duty by serving also as test coverage metrics. They are stated without further elaboration here:

Encapsulation Metrics

E1   Method Cohesion: number of groups of instance variables used on only one method.
E2   Public/Private Ratio: percentage of public data members.
E3   Public Access: number of external accesses to public data members.

Inheritance Metrics

I1   Root Classes: number of root classes.
I2   Class Fan-In: number of classes from which a class is derived.

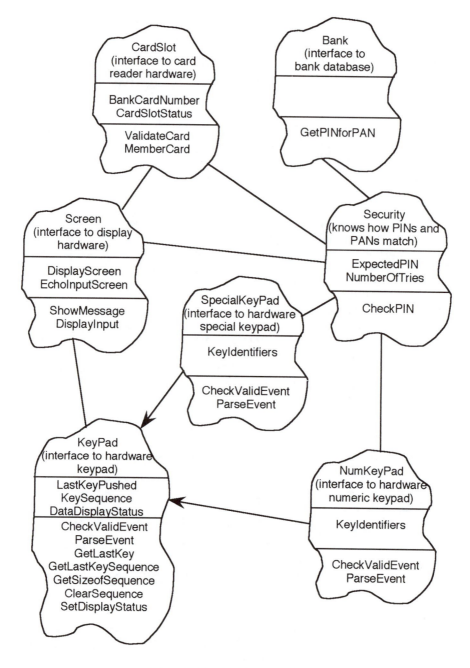

Figure 15.14 Partial Class Hierarchy

I3   Class Fan-Out: number of classes derived from a class.
I4   Tree Depth: depth of inheritance tree.

Polymorphism Metrics

P1   Overloaded Message Ratio: percent of messages not sent to overloaded objects.
P2   Dynamic Message Ratio: percent of messages for which target is determined at execution-time.
P3   Class Bounce: number of "yo-yo" paths in a class due to dynamic binding.
P4   System Bounce: number of "yo-yo" paths in a system due to dynamic binding.

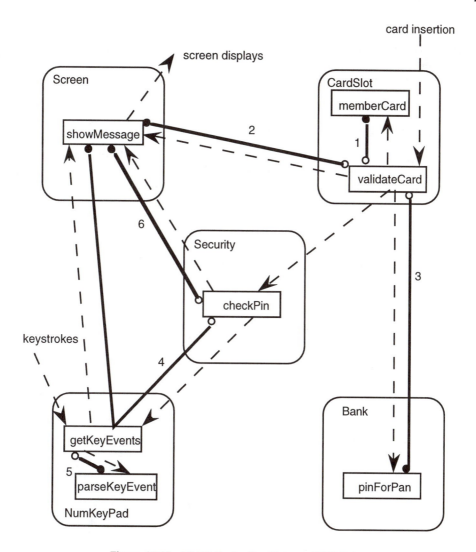

Figure 15.15 MM-Paths for CardEntry and PIN Entry

Complexity Metrics

C1   Method Cyclomatic Complexity: ordinary cyclomatic complexity on a per method basis.
C2   Total Method Complexity: sum of cyclomatic complexities of all methods in a class.
C3   Class Response: sum of the number of methods implemented within a class and the number of
     methods used by an object not due to inheritance.
C4   Object Coupling: number of non-inheritance couples to external classes.
C5   Class Complexity: cyclomatic complexity of the directed graph formed by merging individual
     method graphs into a class state machine graph.
C6   Nominal Number of Functions: count of the non-inherited functions in a class.
C7   Nominal Number of Procedures: count of the non-inherited procedures in a class.
C8   Nominal Number of Methods: count of the non-inherited methods in a class. (C8 = C6 + C7)
C9   Total Number of Functions: count of the non-inherited and inherited functions in a class.
C10 Total Number of Procedures: count of the non-inherited and inherited procedures in a class.
C11 Total Number of Methods: count of the non-inherited and inherited methods in a class.
     (C11 = C9 + C10)

These metrics are defined such that higher values imply more testing. Most of these metrics pertain to integration testing: only the E1 and C1 metrics apply to unit testing, and only the P4 metric applies to system testing.

EXERCISES

1. Compare and contrast an event trace (Figure 15.10) with the call graph (Figure 13.2) used with traditional software.
2. Object reuse implies that objects will be composed with other objects. Revisit the integration testing strategies in Chapter 13 and decide which are appropriate choices for object reuse.
3. Would a system test case for a thread be any different in an object-oriented vs. a traditional implementation? Explain your answer.

Chapter 16

Interaction Testing

Faults and failures due to interaction are the bane of testers. Their subtlety makes them difficult to recognize and even more difficult to reveal by testing. These are deep faults, ones that remain in a system even after extensive thread testing. Unfortunately, faults of interaction most frequently occur as failures in delivered systems that have been in use for some time. Typically they have a very low probability of execution, and they occur only after a large number of threads have been executed. Most of this chapter is devoted to describing forms of interaction, not to testing them. As such, it is really more concerned with requirements specification that with testing. The connection is important: knowing how to specify interactions is the first step in detecting and testing for them. This chapter is also a somewhat philosophical and mildly mathematical discussion of faults and failures of interaction; we cannot hope to test something if we don't understand it. We begin with an important addition to our five basis constructs, and use this to develop a taxonomy of types of interaction. Next, we develop a simple extension to conventional Petri nets that reflects the basis constructs, and then we illustrate the whole discussion with the SATM and Saturn Windshield Wiper systems, and sometimes with examples from telephone systems. We conclude by applying the taxonomy to an important application type: client-server systems.

16.1 CONTEXT OF INTERACTION

Part of the difficulty of specifying and testing interactions is that they are so common. Think of all the things that interact in everyday life: people, automobile drivers, regulations, chemical compounds, and abstractions, to name just a few. We are concerned with interactions in software controlled systems (particularly the unexpected ones), so we start by restricting our discussion to interactions among our basis system constructs: actions, data, events, ports, and threads.

One way to establish a context for interaction is to view it as a relationship among the five constructs. If we did this, we would find that the relation InteractsWith is a reflexive relationship on each entity (data interacts with data, actions with other actions, and so on). It also is a binary relationship between data and events, data and threads, and events and threads. The data modeling approach isn't a dead-end, however. Whenever a data model contains such pervasive relationships, that is a clue that an important entity is missing. If we add some tangible reality to our fairly abstract constructs, we get a more useful framework for our study of interaction. The missing element is location, and location has two components: time and position. Data modeling provides another choice: we can treat location as sixth basic entity, or as an attribute of the other five. We choose the attribute approach here.

What does it mean for location (time and position) to be an attribute of any of the five basis constructs? This is really a short-coming of nearly all requirements specification notations and techniques. (This is probably also the reason that interactions are seldom recognized and tested.) Information about location is usually created when a system is implemented. Sometimes location is mandated as a requirement — when this happens, the requirement is really a forced implementation choice. We first clarify the meaning of the components of location: time and position.

We can take two views of time: as an instant or as a duration. The instantaneous view lets us describe when something happens — it is a point when time is an axis. The duration view is an interval on the time axis. When we think about durations, we usually are interested in the length of the time interval, not the endpoints (the start and finish times). Both views are useful. Because threads execute, they have a duration; they also have points in time when they execute. Similar observations apply to events. Often events have very short durations, and this is problematic if the duration is so short that the event isn't recognized by the system.

The position aspect is easier. We could take a very tangible, physical view of position and describe it in terms of some coordinate system. Position can be a three dimensional Cartesian coordinate system with respect to some origin, or it could be a longitude-latitude-elevation geographic point. For most systems, it is more helpful to slightly abstract position into processor residence. Taken together, time and position tell the tester when and where something happens, and this is essential to understand interactions.

Before we develop our taxonomy, we need some ground rules about threads and processors. For now, a processor is something that executes threads, or a device where events occur.

1. Since threads execute, they have a strictly positive time duration. We usually speak of the execution time of a thread, but we might also be interested in when a thread occurs (executes). Since actions are degenerate cases of threads, actions also have durations.
2. In a single processor, two threads cannot execute simultaneously. This resembles a fundamental precept of physics: no two bodies may occupy the same space at the same time. Sometimes threads appear to be simultaneous, as in time sharing on a single processor; in fact, time shared threads are interleaved. Even though threads cannot execute simultaneously on a single processor, events can be simultaneous. (This is really problematic for testers.)
3. Events have a strictly positive time duration. When we consider events to be actions that execute on port devices, this reduces to the first ground rule.
4. Two (or more) input events can occur simultaneously, but an event cannot occur simultaneously in two (or more) processors. This is immediately clear if we consider port devices to be separate processors.
5. In a single processor, two output events cannot begin simultaneously. This is a direct consequence of output events being caused by thread executions. We need both the instantaneous and duration views of time to fully explain this ground rule. Suppose two output events are such that the duration of one is much greater than the duration of the other. The durations may overlap (because they occur on separate devices), but the start times cannot be identical, as shown in Figure 16.1. There is an example of this in the SATM system, when a thread causes screen 15 to be displayed and then ejects the ATM card. The screen is still being displayed when the card eject event occurs. (This may be a fine distinction; we could also say that port devices are separate processors, and that port output events are really a form of inter-processor communication.)

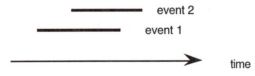

Figure 16.1 Overlapping Events

6. A thread cannot span more than one processor. This convention helps in the definition of threads. By confining a thread to a single processor, we create a natural endpoint for threads; this also results in more simple threads rather than fewer complex threads. In a multi-processing setting, this choice also results in another form of quiescence — trans-processor quiescence.

Taken together, these six ground rules force what we might call "sane behavior" onto the interactions in the taxonomy we define in section 16.3.

16.2 A PETRI NET MODEL FOR INTERACTIONS

The basic Petri nets we studied in Chapter 4 need two slight enhancements. The first makes them correspond more closely to our five basis system constructs, and the second deals with Petri net markings that express event quiescence. Taken together, these extensions result in an effective, operational view of software requirements; elsewhere they are known as OSD nets (for Operational Software Development) [Jorgensen 89].

Definition
An ***OSD net*** is a tripartite directed graph (P, D, S, In, Out) composed of three sets of nodes, P, D, and S, and two mappings, In and Out, where

- P is a set of port events
- D is a set of data places
- S is a set of transitions
- In is a set of ordered pairs from (P ∪ D) × S
- Out is a set of ordered pairs from S × (P ∪ D)

OSD nets express four of our five basis system constructs; only ports are missing. The set S of transitions corresponds to ordinary Petri net transitions, which are interpreted as actions. There are two kinds of places, port events and data places, and these are inputs to or outputs of transitions in S as defined by the input and output functions In and Out. A thread is a sequence of transitions in S, so we can always construct the inputs and outputs of a thread from the inputs and outputs of the transitions in the thread. OSD nets are graphically represented in much the same way as ordinary Petri nets, the only difference is the use of triangles for port event places. In the OSD net in Figure 16.2 there are four transitions, s7, s8, s9, and s10, two port input events, p3 and p4, and three data places, d5, d6, and d7; there are no port output events.

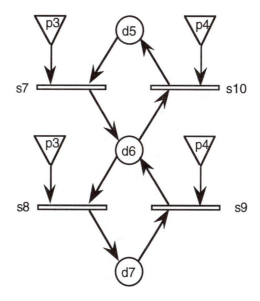

Figure 16.2   An OSD Net

This is the OSD net that corresponds to the finite state machine we developed for the dial portion of the Saturn Windshield Wiper system in Chapter 15 (see Figure 15.3). The components of this net are described in Table 1.

Markings for an OSD net are more complicated because we want to be able to deal with event quiescence.

Definition
A ***marking M of an OSD net (P, D, S, In, Out)*** is a sequence M = <m1, m2, ...> of p-tuples, where p = k + n, and k and n are the number of elements in the sets P and D, and individual entries in a p-tuple indicate the number of tokens in the event or data place.

Table 1 — OSD Elements in Figure 16.2

Element	Type	Description
p3	port input event	rotate dial clockwise
p4	port input event	rotate dial counter-clockwise
d5	data place	dial at position 1
d6	data place	dial at position 2
d7	data place	dial at position 3
s7	transition	state transition: d5 to d6
s8	transition	state transition: d6 to d7
s9	transition	state transition: d7 to d6
s10	transition	state transition: d6 to d5

By convention, we will put the data places first, followed by the input event places, and then the output event places. An OSD net may have any number of markings; each corresponds to an execution of the net. Table 2 shows a sample marking of the OSD net in Figure 16.2.

Table 2 — A Marking of the OSD Net in Figure 16.2

tuple	(p3,p4,d5,d6,d7)	Description
m1	(0, 0, 1, 0, 0)	initial condition, in state d5
m2	(1, 0, 1, 0, 0)	p3 occurs
m3	(0, 0, 0, 1, 0)	in state d6
m4	(1, 0, 0, 1, 0)	p3 occurs
m5	(0, 0, 0, 0, 1)	in state d7
m6	(0, 1, 0, 0, 1)	p4 occurs
m7	(0, 0, 0, 1, 0)	in state d6

The rules for transition enabling and firing in an OSD net are exact analogs of those for traditional Petri nets; a transition is enabled if there is at least one token in each input place, and when an enabled transition fires, one token is removed from each of its input places, and one token is placed in each of its output places. Table 3 follows the marking sequence given in Table 2, showing which transitions are enabled and fired.

Table 3 — Enabled and Fired Transitions in Table 2

tuple	(p3,p4,d5,d6,d7)	Description
m1	(0, 0, 1, 0, 0)	nothing enabled
m2	(1, 0, 1, 0, 0)	s7 enabled; s7 fired
m3	(0, 0, 0, 1, 0)	nothing enabled
m4	(1, 0, 0, 1, 0)	s8 enabled; s8 fired
m5	(0, 0, 0, 0, 1)	nothing enabled
m6	(0, 1, 0, 0, 1)	s9 enabled; s9 fired
m7	(0, 0, 0, 1, 0)	nothing enabled

The important difference between OSD nets and traditional Petri nets is that event quiescence can be broken by creating a token in a port input event place. In traditional Petri nets, when no transition is enabled, we say that the net is deadlocked. In OSD nets, when no transition is enabled, the net is at a point of event quiescence. (Of course, if no event occurs, this is the same as deadlock.) Event quiescence occurs four times in the thread in Table 3; at m1, m3, m5, and m7.

The individual members in a marking can be thought of as snapshots of the executing OSD net at discrete points in time; these members are alternatively referred to as time steps, p-tuples, or marking vectors. This lets us think of time as an ordering that allows us to recognize "before" and "after". If we attach instantaneous time as an attribute of port events, data places, and transitions, we obtain a much clearer picture of thread behavior. One awkward part to this is how to treat tokens in a port output event place. Port output places always have outdegree = 0; in an ordinary Petri net, there is no way for tokens to be removed from a place with a zero outdegree. If the tokens in a port output event place persist, this suggests that the event occurs indefinitely. Here again, the time attributes resolve the confusion; this time we need a duration of the marked output event. (Another possibility is to remove tokens from a marked output event place after one time step; this works reasonably well.)

16.3 A TAXONOMY OF INTERACTIONS

The two aspects of location, time and position, form the starting point of a useful taxonomy of interaction. There are interactions that are completely independent of time; for example, two data items that interact exhibit their interaction regardless of time. There are also time dependent interactions, as when something is a prerequisite for something else. We will refer to time-independent interactions as static, and time dependent interactions as dynamic. We can refine the static/dynamic dichotomy with the distinction between single and multiple processors. These two considerations yield a two dimensional plane (as shown in Figure 16.3) with four basic types of interactions:

- static interactions in a single processor
- static interactions in multiple processors
- dynamic interactions in a single processor
- dynamic interactions in multiple processors

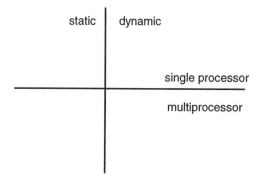

Figure 16.3   Types of Interactions

We next refine these basic four types using the notion of duration. Threads and events have durations (because they execute), hence they cannot be static. Data, on the other hand, is static, but we need to be careful here. Consider two examples, the triangle type that corresponds to the triplet (5, 5, 5) of sides, and the balance of a checking account. The triangle type is always equilateral — time will never change geometry, but the balance of a bank account is likely to change in time. If it does, the change is due to the execution of some thread, and this will be a key consideration.

16.3.1 STATIC INTERACTIONS IN A SINGLE PROCESSOR

Of the five basis constructs, only two have no duration — ports and data. Since ports are physical devices, we can view them as separate processors, and thereby simplify our discussion. Port devices interact in physical ways, such as space and power consumption, but this is usually not important to testers. Data items interact in logical ways (as opposed to physical), and these are important to testers. In an informal way, we often speak of corrupt data, and of maintaining the integrity of a database. We sometimes get a little more precise, and speak of incompatible, or even inconsistent data. We can be very specific if we borrow some terms from Aristotle. (We finally have a chance to use the propositional logic discussed in Chapter 3.) In the following definitions, let p and q be propositions about data items. As examples, we might take p and q to be:

p: AccountBalance = $10.00
q: Sales < $1800.00

Definition:
Propositions p and q are

- *contraries* if they cannot both be true
- *sub-contraries* if they cannot both be false
- *contradictories* if they exactly one is true
- q is a *sub-altern* of p if the truth of p guarantees the truth of q

These relationships are known to logicians as the Square of Opposition, which is shown in Figure 16.4, where p, q, r, and s are all propositions.

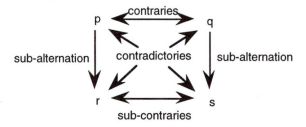

Figure 16.4 The Square of Opposition

Aristotelian logic seems arcane for software testers. Here are some situations that are exactly characterized by data interactions in the square of opposition:

1. When the pre-condition for a thread is a conjunction of data propositions, contrary or contradictory data values will prevent thread execution.
2. Context sensitive port input events usually involve contradictory data.
3. Case statement clauses are contradictories.
4. Rules in a decision table are contradictories.

Static interactions in a single processor are exactly analogous to combinatorial circuits; they are also well-represented by decision tables and unmarked OSD nets. Features in telephone systems are good examples of interaction [Zave 93]. One example is the logical conflict between Calling Party Identification service and unlisted directory numbers. With Calling Party Identification, the directory number of the source of a telephone call is provided to the called party. A conflict occurs when a party with an unlisted directory number makes a call to a party with Calling Party Identification. Which takes precedence — the calling party's desire for privacy or the called party's right to know who is placing an incoming call? These two features are contraries: they cannot both be satisfied, but they could both be waived. Call Waiting Service and Data Line Conditioning are also contrary features. When a business (or home computing enthusiast) pays for a specially conditioned data line, calls on that line are frequently used for the transmission of formatted binary data. If such a line also has Call Waiting service and a call is made to the line that is already in use, a call waiting tone is superimposed onto the pre-existing connection. If the connection had been transmitting data, the transmission would be corrupted by the call waiting tone. In this case, the resolution is easier. The customer disables the Call Waiting service before making data transmission calls.

16.3.2 STATIC INTERACTIONS IN MULTIPLE PROCESSORS

The location of data helps resolve the contraries in the telephone system examples. We would expect that the data for Call Waiting and Data Line Conditioning to be located in the same processor, since both refer to the same subscriber line. Thus the software controlling calls for that line could check for contrary line data. This in an unreasonable expectation for the Calling Party Identification problem, however. Suppose the calling party is a line in an office remote from the office that serves the line with Calling Party Identification. Since these data are in separate locations (processors), neither knows about the other, so their contrary nature can only be detected when they are connected by a thread. To be very precise, we can say that the contrary relationship exists as a static interaction across multiple processors, and it becomes a failure when executing threads in the two telephone offices (processors) interact.

Call Forwarding provides a better example of a static, distributed interaction. Suppose we have three telephone subscribers in separate cities:

Subscriber A is in Grand Rapids, Michigan,
Subscriber B is in Phoenix, and
Subscriber C is in Baltimore.

We further suppose that each subscriber has Call Forwarding service, and that calls are forwarded as follows: calls to A are forwarded to B, calls to B are forwarded to C, and calls to C are forwarded to A.

This call forwarding data is contrary — they cannot all be true. Call Forwarding data is local to the telephone office that provides the service; it is set by a thread when a subscriber defines a new forwarding destination. This means that none of the offices knows of call forwarding data in the other offices; we have distributed contraries. This is a fault, but it does not become a failure until someone (other than A, B, or C) places a call to any phone in this call forwarding loop. Such a call, say to subscriber B, generates a call forwarding thread in B's local telephone office, which results in a call to C's directory number. This generates another thread in C's telephone office, and so on. For now, please note that the existence of the connecting threads moves us out of the static quadrants and into dynamic interactions. The potential failure still exists, its just in a different part of our taxonomy.

The bottom line is that static interactions are essentially the same, whether they are centralized into a single processor, or distributed among multiple processors. (They are harder to detect when they are distributed, however.) Another common form of static interactions occurs with weak relationships and functional dependencies in a data base (centralized or distributed). Both of these interactions are forms of sub-alternation.

16.3.3 DYNAMIC INTERACTIONS IN A SINGLE PROCESSOR

Moving to the dynamic quadrants means we consider the implications of time for interactions. Among other things, this means we must expand from the data only interactions to interactions among data, events, and threads. We also must shift from the strictly declarative relationships in the Square of Opposition to a more imperative view. The notion of n-connectedness in a directed graph (see Chapter 4) serves perfectly. Figure 16.5 shows the four forms of n-connectedness in a directed graph.

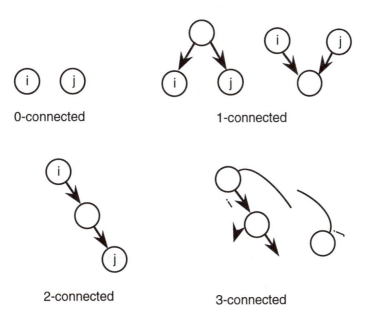

0-connected   1-connected

2-connected   3-connected

Figure 16.5 Forms of n-Connectedness

Even the data-data interactions exhibit forms of n-connectedness. Data that are logically independent are 0-connected, and sub-alternates are 2-connected. The other three relationships, contraries, contradictories, and sub-contraries, all pertain to 3-connected data, because each of these is a bi-directional relationship.

There are six potential pairs of concepts that can interact: data-data, data-events, data-threads, events-events, events-threads, and threads-threads. Each of these is further qualified by four degrees of n-connectedness, resulting in twenty-four elements to our taxonomy for this quadrant. Take some time to think through these interactions. Here are four examples:

1-connected data with data:	occurs when two or more data items are inputs to the same action.
2-connected data with data:	occurs when a data item is used in a computation (as in dataflow testing).
3-connected data with data:	occurs when data are deeply related, as in repetition and semaphores.
1-connected data with events:	context sensitive port input events.

We don't need to analyze all twenty-four possibilities because faults of interaction only become failures when threads establish some connection. The faults are latent, and when a thread makes a connection, the latent fault becomes a failure. Threads can only interact in two ways, via events or via data. We will see this more clearly using OSD nets after we make another definition.

Definition
In an OSD net, the ***external inputs*** are the places with indegree = 0, and the ***external outputs*** are the places with outdegree = 0.

In the OSD net in Figure 16.6, p1 and p2 are the only external inputs, and p5, p9, and p10 are the only external outputs.

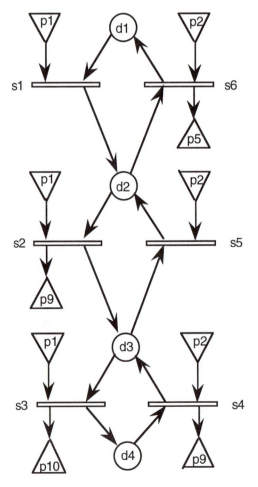

Figure 16.5 External Inputs and Outputs in an OSD Net

Now we are at a key point: we can represent the interaction among threads by the composition of their OSD nets. We do this as follows: each thread has it's own (unique) OSD net, and within each OSD net, the places and transitions have symbolic names. In one sense, these names are local to the thread, but in a larger sense (when they are composed), local names must be resolved into global synonyms. Suppose, for example, that in one SATM thread, a keystroke on the Cancel key is named as port output event p2, and in another thread the same event is called p6. When these two threads are composed, the synonyms must be collapsed onto a single name. (Earlier, we noted that it was good practice to use physical names for port events rather than their logical names; synonym resolution is the reason for this recommendation.) Once synonyms are resolved, the individual threads are drawn as OSD nets. Since threads interact only with respect to their external inputs and outputs, we next identify the sets of external inputs and outputs of each thread. The intersection of these sets contains the events and places at which the composed threads can interact. This process is illustrated in Figures 16.7 and 16.8.

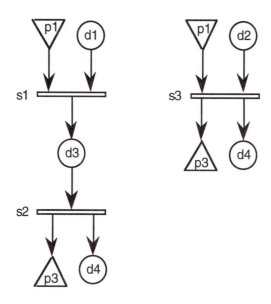

Figure 16.7 Two OSD Threads

Thread 1 is the sequence <s1, s2>, and thread 2 is the sequence <s3>. The external inputs of these threads are the sets EI1 = {p1, d1} and EI2 = {p1, d2}, and the external outputs of these threads are the sets EO1 = {p3, d4} and EO2 = {p3, d4}. Intersecting these, we get the sets EI = EI1 ∩ EI2 = {p1} and EO = EO1 ∩ EO2 = {p3, d4}. The sets EI and EO contain the external inputs and outputs at which threads 1 the 2 may possibly interact. Notice that the external inputs and outputs of the composed threads are the sets EI1 ∪ EI2 and EO1 ∪ EO2. External events will always be preserved as external, but external data may not. It is possible for output data of one thread to be input data to another thread. (This happens in the call forwarding loop.)

We can formalize this process into another definition. Let T1 and T2 be two OSD threads in which synonym places have been resolved, and with external input and output sets EI1, EI2, EO1, and EO2. Furthermore, let T be the composition of threads T1 and T2, where EI = EI1 ∩ EI2 and EO = EO1 ∩ EO2 are the external input and output sets of the composed thread T.

Definition
The threads T1 and T2 are:

- **0-connected** if EI1 ∩ EI2 = ∅, EO1 ∩ EO2 = ∅, EI1 ∩ EO2 = ∅, and EO1 ∩ EI2 = ∅
- **1-connected** if either EI ≠ ∅ or EO ≠ ∅
- **2-connected** if either EI1 ∩ EO2 ≠ ∅ or EI2 ∩ EO1 ≠ ∅
- **3-connected** if both EI1 ∩ EO2 ≠ ∅ and EI2 ∩ EO1 ≠ ∅

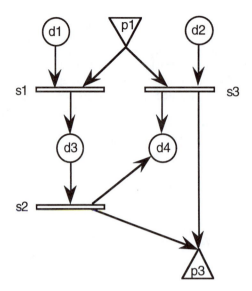

Figure 16.7 Composition of OSD Threads

Compare this with the definition of n-connectedness in Chapter 4. There we were concerned with a relationship among pairs of nodes; here we are concerned with a relationship among threads. We can eliminate these somewhat overlapping definitions by constructing a rather elaborate directed graph in which nodes are threads from which the external inputs and outputs have been deleted, and edges connect threads according to the deleted external input and output places. Figure 16.9 shows such a graph for the composition in Figure 16.8. Notice we see directly that the threads are 1-connected via the input place p1 and via the output places p3 and d4.

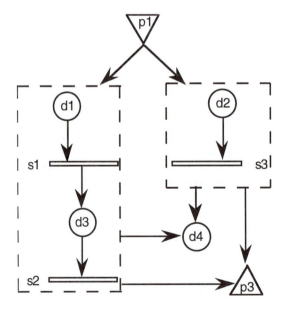

Figure 16.9 n-Connected Threads

The definition of n-connectedness exactly addresses the ways in which threads can interact in the dynamic, single processor quadrant. Only one thing is missing: just as with n-connectedness in an ordinary directed graph, the connectivity can be established by chains of threads rather that by adjacent threads as we have done here. (Imagine a call-forwarding loop that involves a dozen phone subscribers in as many states.) In my personal testing experience, many of the problems described in field trouble reports turn out to be unexpected instances of 1-, 2-, or 3-connectedness among threads that were thought to be 0-connected.

The two forms of 1-connectedness among threads deserve special comment. When two threads are connected via a common input (event or data), the interaction is the classical form of Petri net conflict. (In Figure 16.8, threads 1 and 2 are 1-connected via the port input event p1; this is also an example of a context sensitive port input event.) If we imagine a marking in which the first transitions in each thread are both enabled, then firing one of them consumes the token from the common input place, and this disables the other. When two threads are 1-connected by an output place (again either an event or data), no conflict occurs, but there is an interesting ambiguity. The common output place is marked when one of the threads executes, but we usually don't know which one. This can happen in the SATM system when screen 10 (Temporarily unable to process withdrawals) is displayed. It could be displayed because the ATM has no more cash, or because there is a malfunction in the withdrawal door. This form of output cause ambiguity is very common in field trouble reports. Many times it is due to an unexpected interaction among threads, some of which may have executed long before others.

Since port events cannot be both inputs and outputs, the only way threads can be 2-connected is via data places; and since 3-connectedness is bi-directional 2-connectedness, threads can only be 3-connected via data places. In a sense, this simplifies interactions, because the number of possibilities is reduced. The real problem with interaction via data is that long intervals of time can be involved. We can add a small refinement here: the difference between read-only data, and read-write data. Read-only data never changes, so we could say it has an infinite (or indefinite) duration. Read-write data obviously changes upon a write, so it has a duration — the interval between successive writes. The real problem with this is that seldom used (written) data may be the connection that causes two threads to be 2- or 3-connected, and the long time separation between the first and second threads can be very difficult to diagnose and difficult to cause with a test case.

There are several dynamic interactions in the SATM system. First, notice that we are dealing with one ATM terminal, so we are concerned with dynamic interactions in a single processor. Technically there are two processors, because the SATM system gets the account information from the central bank, but we can treat this interaction as though the bank is a port device. There are several context sensitive port input events in the SATM system; since we discussed these at length in Chapter 14, we move on to 1- and 2-connected interactions among threads.

It's easy to devise threads that make deposits to and withdrawals from a given bank account. These are 1- and 2-connected via the data place for the account balance. Withdrawal threads that attempt to withdraw more than, and less than, the existing balance are 1-connected to the balance place. A successful withdrawal (in which the requested amount is less than the balance) clearly changes the balance, so the before and after instances of the balance place are 2-connected via the withdrawal thread. If we add a deposit thread, we obtain even richer interactions, and the key to all of this is the time order in which they execute.

There is another subtlety in the foregoing discussion; it has to do with how we describe such interacting threads. One possibility is to rely on specific values, both for pre-conditions and for amounts entered in the input portion of the threads. With the explicit approach, we might postulate, as a pre-condition, a balance of $50.00, and define thread T1 as a withdrawal of $40.00, and thread T2 as a withdrawal of $60.00. Superficially this is easy — thread T2 will not execute, and thread T1 will. We could be more precise by defining two port inputs for the withdrawal amount: p1 is withdrawal amount = $40.00, and p2 is withdrawal amount = $60.00. With these, thread T1 will contain a port event to display screen 11 (take cash), and T2 will contain a port event to display screen 8 (insufficient funds). Here is where the subtlety comes in. By being more precise, we also remove the conflict, because we have stated in advance which port output will occur. When do these values exist: when the thread is described (specified) or when it actually executes? The explicit approach is commonly used by testers, but it doesn't work well for requirements specification because of the pre-disposition. Alternatively, we could be more general, and say that thread T1 is a withdrawal of an amount less than the balance, and thread T2 is a withdrawal of an amount greater than the balance, and not state the balance until execution time. (This is a good choice when executable specifications are used as a rapid prototype.) The problem with the latter choice is that testers cannot provide the expected output portions of a test case. The subtlety hinges on when the path of a thread is determined: before it begins to execute, as in a test case, or as it executes, as in a rapid prototype. We will revisit this discussion in Section 16.4 when we discuss the connection between interaction, composition, and determinism. For now, testers might relish the idea that they can control the destiny of threads, but specifiers cannot.

16.3.4 DYNAMIC INTERACTIONS IN MULTIPLE PROCESSORS

Dynamic interactions among multiple processors are the most complex in our taxonomy. Because threads and events can execute simultaneously, strictly sequential, deterministic behavior is replaced by concurrent behavior. In the words of Robin Milner, "concurrency inflicts non-determinism" [Milner 93]. The added complexity is also seen in the models mandated by each quadrant: decision tables suffice for static interactions, and finite state machines express dynamic interactions on a single processor. Dynamic interactions on multiple processors need the expressive power of communicating finite state machines or some form of Petri nets. We will see these interactions in the Saturn Windshield Wiper system.

When we viewed the Saturn Windshield Wiper system in terms of objects in Chapter 15, we developed a finite state machine for each object. Take a moment to review that discussion. One of the problems we had was that, by themselves, the lever and dial machines could not determine all of the wiper speeds (port output events). When we composed the lever and dial objects, their interaction defined the port events when the lever is in the Intermittent state. In the object-oriented view, we substituted messages for port events, and let the wiper object deal with all the port events. Here we will use OSD nets to compose the lever and dial finite state machines, and this composition will exactly describe the interaction. Figures 16.2 and 16.6 are the OSD net equivalents of the dial and lever finite state machines from Chapter 15. The OSD transitions, places, and events used in Figure 16.10 are summarized in Table 4.

Table 4   OSD Windshield Wiper Elements

Element	Description
s1	transition OFF to INT
s2	transition INT to LO
s3	transition LO to HI
s4	transition HI to LO
s5	transition LO to INT
s6	transition INT to OFF
s7	transition 1 to 2
s8	transition 2 to 3
s9	transition 3 to 2
s10	transition 2 to 1
s11	provide 6 strokes per minute
s12	provide 12 strokes per minute
s13	provide 20 strokes per minute
d1	lever at Off
d2	lever at INT
d3	lever at LO
d4	lever at Hi
d5	dial at 1
d6	dial at 2
d7	dial at 3
p1	move lever up one position
p2	move lever down one position
p3	move dial up one position
p4	move dial down one position
p5	provide 0 strokes per minute
p6	provide 6 strokes per minute
p7	provide 12 strokes per minute
p8	provide 20 strokes per minute
p9	provide 30 strokes per minute
p10	provide 60 strokes per minute

To cast a finite state machine into an OSD net, states become data places and state transitions become OSD transitions. The events that cause state transitions become port input events, and the outputs associated with a state transition become port output events. In the lever OSD net (Figure 16.6), transitions to the Off, LO and Hi states require no interaction with the dial OSD net to determine the associated port output events (p5, p9, and p10). Also, transitions to the INT state (s1 and s5) have no port output events. In the dial OSD net (Figure 16.2), the three dial positions are the three data places, and the dial events (p3 and p4) are inputs that cause transitions. The dial OSD net has no port output events, because these are never outputs of transitions in the dial OSD net.

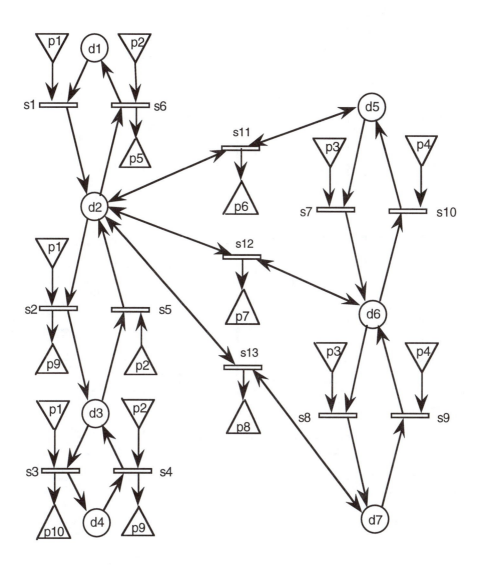

Figure 16.10   OSD Net for the Windshield Wiper System

The interaction between the lever and the dial OSD nets is shown in Figure 16.10. It entails places d2, d5, d6, and d7, transitions s11, s12, and s13, and port events p6, p7, and p8., which are the INT state, the dial position states, and the three intermittent wiper speeds. The edges with arrowheads at each end (e.g., between d2 and s11) indicate that the places are inputs to and outputs of the associated transitions. This seems a little artificial, but it makes the markings work smoothly.

We can execute the OSD net in Figure 16.10, but we need to devise (or rationalize) an initial marking. Notice that none of the places is an external input. This means we must arbitrarily determine some starting position for the dial and lever. The physical reality is that both devices can be in exactly one position at a time (a form of contraries), thus exactly one of d1, d2, d3, and d4 is always marked, and similarly for d5, d6, and d7. We will assume that the car is shipped with the lever in the off position and the dial at position 1. Table 5 shows the marking sequence for the following scenario:

User Input	Expected Output
lever up one position	6 strokes per minute
lever up one position	30 strokes per minute
dial up one position	30 strokes per minute
lever down one position	12 strokes per minute
lever down one position	0 strokes per minute

Table 5   Marking for Sample Scenario

M	d1	d2	d3	d4	d5	d6	d7	p1	p2	p3	p4	p5	p6	p7	p8	p9	p10	Description
0	1				1													Off, 1
1	1				1			1										lever up, s1 enabled
2		1			1													s1 fired, s11 enabled
3		1			1								1					s11 fired, s11 enabled
4		1			1			1										lever up, s2 and s11 enabled
5			1		1											1		s2 fired
6			1		1					1								dial up, s7 enabled
7			1			1												s7 fired
8			1			1			1									lever down, s5 enabled
9		1				1												s5 fired, s12 enabled
10		1				1								1				s12 fired
11		1				1			1									lever down, s6 enabled
12	1					1					1							s6 fired

The OSD net of the full Saturn Windshield Wiper system in Figure 16.10 just begins to show the complexity of dynamic interactions among multiple processors. For starters, consider cyclomatic complexity: it is 3 for the lever OSD net, 2 for the dial OSD net, and 20 for the full OSD net. The jump in complexity is directly attributable to the interactions. Now, consider the complexities that result from the various strictly sequential markings of this net, and then the contribution to complexity when concurrent execution is allowed.

Some of this becomes clear if you carefully follow the marking sequence in Table 5 for the OSD net in Figure 16.10. First notice that there are several points of event quiescence, such as at marking steps m0 and m2. The net at steps m3 and m5 needs some explanation. Basically, we need to clarify the nature of the port output events (the wiper speeds). When a port output occurs, what is its duration? Does it continue to provide wiper strokes, or must it be executed periodically? Both of these styles are shown in Figure 16.10. At step m3, when transition s11 fires, it remarks its input places (d2 and d5) and executes p6 (six strokes per minute). Since no other transition is enabled, we can picture s11 as continuously firing until something else (an event) happens. This is a strange form of event quiescence, but it is clearly a steady state of the system. The other form is shown at marking step m5, where transition s2 has fired, resulting in port output p9 (30 strokes per minute). Here we picture p9 as having a duration that lasts as long as d3 is marked. While p9 is operating, the user can cause dial port events (steps 6 and 7) with no effect on the wiper strokes. The possible markings, then, give us additional insight into the complexity of these interactions.

The role of time adds the last increment of complexity. Consider the time interval between port input events and what we might call the reaction time of the system. The highest wiper speed is 60 strokes per minute, and a driver can easily move the lever from the Off position to the Hi position in less than one second. What happened to the intervening port events (p9 and one of p6, p7, and p8)? The model is incomplete on this detail. Markings let us deal with simultaneity: if two events (or transitions) occur at exactly the same point in time, we can easily show this by marking their corresponding positions in the marking vector. We can also amend the firing rules to allow simultaneous transition firings as long as the transitions are in different processors. We can represent all of this with diagrams similar to the timing diagrams used to describe electronic circuits. (They are also similar to music notation, in which each voice has its own clef. Music also has a notion of time steps, the measures of equal time duration. Tables 6 and 7 show two possible ways to present the concurrent behavior of the marking in Table 5.

Table 6   Concurrent Behavior of the Sample Scenario

time	0	1	2	3	4	5	6	7	8	9	10	11	12
lever													
d1	1	1											
d2					1	1							1
d3							1	1	1	1	1		
d4													
s1			1										
s2						1							
s3													
s4													
s5													
s6												1	
p1		1			1								
p2										1			
dial													
d5	1	1	1	1	1	1	1	1					
d6									1	1	1	1	
d7													
s7								1					
s8													
s9													
s10													
p3							1						
p4													
wiper													
s11													
s12													
s13													
p5													
p6			1	1	1								
p7													1
p8													
p9							1	1	1	1	1	1	
p10													
time	0	1	2	3	4	5	6	7	8	9	10	11	12

Table 7 Condensed Version of Table 6

		time	0	1	2	3	4	5	6	7	8	9	10	11	12
lever		data	d1	d1		d2	d2		d3	d3	d3	d3	d3		d2
		trans			s1			s2						s5	
		input		p1			p1						p2		
		output							p9	p9	p9	p9	p9	p9	
dial		data	d5	d5	d5	d5	d5	d5	d5	d5		d6	d6	d6	d6
		trans									s7				
		input							p3						
		output													
wiper		data													
		trans													
		input													
		output				p6	p6	p6							p7

We can extend the SATM system to exhibit dynamic interactions among multiple processors. For now, suppose we have several SATM terminals connected to the central bank in a network. Suppose also that several people have card and PIN access to the same account, and that they frequently (even simultaneously) make deposits to and withdrawals from their joint account. This situation clearly involves concurrent execution of threads in multiple processors, and the deposit and withdrawal threads are 1-, 2-, or 3-connected via the balance data place. The difficulty hinges on how the balance data place is treated in the ATM network. Is it centralized data that is (nearly) immediately updated by remote ATM terminals? If so, the distributed threads interact in real time. In fact, most ATM networks send copies of the balance data on an as-requested basis to remote ATM terminals. At a given terminal, the balance data becomes local data, and always reflects transactions that occur at that location. At some time during the day, the terminals are polled, and the local balances are resolved to create a new centralized balance. This global-local-global practice eliminates the difficult time-based interactions among the distributed threads.

16.4 INTERACTION, COMPOSITION, AND DETERMINISM

The question of non-determinism looms as a backdrop to deep questions in science and philosophy. Einstein didn't believe in non-determinism; he once commented that he doubted that God would play dice with the universe. Non-determinism generally refers to consequences of random events, asking in effect, if there are truly random events (inputs), can we ever predict their consequences? The logical extreme of this debate ends in the philosophical/theological question of free will versus pre-destination. Fortunately for testers, the software version of non-determinism is less severe. You might want to consider this section to be a technical editorial. It is based on my experience and analysis using the OSD framework. I find it yields reasonable answers to the problem of non-determinism; you may too.

Let's start with a working definition if determinism; here are two possibilities:

1. A system is deterministic if, given its inputs, we can always predict its outputs.
2. A system is deterministic if it always produces the same outputs for a given set of inputs.

Since the second view (repeatable outputs) is less stringent than the first (predictable outputs), we'll use it as our working definition. Then a non-deterministic system is one in which there is at least one set of inputs that results in two distinct sets of outputs. It's easy to devise a non-deterministic finite state machine; Figure 16.11 is one example.

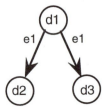

Figure 16.11 A Non-deterministic Finite State Machine

When the machine in Figure 16.11 is in state d1, if event e1 occurs, there is a transition either to state d2 or to d3.

If it is so easy to create a non-deterministic finite state machine, why all the fuss about determinism in the first place? (It turns out that we can always find a deterministic equivalent to any non-deterministic finite state machine anyway.) Recall that, in Chapter 12 we took great pains to separate the reality of a system from models of the system's behavior. Finite state machines are models of reality; they only approximate the behavior of a real system. This is why it is so important to choose an appropriate model — we would like to use the best approximation. Roughly speaking, decision tables are the model of choice for static interactions, finite state machines suffice for dynamic interactions in a single processor, and some form of Petri net is needed for dynamic interactions in multiple processors. Before going on, we should indicate instances of non-determinism in the other two models. A multiple hit decision table is one in which the inputs (variables in the condition stub) are such that more than one rule is selected. In Petri nets, non-determinism occurs when more than one transition is enabled. The choice of which rule executes or which transition fires is made by an external agent. (Notice that the choice is actually an input!)

Our question of non-determinism reduces to threads in an OSD net, and this is where interactions, composition, and determinism come together. To ground our discussion in something "real", consider the SATM threads we used earlier:

T1: withdraw $40.00
T2: withdraw $60.00
T3: deposit $30.00

Threads T1, T2, and T3 interact via a data place for the account balance, and they may be executed in different processors. The initial balance is $50.00.

Begin with thread T1; if no other thread executes, it will execute correctly, leaving a balance of $10.00. Suppose we began with thread T2; we should really call it "attempt to withdraw $60.00", because, if no other thread executes, it will result in the insufficient funds screen. We should really separate T2 into two threads, T2.1 which is a successful withdrawal that ends with the display of screen 11 (take cash), and T2.2 which is a failed withdrawal that ends with the display of screen 8 (insufficient funds). Now let's add some interaction with thread T3. Threads T2 and T3 are 2-connected via the balance data place. If T3 executes before T2 reads the balance data, then T2.1 occurs, otherwise T2.2 occurs. The difference between the two views of determinism is visible here: When the OSD net of T2 begins to execute, we cannot predict the outcome (T2.1 or T2.2), so by the first definition, this is non-deterministic. By the second definition, however, we can recreate the interaction (including times) between T2 and T2. If we do, and we capture the behavior as a marking of the composite OSD net, we will satisfy the repeatable definition of determinism.

We now have a mild resolution to the question of determinism, at least as it applies to testing threads that are expressed as OSD nets. We can go so far as to say that a thread is locally non-deterministic, in the sense that its outcome cannot be predicted with information local to the thread. We also saw this in the windshield wiper system. If we were confined to the lever finite state machine, we cannot determine the output when the lever moves to the Intermittent position, because we don't know the dial position. In a global sense, however, non-determinism vanishes, because all the inputs are known. The implication for testers is that, when testing threads with external inputs (particularly data places), it is important to test the interaction with all other threads that can be n-connected via external inputs.

16.5 CLIENT-SERVER TESTING

Client-server systems are difficult to test because they exhibit the most difficult form of interactions, the dynamic ones across multiple processors. Here we can enjoy the benefits of our strong theoretical development. Client-server systems always entail at least two processors, one where the server software exists and executes, and one (usually several) where the client software executes. The main components are usually a database management system, application programs that use the database, and presentation programs that produce user-defined output. The position of these components results in the fat server vs. fat client distinction [Lewis 94] (see Figure 16.12).

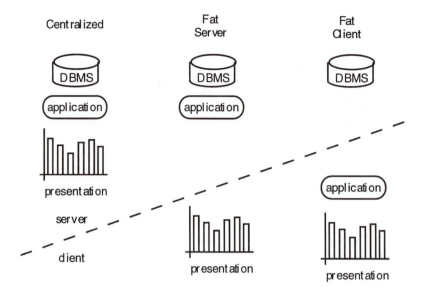

Figure 16.12 Fat Clients and Servers

Client-server systems also include a network to connect the clients with the server, the network software, and a graphical user interface (GUI) for the clients. To make matters worse, we can differentiate homogeneous and heterogeneous CS systems in terms of client processors that are identical or diverse. The multiple terminal version of the SATM system would be a fat client system, since the central bank does very little of the transaction processing.

In our formulation of OSD threads, we confined a thread to a processor. With client-server systems, we need a term for a sequence of threads that crosses the client-server boundary; call it a CS transaction. A typical CS transaction begins with a request (or query) at a client processor. The request is transmitted over the network (where it might be scheduled) to the server, where some application program processes it using the database management system. The results are transmitted over the network to the client, where they are mapped to a user-defined output format. If something goes wrong in a CS transaction, there's a lot of room for finger pointing: clients blame the server, servers blame the clients, and both blame the network.

The threads in the DBMS portion of CS transactions are all of the static sequential type, and since this is likely to be either a commercial product or a very stable application, there is not much need for testing here. Should testing be necessary, it will almost always be strictly functional, because we rarely have the source code of commercial applications. Threads in the server applications also exhibit primarily static sequential interactions, and these too are likely to be in stable, existing applications. The applications will probably be more error prone (failure prone is better) than the DBMS. The network software portion of a CS transaction is also likely to be a commercial application, hence most CS transaction testing will occur on the client processor(s). The most interesting (from a testing standpoint) is the GUI portion. The user portion of a CS transaction is typically built within a commercial application program that allows the user to develop in terms of a WIMP interface (Windows, Icons, Menus, and Pull-downs), and this is where the fun begins. Clients are free to move in arbitrary ways across multiple windows, yet the results must be compatible. In our terminology, we can view a window as a finite state machine, and inter-window moves will correspond to communicating finite state machines. All the actions available to a user in a window are port input events, and the results of these actions are port output events. The client portions of a CS transaction are therefore threads that exhibit dynamic interactions across multiple processors (the windows), which we know to be the most complex.

This framework at least gives the CS tester a rigorous approach that supports testing strategies that can be measured in terms of coverage metrics. The notion of operational profiles (see Chapter 14) is very appropriate, since testing all possible interactions could be very time consuming. Another advantage to this framework is that, once a client thread is satisfactorily tested, the only further concern is its interaction with other threads. This should be an important step, because there is a lot of potential for n-connectivity among the threads of separate clients, very much like the SATM scenario in which several people conducted deposits and withdrawals on the same account.

EXERCISES

1. Figure 16.4 has a nice connection with set theory. Take the propositions p, q, r, and s to be the following set theory statements about some sets S and P:

   p: $S \subseteq P$
   q: $S \cap P = \varnothing$
   r: $S \cap P \neq \varnothing$
   s: $S \not\subseteq P$

   Convince yourself that the relationships in the Square of Opposition apply to these set theory propositions.

2. Find and discuss examples of n-connectivity for the events in Table 4.

3. The Central ATM system (CATM) is the "other side" of the SATM system; it supports the following activities:
   a. Open and Close bank accounts.
   b. Maintain daily balances of accounts to reflect the twice daily postings of SATM transactions. These occur at 9:00 am and 3:00 pm.
   c. Provide Expected PIN and account balance information to an SATM terminal.
   d. Apply a service charge ($1.00) to any account that shows more than three ATM transactions in a given day.
   Consider the CATM and SATM functions, and allocate these to Fat Server and Fat Client formulations.

4. List examples of the various kinds of interactions you can find in the combined CATM/SATM system. Decide whether these interactions are affected by the fat server vs. the fat client formulations.

References

[Agresti 86]   Agresti, W. W., *New Paradigms for Software Development*   IEEE Computer Society Press, Washington DC, 1986

[Beizer 84]   Boris Beizer *Software System Testing and Quality Assurance* Van Nostrand Reinhold, New York, 1984

[Bieman 94]   J. M. Bieman and L. M. Ott "Measuring functional cohesion" *IEEE Transactions on Software Engineering*, vol. SE-20, no.8, pp. 644-657, Aug. 1994.

[Binder 94a]   Robert V. Binder "Introduction to Special Section on Object-Oriented Software Testing" *Communications of the ACM,* vol. 37, no. 9, p. 28, September 1994.

[Binder 94b]   Robert V. Binder "Design for Testability in Object-Oriented Systems" *Communications of the ACM*, vol. 37, no. 9, pp. 87-101, September 1994.

[Boehm 88]   Boehm, B. W., "A spiral model for software development and enhancement" *IEEE Computer*, vol. 21, no. 6, IEEE Computer Society Press, Washington DC, pp. 61-72, May 1988.

[Brown 75]   J. R. Brown and M. Lipov "Testing for Software Reliability" *Proceedings of the International Symposium on Reliable Software* Los Angeles, pp 518-527, April 1975.

[Chellappa 87]   Mallika Chellappa "Nontraversible Paths in a Program" *IEEE Transactions on Software Engineering,* vol. SE-13, no. 6, pp. 751-756, June 1987.

[Clarke83]   Lori A. Clarke and Debra J. Richardson "The Application of Error Sensitive Strategies to Debugging" *ACM SIGSOFT Software Engineering Notes,* vol. 8 no. 4, August 1983.

[Clarke 84]   Lori A. Clarke and Debra J. Richardson "A Reply to Foster's 'Comment on "The Application of Error Sensitive Strategies to Debugging" *ACM SIGSOFT Software Engineering Notes*, vol. 9 no. 1, January 1984.

[Clarke 89]   Lori A. Clarke, Andy Podgurski, Debra J. Richardson, and Steven J. Zeil "A formal evaluation of data flow path selection criteria" *IEEE Transactions on Software Engineering*, vol. SE-15, no.11, pp. 1318-1332, November, 1989.

[Elmendorf 73]   William R. Elmendorf "Cause-Effect Graphs in Functional Testing" Poughkeepsie, NY; IBM System Development Division TR-00.2487, 1973

[Gallagher 91]   K. B. Gallagher and J. R. Lyle "Using program slicing in software maintenance" *IEEE Transactions on Software Engineering*, vol. SE-17, no.8, pp. 751-761, August, 1991.

[Gruenberger 73]   F. Gruenberger "Program Testing, The Historical Perspective" *Program Test Methods*, edited by William C. Hetzel, Prentice-Hall, 1973, pp 11-14.

[Harel 88]   Harel, David "On Visual Formalisms" *Communications of the ACM*, vol. 31 no. 5, pp. 514-530, May 1988.

[Henderson-Sellers 90]   Henderson-Sellers, Brian and Edwards, J.M. "The object-oriented systems life cycle" *Communications of the ACM*, vol. 33 no. 9, pp. 142-159, September. 1990.

[Hetzel88]   Bill Hetzel *The Complete Guide to Software Testing, Second Edition*, QED Information Sciences, Inc., Wellesley, MA 1988.

[Huang 79]   J. C. Huang "Detection of dataflow anomaly through program instrumentation" *IEEE Transactions on Software Engineering* SE-5; pp. 226-236 (1979).

[IEEE 83]   IEEE Computer Society *IEEE Standard Glossary of Software Engineering Terminology*, ANSI/IEEE Std. 729-1983

[IEEE 93]   IEEE Computer Society *IEEE Standard Classification for Software Anomalies*, IEEE Std. 1044-1993.

[Inglis 61]   Stuart J. Inglis *Planets, Stars, and Galaxies*, 4th Edition, Wiley and Sons, New York, 1961.

[ISO 91]   International Organization for Standardization *Data elements and interchange formats—Information interchange—Representation of dates and times*, International Standard ISO 8601:1988, Technical Corrigendum 1, Switzerland, 1991.

[Jorgensen 89]   Paul C. Jorgensen "An Operational Common Denominator to the Structured Real-Time Methods" *Proceedings of the Fifth Structured Techniques Association (STA-5) Conference*, Chicago, May 11, 1989.

[Jorgensen 94]	Paul C. Jorgensen "System Testing with Pseudo-Structures" *American Programmer*, vol. 7, no. 4, pp. 29-34, April 1994
[Jorgensen 94]	Paul C. Jorgensen and Carl Erickson "Object-Oriented Integration Testing" *Communications of the ACM*, vol. 37, no. 9, pp. 30-38, September 1994.
[Lewis 94]	Ted Lewis and Michael Evangelist "Fat Servers vs. Fat Clients: The Transition from Client-Server to Distributed Computing" *American Programmer*, vol. 7 no. 11, pp. 2-9, November 1994.
[McCabe 76]	Thomas J. McCabe "A Complexity Metric" *IEEE Transactions on Software Engineering*, SE-2, 4, (December 1976) pp. 308-320.
[McCabe 82]	Thomas J. McCabe "Structural Testing: A Software Testing Methodology Using the Cyclomatic Complexity Metric" National Bureau of Standards (now NIST) Special Publication 500-99, Washington 1982
[McCabe 87]	Thomas J. McCabe "Structural Testing: A Software Testing Methodology Using the Cyclomatic Complexity Metric" McCabe and Associates, Baltimore, 1987
[Miller 77]	E. F. Miller *Tutorial: Program Testing Techniques*, at COMPSAC'77 IEEE Computer Society, 1977
[Miller 91]	Edward F. Miller, Jr. "Automated Software Testing: A Technical Perspective" *American Programmer*, vol. 4 no. 4, pp. 38 - 43, April 1991.
[Mosley 93]	Daniel J. Mosley *The Handbook of MIS Application Software Testing* Yourdon Press, Prentice Hall, Englewood Cliffs, NJ, 1993
[Myers 79]	Glenford J. Myers *The Art of Software Testing* New York, Wiley Interscience, 1979.
[Pirsig 73]	Robert M. Pirsug *Zen and The Art of Motorcycle Maintenance* Bantam Books, New York, 1973.
[Poston 90]	Robert M. Poston *T: Automated Software Testing Workshop* Programming Environments, Inc. Tinton Falls, NJ, 1990
[Poston 91]	Robert M. Poston "A Complete Toolkit for the Software Tester" *American Programmer*, vol. 4 no. 4, pp 28-37, April 1991. Reprinted in *CrossTalk*, a USAF publication.
[Pressman 82]	Roger S. pressman *Software Engineering: A Practitioner's Approach* New York, McGraw-Hill, 1982.
[Rapps 85]	S. Rapps and E. J. Weyuker "Selecting software test data using data flow information" *IEEE Transactions on Software Engineering*, vol. SE-11, no. 4, pp. 367-375, April, 1985.

[Rosen 91]   Kenneth H. Rosen _Discrete Mathematics and Its Applications_ McGraw-Hill, New York, 1991

[Rumbaugh 91]   James Rumbaugh, Michael Blaha, William Premerlani, Frederick Eddy, William Lorensen _Object-Oriented Modeling and Design_ Prentice-Hall, Englewood Cliffs, NJ, 1991

[Schach 93]   Stephen R. Schach_Software Engineering_, 2nd Edition Richard D. Irwin, Inc. and Aksen Associates, Inc., 1993

[Topper 93]   Andrew Topper, Daniel J. Ouellette, and Paul C. Jorgensen _STRUCTURED METHODS: Merging Models, Techniques, and CASE_, McGraw-Hill, 1993.

[Weiser 84]   M. D. Weiser "Program slicing" _IEEE Transactions on Software Engineering_, vol. SE-10, no. 4, pp. 352-357, April, 1988.

[Zave 93]   Pamela Zave "Feature Interactions and Formal specifications in Telecommunications" _IEEE Computer_, August, 1993

Index

A

Adjacency matrix 43
Alternative life cycle models 160
ASF. *See* atomic system function
Atomic System Function 185
  of objects 219

B

Basis Concepts 193
  action 194
  data 193
  port 194
  thread 194
Basis Path Testing 114
Black Box Testing. *See* functional
  testing
Boundary value analysis 57
Boundary value testing 57
Builds 162

C

Cause-Effect graphing. *See* Deci-
  sion tables
Chain 110
Clear Box Testing. *See* Structural
  testing
Client-Server Testing 243
Commission Problem 20
Composition 160
Condensation Graph 44
Contradiction 38
Contradictories 232
Contraries 232
Correctness 6
Cyclomatic complexity 116

D

Data flow testing 123
DD-Path. *See* decision-to-decision
  path
DD-Path graph 111
Decision table 81
  action entry 82
  action stub 82

condition entry 82
condition stub 82
Don't Care entry 82
extendeded Entry 82
Limited Entry 82
rule 82
test cases 82
Decision-to-decision path 109
Declarative language 45
Decomposition tree 177
Define/reference anomalies 123
Define/Use Testing 123
  defining node 123
  usage node 124
    computation use 124
    predicate use 124
Definition-use. *See* path: definition-
  use path
Determinism. *See* Non-determinism
Directed graph 45
  adjacency matrix 46
  incidence matrix 42, 46
  N-Connectedness 47
  outdegree 46
  path 47
  reachability matrix 47
  semi-path 47
  sink node 46
  source node 46
  strong component 48
  transfer node 46
Domain 57
Du-path. *See* path: definition-use
  path
Du-path Test Coverage Metrics 129
  All C-uses/Some P-uses 130
  All definitionss 129
  All du-paths 130
  All P-uses/Some C-uses 129
  All-uses 129

E

Empty set 28
Equivalence Class Testing 71

strong 72
traditional 73
weak 72
Equivalence relation 36
Error 3
Essential Complexity 118
Event 194
Event quiescence 218

F

Failure 3
Fault 3
taxonomy of 10
Finite State Machine 50
state 50
transition 50
Function 32
composition 33
domain 32
into 33
many-to-one 33
one-to-one 33
onto 33
range 32
Functional decomposition 160, 177
Functional Testing 7

G

Graph 41
component 44
connectedness 44
cyclomatic number 44
directed 45
edge 41
node 41
path 43

H

Hybrid testing 149

I

Imperative language 45
Incident 4
Integration testing
call graph based
neighborhood 182
pairwise 182
decomposition based
big bang 180
bottom-up 181
sandwich 181
top-down 180
path based 183
Interaction, taxonomy of 231
dynamic 231
multiple processor 231
single processor 231
static 231

L

Life cycle models
evolutionary development 161
fountain 164
incremental development 161
operational specification 163
rapid prototyping 163
spiral 161
traditional. *See* Life cycle models:
waterfall
waterfall 159
Linear graph 41. *See also* graph
Location 227
position 228
time 228
Lock, Stock, and Barrel problem. *See*
Commission Problem
Logical Equivalence 37
Logical operator 37
conjunction 37
disjunction 37
exclusive-or 37
if-then 37
negation 37

M

McCabe, Thomas 114
Message 184
Message quiescence 218
Miller, E. F. 112
MM-Path 184
of objects 218
MM-Path graph 185
Module execution path 183
multiple fault assumption 67

N

N-connectedness 233
NextDate function 19
Node
degree 42
Non-determinism 242

O

Object Composition 215
Object-oriented Testing 223
  complexity metrics 225
  encapsulation metrics 223
  inheritance metrics 223
  polymorphism metrics 224
OMT 30
Operational Profiles 210
Oracle 5
Ordering relation 36
OSD net 229
  event quiescence 230
  external inputs 234
  external outputs 234
  graph 229
  marking 229

P

Path
  definition-clear path 124
  definition-use path 124
  feasible path 117
  infeasible paths 120
Path testing 107
  DD-Path testing 112
  loop coverage 113
  multiple condition 113
  Predicate Testing 112
  Statement Testing 112
PDL. *See* program design language
Petri net 52
  marked 52
  place 52
  transitions 52
    enabled 52
    fired 53
Post conditions 5
Pre-conditions 4
Probability 38
Program design language 171
Program graph 49, 107
Program slices. *See* slice
Progression testing 212
Proposition 36

R

Range 57
Reference Testing 5
Regression testing 212

S

Relation 34
  cardinality 35
  participation 35
Robustness testing 59

SATM system 22
Saturn Windshield Wiper Control-
  ler 24
Set
  definition 28
  empty set 28
  set operations 29
    Cartesian product 29
    complement 29
    intersection 29
    relative complement 29
    symmetric difference 29
    union 29
  Venn diagram 29
Set Identities 32
Set Partition 31
Set Relations 31
  equality 31
  proper subset 31
  subset 31
Set theory 27
  element 27
  member 27
Single fault assumption 58
Sink node 183
Slice 131
Software anomaly 10
Source node 183
Special value testing 60
Square of Opposition 232
StateCharts 30
Strongly connected graph 114
Structural Testing 8
Sub-altern 232
Sub-contraries 232

T

Tautology 38
Test 4
Test Case 4
Test Coverage Analyzer 114
Test coverage metrics 112
Testing
  integration 160
  levels of 10, 159

progression 161
regression 161
system 160
unit 159
Testing method
coverage of 145
net redundancy of 145
redundancy of 145
Thread 173, 191
integration 192
system 193
unit 192
Thread graph 193
Thread testing
functional strategies 201
data-based 204
event-based 203
port-based 203
pseudo-structural strategies 210

structural strategies 200
bottom-up threads 200
edge coverage 201
node coverage 201
Triangle Problem 15
Truth set 39

V

Vector space 122
Venn diagram 29

W

White Box Testing. *See* Structural
testing
Worst Case Testing 60

Y

YesterDate problem 25

Z

Zipf's Law 19, 210